The Black Family
REUNION
COOKBOOK

RECIPES & FOOD MEMORIES™
from The National Council of Negro Women, Inc.

A FIRESIDE BOOK
Published by Simon & Schuster
New York   London   Toronto   Sydney   Tokyo   Singapore

FIRESIDE
Simon & Schuster Building
Rockefeller Center
1230 Avenue of the Americas
New York, New York 10020

Libby Clark, Food Editor   Varnette P. Honeywood, Cover Artist
Janet Cheatham Bell, Writer   Jessica B. Harris, Food Consultant
Acuff/Pollard, Text Design

First Fireside Edition 1993
Published by arrangement with The Wimmer Companies, Inc.
4210 B. F. Goodrich Boulevard
Memphis, Tennessee 38118

FIRESIDE and colophon are registered trademarks
of Simon & Schuster Inc.

Manufactured in the United States of America

ISBN: 0-671-79629-1

Any inquiries should be directed to
THE NATIONAL COUNCIL OF NEGRO WOMEN, INC.
1667 K Street, NW, Suite 700, Washington, DC 20006

THE WIMMER COMPANIES
1-800-727-1034

INTRODUCTION

Through choosing this cookbook, you are embarking on a process that goes beyond the preparation of food. You are partaking in centuries of history, tradition and culture. You are continuing an important legacy that is central to the fabric of African-American life. Through your participation, you are an advocate of a very simple pleasure in life that cannot be overlooked in its importance.

The sharing of good food among loved ones and good friends not only gives us sustenance but also strength to meet life's challenges. During decades of public life, I have seen more problems settled in a dining room than in a conference room. A good meal creates a special fellowship that can break down barriers. And, of course, some of my fondest memories of family and relationships revolve around the table or in the beckoning warmth and aroma of the kitchen.

Where family values are strong, the health of the community is likewise. These values, as simple as they may sound, are fostered by the rituals that bind us together as families, as neighbors and as citizens.

In the tradition of Mary McLeod Bethune, the National Council of Negro Women has made the issues that impact African-American family life our highest priorities. Through our Black Family Reunion Celebrations around the country, we have brought together millions of people — families of all compositions. Our celebrations have been lauded for creating new community energy and fostering self-help approaches to many contemporary concerns. Together we can become a more caring community, the greater extended family. The Black Family Reunion Celebration, like this cookbook, underscores the wealth of resources and the diversity in African-American culture that is so positive and life-affirming.

We have titled this **THE BLACK FAMILY REUNION COOKBOOK**, drawing upon the rich experiences, and traditional values of the family. On a personal note, the book is to inspire the reunion of the greater NCNW family — our membership, sections and affiliates, plus our celebrity friends and role models who have all contributed treasured recipes and Food Memories™ on these pages. We are indeed, deeply grateful. I hope you and your family will find enjoyment and inspiration and make each meal together a celebration.

Dorothy Height

Dorothy I. Height
President and CEO
National Council of Negro Women, Inc.

Publisher's Note

Dr. Dorothy I. Height has been called by many a "living link" to the greatest sociological development in 20th Century America—the Civil Rights Movement. A member of the leadership which included Dr. Martin Luther King, Roy Wilkins, Whitney Young and others, Dr. Height is the last remaining active head of a national organization from that era. Just as she was inspired into a life of public service after first meeting her mentor, the legendary educator and human rights activist Mary McLeod Bethune, Dr. Height has continued this legacy by being a shining example to many of what can be achieved against seemingly insurmountable odds.

During a public life that has spanned nearly six decades, Dr. Height has worked tirelessly at all levels against hunger and malnutrition, underemployment, teenage pregnancy, substance abuse, substandard housing, and illiteracy and inferior education. She has made the issues that affect the quality of life for families her priority. Under her leadership at the National Council of Negro Women, the Black Family Reunion Celebration has grown into a nationwide movement. It has demonstrated the value of building upon the strengths of the African-American family, its traditional values, culture and diversity.

Dr. Height's recognition of the significance of mealtime became evident to us in her commitment to this cookbook. We trust this project will enable all people to recognize the power of breaking bread in the building of families and communities.

The Black Family Reunion Cookbook
Dedicated to Mary McLeod Bethune
Founder of The National Council of Negro Women
July 10, 1875 - May 18, 1955

Mary McLeod Bethune was born to former slave parents the fifteenth of seventeen children in Mayesville, South Carolina. She would become one of the most significant forces of her era in the emerging struggle for civil rights.

Mary McLeod Bethune, who first achieved prominence as an educator, started what became Bethune-Cookman College with five girls, her son, faith in God and $1.50. Her work brought her into contact with important political and financial figures. Mrs. Bethune's arena of influence soon extended to the national government, where she became an advisor to Presidents Coolidge and Hoover at the National Child Welfare Commission. But it was under President Roosevelt as Director of Negro Affairs from 1936 - 1944 that Mrs. Bethune reached a position to impact policy, especially as it related to employment, housing and personal freedom.

As titular head of the "Black Cabinet" in the Roosevelt Administration, Mrs. Bethune organized three major national conference of Black leaders to establish concrete policy guidelines for the improvement of life for African-Americans. Recommendations from these conferences were submitted to President Roosevelt accompanied by Mrs. Bethune's urgings for implementation.

In the struggle for human rights, Mrs. Bethune dreamed of an organization that could tap the resources of America's women to effect change on local, national and international levels. On December 5, 1935, Mrs. Bethune convened a group of notable Black women leaders who represented a spectrum of national women's organizations to form the National Council of Negro Women.

Mrs. Bethune is the first African-American or woman of any race to be honored with a monument in a public park in the nation's capital. The Bethune Memorial in Lincoln Park was dedicated by the National Council of Negro Women on July 10, 1974.

Just prior to her death, Mrs. Bethune dictated to an editor of *Ebony* magazine her "Last Will and Testament," which outlined the meaning of her life and her hopes for her people. Known as the Bethune Legacy, this document is recognized internationally as a truly great literary work and as a defining element to the mission of the National Council of Negro Women.

The Bethune Legacy is inscribed on the base of the Bethune Memorial and is reproduced on the pages of this cookbook for all to share the vision and inspiration of Mary McLeod Bethune.

BLACK FAMILY REUNION PLEDGE

Because we have forgotten our ancestors, our children no longer give us honor.

Because we have lost the path our ancestors cleared kneeling in perilous undergrowth, our children cannot find their way.

Because we have banished the God of our ancestors, our children cannot pray.

Because the old wails of our ancestors have faded beyond our hearing, our children cannot hear us crying.

Because we have abandoned our wisdom of mothering and fathering, our befuddled children give birth to children they neither want nor understand.

Because we have forgotten how to love, the adversary is within our gates, and holds us up to the mirror of the world, shouting, "Regard the loveless."

Therefore, we pledge to bind ourselves to one another

To embrace our lowliest,

To keep company with our loneliest,

To educate our illiterate,

To feed our starving,

To clothe our ragged.

To do all good things, knowing that we are more than keepers of our brothers and sisters. We are our brothers and sisters.

In honor of those who toiled and implored God with golden tongues, and in gratitude to the same God who brought us out of hopeless desolation.

We make this pledge.

Dr. Maya Angelou

*Written expressly for the National Council of Negro Women
Black Family Reunion Celebration on May 14, 1986.*

TABLE OF CONTENTS

DEVELOPMENT TEAM

Janet Cheatham Bell is president and owner of Sabayt Publications, Inc., Chicago, publishers of the *Famous Black Quotations* bookstore sidelines. Prior to establishing her own business, Bell was a senior editor of literature textbooks for Ginn and Company, Boston. She has also been a curriculum consultant for the Indiana Department of Education, research associate for the Multi Ethnic Education Resource Center at Stanford University, and associate editor of *The Black Scholar*.

Libby Clark is Food Editor of *The Los Angeles Sentinel* and a syndicated food columnist for Amalgamated Publishers, Inc. New York. She has traveled extensively throughout the African diaspora to discover cultural ties and food preparation similarities of Blacks in Africa, America, the Caribbean, and Brazil. She is a three times Life Member of the National Council of Negro Women.

Jessica B. Harris lives in New York City and is a professor of French and English at Queens College. She is the author of **Hot Stuff**: *In Praise of the Piquant*, **Iron Pots and Wooden Spoons**: *Africa's Gift to New World Cooking* and **Sky Juice and Flying Fish**: *Traditional Caribbean Cooking*.

Varnette P. Honeywood is an artist of exceptional talent. Her work is a vivid reflection of her deep love and sensitivity for the Black experience. Honeywood received training in art at Spelman College in Atlanta, Georgia. Her original paintings and collages are included in numerous public and private collections. Honeywood lives and works in Los Angeles.

BREAD SPECIALTIES

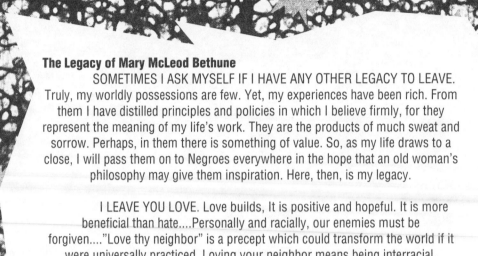

The Legacy of Mary McLeod Bethune

SOMETIMES I ASK MYSELF IF I HAVE ANY OTHER LEGACY TO LEAVE. Truly, my worldly possessions are few. Yet, my experiences have been rich. From them I have distilled principles and policies in which I believe firmly, for they represent the meaning of my life's work. They are the products of much sweat and sorrow. Perhaps, in them there is something of value. So, as my life draws to a close, I will pass them on to Negroes everywhere in the hope that an old woman's philosophy may give them inspiration. Here, then, is my legacy.

I LEAVE YOU LOVE. Love builds, It is positive and hopeful. It is more beneficial than hate....Personally and racially, our enemies must be forgiven...."Love thy neighbor" is a precept which could transform the world if it were universally practiced. Loving your neighbor means being interracial, interreligious, and international.

I LEAVE YOU HOPE . . . . Yesterday, our ancestors endured the degradation of slavery, yet they retained their dignity. Today, we direct our economic and political strength toward winning a more abundant and secure life. Tomorrow, a new Negro, unhindered by race taboos and shackles, will benefit from more than 330 years of ceaseless striving and struggle. Theirs will be a better world. This I believe with all my heart.

About this fabric

Wax Hollandais (black and gold with print) [WAX-OH-LAHN-DAY]
One of the most valuable of the printed fabrics found in West Africa, wax fabrics, ironically, come from Europe. Originally they were produced by using batik techniques. This design shows the fly whisk which is a symbol of power for some African peoples.

EMANCIPATION PROCLAMATION BREAKFAST CAKE

⅓	cup Butter Flavor Crisco
⅓	cup sugar
1	egg
2	cups all-purpose flour
1	tablespoon baking powder
½	teaspoon salt
¼	teaspoon cinnamon
⅓	cup milk
1½	cups blueberries, fresh or frozen
¼	cup honey
	Grated peel of one orange
	Grated peel of one lemon

1. Heat oven to 400°F. Grease 9-inch pie plate.
2. Combine Butter Flavor Crisco and sugar in large bowl. Beat at medium speed of electric mixer until creamy. Beat in egg.
3. Combine flour, baking powder, salt and cinnamon. Add alternately with milk to creamed mixture. Fold in blueberries.
4. Pat dough out to ½-inch thickness on lightly floured surface. Cut into nine 3-inch rounds. Place one in center of pie plate. Arrange eight, tilted and overlapping, around center dough circle. Spread with honey. Sprinkle with orange and lemon peel.
5. Bake at 400°F for 20 to 24 minutes or until dough in center is thoroughly baked. Serve warm or at room temperature.

8 servings

HERITAGE RECIPE

Basket Dinners
As a small child growing up in the South, my fondest memories are of the basket dinners served at our church. Each family prepared food and brought it to the meetings on a designated Sunday, usually in June, July or August. The food was delicious, usually fried chicken, barbe-cued pork and goat and all kinds of desserts, including homemade ice cream. It was a delight for us kids to turn the handle of the ice cream freezer because it meant we would get the dasher to lick from after the cream was frozen. In my home state we have com-memorated the Emancipation Procla-mation on the 8th of August, or the closest weekend to that date, with basket dinners. Former slaves and descendants of slaves would come from around the country for this grand day of celebration.

Mayme L. Brown
Williamsburg, VA

3

Grandma's Helping Hand

When I was 7 years old, my grandmother started teaching me how to cook. We had 12 people in our family and she needed all the help she could get!

I was so small she gave me my own special stool to help me reach the table. I remember standing on that stool trying to roll out biscuit dough that was so big I could never do it by myself. I would try so hard but only end up with flour everywhere! I'll never forget how grandma would come over, put her arm around my shoulders and say, "It's all right, sugar, you'll be big enough some day." She never got upset with me for being too small. Every time I make biscuits I remember those early days with my grandmother. And even though I'm big enough now to roll out the dough by myself, I can still feel grandma standing next to me...helping me.

Pearletha Nelson
NCNW Ohio State Project Coordinator/
Legacy Life Member
Lorain, OH

BENNE SEED WAFERS

1	cup firmly packed brown sugar
¼	cup butter or margarine (½ stick)
1	egg, beaten
½	cup all-purpose flour
⅛	teaspoon baking powder
¼	teaspoon salt
1	cup toasted* sesame seeds
1	teaspoon freshly squeezed lemon juice
½	teaspoon vanilla

1. Heat oven to 325°F. Grease baking sheet.
2. Combine brown sugar and butter in medium bowl. Beat until creamy. Stir in egg, flour, baking powder and salt. Stir in sesame seeds, lemon juice and vanilla. Drop by teaspoonfuls onto baking sheet, 2 inches apart.
3. Bake at 325°F for 15 minutes, or until wafers are brown around edges. Allow wafers to cool one minute before removing to cooling rack.

Note: Benne is a West African word for sesame which is still in common daily usage in South Carolina. Legend has it that eating sesame seeds brings good luck.

50 wafers

*Toast sesame seeds in heavy cast iron skillet on low heat, stirring until they turn golden brown, about 7 to 10 minutes. (NOTE: be careful. The transition from toasted brown to black is almost instantaneous.) When toasted, remove from the skillet and place in small bowl until needed.

HERITAGE RECIPE

4

ANGEL BISCUITS

1	package active dry yeast
2	tablespoons warm water
5	cups all-purpose flour
⅓	cup sugar
1	tablespoon baking powder
1	teaspoon baking soda
1	teaspoon salt
1	cup Crisco Shortening
2	cups buttermilk

1. Dissolve yeast in warm water.
2. Combine flour, sugar, baking powder, baking soda and salt in large bowl. Cut in Crisco using pastry blender (or 2 knives) until all flour is blended in to form pea-size chunks. Stir in yeast mixture and buttermilk. Place in large bowl. Cover with plastic wrap. Refrigerate overnight.
3. Heat oven to 400°F.
4. Roll or pat dough to ½-inch thickness on well floured surface. Cut with floured 1¾ to 2-inch biscuit cutter. Place on ungreased baking sheet.
5. Bake at 400°F for 10 to 12 minutes or until lightly browned.

4 dozen biscuits

NICE AND EASY ROLLS

2	cups self-rising flour
1	cup milk
¼	cup regular mayonnaise

1. Heat oven to 425°F. Grease twelve (about 2½-inch) muffin cups.
2. Combine flour, milk and mayonnaise in medium bowl. Stir just until dry ingredients are moistened. Divide dough equally between muffin cups.
3. Bake at 425°F for 20 minutes. Serve warm or at room temperature.

12 rolls

Sunday Rolls

When I was young I remember my mother making hot rolls. I loved to smell the pungent aroma of the yeast. Our Sunday morning breakfast was always hot, light delicious rolls and fried chicken. I'll always cherish the memory.

Elizabeth Morton Brown
Carson, CA

COCONUT BISCUITS

2	cups all-purpose flour
¾	cup flake coconut, toasted
2	tablespoons sugar
1	tablespoon baking powder
½	teaspoon salt
⅓	cup Crisco Shortening
1	cup milk
½	teaspoon vanilla

1. Heat oven to 425°F. Grease baking sheet.
2. Combine flour, coconut, sugar, baking powder and salt in medium bowl. Cut in shortening using pastry blender (or two knives) to form coarse crumbs.
3. Combine milk and vanilla. Add to dry ingredients. Mix with fork until particles are moistened and cling together. Drop tablespoonfuls onto baking sheet.
4. Bake at 425°F for 12 to 14 minutes.

12 to 16 biscuits

❖

SWEET POTATO BISCUITS

2	cups all-purpose flour
1	tablespoon baking powder
1	teaspoon salt
1	cup mashed sweet potato
2	tablespoons firmly packed brown sugar
½	cup Butter Flavor Crisco, melted
½	teaspoon baking soda
¾	cup buttermilk

1. Heat oven to 425°F. Combine flour, baking powder and salt in large bowl.
2. Combine sweet potato, brown sugar and Butter Flavor Crisco. Beat at low speed of electric mixer until well blended and fluffy.
3. Dissolve baking soda in buttermilk. Stir buttermilk and sweet potato mixture alternately into dry ingredients.
4. Roll dough ½-inch thick. Cut with floured 2-inch round cutter. Place on ungreased baking sheet.
5. Bake at 425°F for 15 to 20 minutes.

12 to 16 biscuits

Sunday Morning Biscuits

Sunday has always been a very special day for me. When I was a little girl I looked forward to Sunday for lots of reasons. Sunday was the day the family would get all dressed up to go to church. It was the day we did not do extra chores and it was a day we had delicious meals all day long. I especially looked forward to Sunday morning breakfast which often featured hot buttered home-made biscuits and syrup. Mama could get me to agree to just about anything when she promised to make biscuits!

Brenda M. Girton
NCNW Vice President
Washington, DC

MONKEY BREAD

⅓	cup sugar	¼	cup lukewarm water
⅓	cup Crisco Shortening	2	eggs, beaten
1	teaspoon salt	4	cups sifted all-purpose flour
1	cup milk, scalded	¼	cup melted butter or
1	cake compressed yeast		margarine

1. Add sugar, Crisco Shortening and salt to hot milk. Stir until shortening melts and sugar dissolves. Cool to lukewarm.
2. Crumble yeast into warm water. Let stand 5 minutes. Combine milk and yeast mixtures.
3. Add eggs and half the flour. Beat well. Add remaining flour. Turn dough onto lightly floured board. Knead until smooth. Place dough in well greased bowl. Cover. Let rise 1½ hours or until double in bulk.
4. Roll dough to ½-inch thickness. Cut into pieces size of small walnut. Roll into balls. Roll each ball in melted butter.
5. Place in 10-inch tube pan. Cover. Let rise until double in bulk. Heat oven to 350°F and bake for 20 minutes. Turn out onto serving plate. Serve hot Do not cut. Pull apart.

10 - 12 servings

JUANITA'S SWEET POTATO MUFFINS

¾	cup skim or lowfat milk	1	tablespoon molasses
½	cup cold mashed sweet	¾	cup all-purpose flour
	potatoes or yams	½	cup whole wheat flour
¼	cup firmly packed brown sugar	½	cup oat bran
1	egg	2½	teaspoons baking powder
3	tablespoons Crisco Oil	1	teaspoon grated orange peel

1. Heat oven to 400°F. Grease twelve medium (about 2½-inch) muffin cups or use paper or foil liners.
2. Combine milk, sweet potatoes, brown sugar, egg, Crisco Oil and molasses in large bowl. Stir until well mixed.
3. Combine all-purpose flour, whole wheat flour, oat bran, baking powder and orange peel. Add to liquid mixture. Stir just until dry ingredients are moistened. Spoon batter into muffin cups.
4. Bake at 400°F for 20 to 25 minutes.

12 muffins

REEDER REFRIGERATOR ROLLS

1	package active dry yeast
½	cup warm water (110 to 115°F)
1	cup milk, scalded
⅔	cup Crisco Shortening
½	cup sugar
2	teaspoons salt
1	cup mashed potatoes
2	eggs
6 - 6½	cups all-purpose flour
	Butter Flavor Crisco, melted, optional

1. Sprinkle yeast over warm water in small bowl. Let stand until softened.
2. Pour scalded milk over Crisco, sugar and salt in large bowl. Stir until Crisco is melted. Stir in mashed potatoes. Add eggs, one at a time, stirring well after each addition. Stir in 1 cup flour. Add softened yeast. Mix well. Stir in enough remaining flour to make soft dough.
3. Turn dough onto lightly floured surface. Cover. Let rest 10 minutes. Knead dough until smooth and elastic.
4. Place dough in greased deep bowl. Turn to bring greased surface to top. Cover tightly. Refrigerate. Dough can be refrigerated for 1 to 3 days.
5. Shape dough into rolls 2 hours before baking. Cover. Let rise until doubled.
6. Heat oven to 425°F. Bake for 15 minutes or until golden brown. Brush with melted Butter Flavor Crisco, if desired.

3 dozen rolls

Church Rolls

My mother made yeast bread every Saturday for Sunday dinner. Often she would send a pan of rolls to a neighbor in need and she always took her rolls to share at church activities. When one of my brothers returned home after he had moved out, he would always ask Mom if she had any of those "church rolls." She always did because she continued to cook homemade bread until all the family had left home.

Annie Kennedy
Barbour
Indian Head, MO

OAT BRAN MUFFINS

2	cups oat bran
¼	cup firmly packed brown sugar
2	teaspoons baking powder
1	cup skim milk
2	egg whites or 2 ounces egg substitute
¼	cup honey or molasses
2	tablespoons safflower oil

1. Heat oven to 400°F. Grease twelve medium (about 2½-inch) muffin cups or use paper or foil liners.
2. Combine oat bran, brown sugar and baking powder in large bowl.
3. Combine milk, egg whites, honey and oil in small bowl. Stir until well blended. Add liquid mixture to dry ingredients. Stir just until dry ingredients are moistened. Fill muffin cups almost full.
4. Bake at 400°F. for 15 to 18 minutes.

12 muffins

WILLIE MAYS' FAVORITE BRAN MUFFINS

1	cup natural bran
1	cup whole wheat flour
1	cup skim milk
2	eggs
1	tablespoon baking powder
3	tablespoons natural honey
½	teaspoon salt
	Favorite fruit (optional)

1. Heat oven to 350°F. Grease twelve medium (2½-inch) muffin cups or use paper or foil liners.
2. Combine all ingredients in large bowl. Stir just until blended. Add favorite fruit, if desired. Spoon into muffin cups
3. Bake at 350°F. for 20 to 25 minutes.

12 muffins

Mae Louise Mays, Wife of Willie Mays, Baseball Player

Discovery Muffins

My oat bran muffins could easily be called "discovery muffins." I attended the National Council of Negro Women's Black Family Reunion several years ago in Washington, D.C. and took advantage of the free medical tests. I discovered that my cholesterol was over 300! When I returned home and consulted the Lipic Clinic about getting my cholesterol down, a part of the recommended treatment was daily consumption of oat bran, prepared as hot cereal or made into muffins. This dietary routine has proven to be adequate medication for the past eight years. I am grateful to the NCNW Black Family Reunion Celebration for providing the testing that alerted me to this dangerous condition.

Olivia Ellis Calloway
St. Louis, MO

FAMILY BISCUITS

2	cups all-purpose flour
1	tablespoon baking powder
1	teaspoon salt
⅓	cup Crisco Shortening
¾	cup milk

◆

1. Heat oven to 425°F.
2. Combine flour, baking powder and salt in large bowl. Cut in Crisco using pastry blender (or two knives) to form coarse crumbs. Add milk. Mix with fork until particles are moistened and cling together. Form dough into ball.
3. Transfer dough to lightly floured surface. Knead gently 8 to 10 times. Roll dough to ½-inch thickness. Cut with floured 2-inch round cutter. Place on ungreased baking sheet.
4. Bake at 425°F for 12 to 14 minutes.

12 to 16 biscuits

◆

Variations:

Drop Biscuits: Prepare biscuits as above, increase milk to 1 cup. Do not knead. Drop from spoon onto ungreased baking sheet. Bake as above.

Whole Wheat Biscuits: Prepare biscuits as above, substitute 1 cup all-purpose flour and 1 cup whole wheat flour for the 2 cups flour. Proceed as above, rolling dough to ⅝-inch thickness.

Buttermilk Biscuits: Prepare biscuits as above, add ¼ teaspoon baking soda to flour mixture. Substitute buttermilk for milk. Proceed as above.

Sour Cream Biscuits: Prepare biscuits as above, substitute 1 cup dairy sour cream for milk. Proceed as above.

Coconut Biscuits: Prepare biscuits as above, add ½ teaspoon vanilla, ¾ cup flake coconut and 2 tablespoons sugar. Proceed as above.

Bacon and Cheese Biscuits: Prepare biscuits as above, omitting salt. Add 1 tablespoon sugar to dry ingredients. Stir in 1 cup cooked, crumbled bacon (about 14 slices) and 1 cup (4 ounces) finely shredded Cheddar cheese after cutting in shortening. About 20 biscuits. (Bacon can be omitted for plain cheese biscuits.)

You Might Make A Friend Along The Way

When I was a little boy, about 7 or 8 years old, I'd come home from school and find my grandmother baking those delicious oversized biscuits. A platter of them would be on top of the stove to keep warm. I'd sneak up to the stove and grab a biscuit then run outside to play. She always caught me, pulled me back by my shirttail and said, "Where are you going?" I'd tell her I was going outside to play. Then she would hand me another biscuit and say, "You'd better take two because you might make a friend along the way."

Phil Mendez
Los Angeles, CA

ANADAMA BREAD

1	cup yellow cornmeal
⅓	cup Crisco Shortening
½	cup molasses
2	teaspoons salt
2	cups boiling water
1	package active dry yeast
¼	cup warm water (110° to 115°)
5 - 6	cups all-purpose flour

1. Combine cornmeal, Crisco, molasses and salt in large bowl. Stir in boiling water. Let cool to lukewarm.
2. Sprinkle yeast over warm water. Let stand until softened.
3. Add 1 cup flour to cornmeal mixture. Beat until very smooth. Add softened yeast. Stir. Add half of remaining flour. Beat until very smooth. Mix in enough remaining flour to make soft dough.
4. Turn dough onto lightly floured surface. Cover. Let rest 10 minutes. Knead dough until smooth and elastic.
5. Place dough in greased deep bowl. Turn to bring greased surface to top. Cover. Let rise in warm place until doubled (about 1 hour).
6. Punch down dough. Divide in half. Shape into loaves. Place in 2 greased 9 X 5 X 3-inch loaf pans. Cover. Let rise until doubled (about 1 hour).
7. Heat oven to 375°F.
8. Bake at 375°F for 30 to 35 minutes or until bread sounds hollow when tapped. Remove from pans. Cool on racks.

2 loaves

HERITAGE
RECIPE

A Secure, Loving Feeling

As a child I would wake up to the delicious, delightful aroma of fresh homemade dough, that had risen overnight, to the warmth of the oven in which rolls were baking. Still, today, the memory of that smell provides me with a secure, loving feeling which will live with me forever.

Charlotte Willerford Brown
New Haven, CT

SWEET POTATO NUT BREAD

½	cup Crisco Shortening	1	teaspoon cinnamon
1¼	cups sugar	1	teaspoon baking soda
2	eggs	½	teaspoon salt
1	cup cold mashed sweet potatoes (about 2 medium sweet potatoes)	⅓	cup water
		½	cup chopped nuts (walnuts or pecans)
1¾	cups all-purpose flour	1½	teaspoons vanilla
1¼	teaspoons nutmeg	½	cup raisins (optional)

1. Heat oven to 375°F. Grease one 9 X 5 X 3-inch loaf pan.
2. Combine Crisco and sugar in large bowl. Beat at low speed of electric mixer until blended. Increase speed to medium. Beat until well mixed. Add eggs one at a time, beating well after each addition. Add sweet potatoes.
3. Combine flour, nutmeg, cinnamon, baking soda and salt. Add alternately with water to creamed mixture at medium-low speed. Add nuts, vanilla and raisins, if used. Spread in pan.
4. Bake at 375°F for 60 to 70 minutes or until toothpick inserted in center comes out clean. Cool in pan 10 minutes. Turn out onto cooling rack.

One loaf

OHIO PORK CAKE

1	cup finely chopped salt pork	1	teaspoon cinnamon
1	cup boiling water	½	teaspoon nutmeg
½	teaspoon baking soda	½	teaspoon allspice
1	cup molasses	½	teaspoon ground cloves
1	cup sugar	3	cups all-purpose flour
1	cup raisins		

1. Heat oven to 375°F. Grease 8-inch square pan.
2. Place chopped salt pork in large bowl. Pour in boiling water. Cool to room temperature.
3. Add baking soda to molasses. Stir until dissolved. Stir molasses, sugar, raisins, cinnamon, nutmeg, allspice and cloves into salt pork. Stir flour in gradually until just blended. Pour into pan.
4. Bake at 375°F for 1 hour to 1 hour 15 minutes or until toothpick inserted in center comes out clean.

One cake

HERITAGE RECIPE

WALNUT BREAD

2	packages active dry yeast
¼	cup warm water
5	cups bread flour
1	tablespoon salt
4	teaspoons sugar
½	cup very finely chopped walnuts
1	cup liquid from non-fat dry milk
2	tablespoons vegetable oil
2	small eggs

1. Mix yeast with warm water. Set aside until dissolved.
2. Combine flour, salt, sugar and walnuts in large bowl.
3. Stir in milk, oil, eggs and yeast. Use electric mixer dough hook attachment on low speed to blend ingredients. Increase speed to medium. Mix 15 minutes. Cover. Let stand 15 minutes.
4. Turn dough out onto lightly floured board. Cut into 6 equal pieces. Flour hands. Knead dough pieces into loaf shapes. Place on baking sheet. Cover. Let rise in warm place until double in bulk.
5. Bake at 375°F for 25 to 30 minutes or until golden brown. Serve hot.

6 loaves

Note: Bread freezes well.

Johnny Rivers, Executive Chef
Walt Disneyworld Resorts

Special Childhood Memories

Every Saturday night when I was growing up, I had to make the dough for Sunday morning rolls. It was my job to make the dough before I went to bed so we could have fresh baked rolls for Sunday morning breakfast. I looked forward to this meal so much that I would go to bed early in hopes that morning would come quicker. The smell would always wake me up early and I would hurry to get ready and go downstairs to a special Sunday treat. Even now the smell of fresh baked rolls gives me that special feeling I had as a young girl on Sunday mornings. I rarely have the time to cook now, but whenever I'm in a restaurant or at a friend's house and I smell the aroma of rolls baking, it reminds me of that special time in my life.

Esther McCall
NCNW Board of Directors
National Chair,
Bethune Recognition Program
New York, NY

Mealtimes Were Happy Times

My family consisted of 18 children and two parents. My most vivid memories of the old times are of mealtimes. Mealtime is a communion time. It's a time when you share joys and sorrows and a time to get close. You miss out if you don't have a formal dinner hour. If you messed around in our house and didn't make mealtimes, my parents decided you didn't want that meal because they insisted that everybody sit together at mealtimes. You were required to report on the progress you were making in what you were doing. It was just a joyful time. There was no scolding allowed at mealtimes. So if you had done something wrong, you would try to think of something interesting to say to get Poppa to forget what you had done wrong earlier in the day.

We also had an early morning prayer service the first Sunday of every month. At four in the morning, everybody got out of bed and

Continued on next page

STUFFED FRENCH TOAST

2 or 4	slices sourdough bread, depending on size, cut 1-inch thick
1	banana
1	egg
¼	cup milk
½	teaspoon vanilla
⅓	cup sugar
1	teaspoon cinnamon
⅓	cup sugar
1	teaspoon cinnamon
	Oil or shortening for frying
	Whipped butter (optional)
	Maple syrup (optional)

1. Cut 2-inch pocket in one side of each bread slice. Cut bananas in half crosswise. Split each piece lengthwise. Remove peel. Stuff 2 pieces in each pocket of bread, depending on size. (If bread slices are small, use 4 and stuff one piece banana in each pocket.)
2. Mix egg, milk and vanilla until well blended.
3. Mix sugar and cinnamon.
4. Heat about 4 inches of oil in deep fryer or deep saucepan to 350°F.
5. Dip stuffed bread into egg and milk mixture, soaking a few minutes to penetrate into bread.
6. Fry about 3 minutes until lightly browned, turning to brown both sides. Drain on paper towels on cake rack.
7. Sprinkle with sugar and cinnamon. Serve immediately. Spread with whipped butter and serve with maple syrup, if desired.

2 servings (For 4 servings, double the amount of bread, bananas, egg, milk and vanilla.)

Johnny Rivers, Executive Chef
Walt Disneyworld Resorts

TROPICAL BANANA BREAD

½   cup Crisco Shortening
1   cup sugar
2   eggs, well beaten
1   cup mashed bananas (2 to 3 medium)
½   cup dairy sour cream
2   cups all-purpose flour
1   teaspoon baking soda
½   teaspoon salt
½   cup chopped pecans or walnuts

1. Heat oven to 350°F. Grease and flour 8½ X 4½ X 2½-inch loaf pan.
2. Combine Crisco and sugar in large bowl. Beat at medium speed of electric mixer until creamed.
3. Add eggs, bananas and sour cream. Beat until well blended.
4. Combine flour, baking soda and salt. Add at low speed of electric mixer. Mix just until blended. Stir in nuts. Spread in pan.
5. Bake at 350°F for 50 to 60 minutes or until toothpick inserted in center comes out clean. Cool in pan 10 minutes. Remove from pan to cooling rack. Cool completely before slicing.

One loaf

Continued

went and kneeled around Momma's and Poppa's bed. The smallest child would have the shortest prayer, "Jesus Wept", and you would graduate up to longer verses. The teenagers said a short prayer. Momma said a longer one and Poppa said the final prayer. The prayer service was over at five, then we were free until a wonderful breakfast was cooked. We would hang around the kitchen to smell the wonderful aromas of the meal Momma was preparing. Momma made everything with love. I loved the care she took to make the meal more palatable. She could make a meager fare taste rich. I still can't make beans the way she could. Momma always cooked enough for someone else. We had one playmate who, when Momma would ask him if he wanted to stay for the meal, would say, "Yes ma'am, thank you. I'd love some if you have a lots."

Ms. Esther Rolle
Actress
Los Angeles, CA

BLUEBERRY COFFEE CAKE

Cake

2⅓	cups all-purpose flour
1⅓	cups plus 2 tablespoons granulated sugar, divided
½	teaspoon salt
¾	cup Crisco Shortening
¾	cup milk
3	eggs, divided
2	teaspoons baking powder

1	teaspoon vanilla
1	cup ricotta cheese
1	tablespoon finely shredded fresh lemon peel
1	cup fresh or frozen blueberries
½	cup chopped walnuts
⅓	cup firmly packed brown sugar
1	teaspoon cinnamon

Confectioners Sugar Icing

1	cup confectioners sugar
1	tablespoon milk

¼	teaspoon vanilla

1. Heat oven to 350°F. Grease 13 X 9 X 2-inch pan.
2. Combine flour, 1⅓ cups granulated sugar and salt in medium bowl. Cut in Crisco using pastry blender (or 2 knives) until crumbly. Reserve 1 cup mixture for topping. Add milk, two eggs, baking powder and vanilla to remaining crumb mixture. Beat at medium speed 2 minutes. Scrape sides of bowl as needed. Spread in pan.
3. Combine remaining 2 tablespoons sugar, remaining egg, ricotta cheese and lemon peel in small bowl. Mix well.
4. Sprinkle berries over batter in pan. Spoon cheese mixture over berries. Spread gently and evenly.
5. Mix reserved crumb mixture, nuts, brown sugar and cinnamon. Sprinkle over cake.
6. Bake at 350°F for 45 minutes or until toothpick inserted in center comes out clean. Cool slightly.
7. Place confectioners sugar in small bowl. Stir in milk one teaspoon at a time until desired drizzling consistency. Stir in vanilla. Drizzle over coffee cake.

12 servings

MOLASSES MUFFINS

1⅔	cups all-purpose flour	½	cup dark molasses
3	tablespoons sugar	2	eggs, lightly beaten
2	teaspoons baking powder	¼	cup Crisco Oil
1	teaspoon ginger	¼	cup milk
½	teaspoon salt		

1. Heat oven to 400°F. Place paper liners in twelve medium (about 2½-inch) muffin cups.
2. Combine flour, sugar, baking powder, ginger and salt in medium bowl. Make "well" in center of mixture.
3. Combine molasses, eggs, Crisco Oil and milk in small bowl. Stir to blend. Pour into "well" in dry ingredients. Stir just until dry ingredients are moistened. Spoon into muffin cups, filling each about ⅔ full.
4. Bake at 400°F for 15 to 17 minutes, or until centers spring back when touched lightly.

12 muffins

Variation:
Orange Raisin Muffins: Follow recipe above, omitting ginger. Add ½ cup raisins and 2 teaspoons grated orange peel to dry ingredients.

MOLASSES BROWN BREAD

1	egg, lightly beaten	¾	cup very hot water
1	cup all-bran or bran bud cereal	1	cup all-purpose flour
½	cup raisins	1	teaspoon baking soda
⅓	cup molasses	½	teaspoon cinnamon
2	tablespoons Butter Flavor Crisco		

1. Heat oven to 350°F. Grease inside of two clean metal food cans, with labels removed. (4½ inches deep X 3 inches wide.)
2. Combine egg, cereal, raisins, molasses and Butter Flavor Crisco in large mixing bowl. Add hot water, stirring until shortening is melted.
3. Combine flour, baking soda and cinnamon. Add to cereal mixture, stirring just until combined. Fill cans two-thirds full.
4. Bake at 350°F for 45 minutes or until toothpick inserted in center comes out clean. Remove from cans. Cool slightly. Slice and serve warm or cool completely on cooling rack. Wrap tightly when cooled.

2 loaves

SWEET 'N LIGHT APRICOT FRITTERS

	Crisco Shortening or Crisco Oil for deep frying	1	tablespoon Crisco Shortening, melted
1	can (16 or 17 ounces) unpeeled apricot halves, well drained	1	cup all-purpose flour
		2	tablespoons granulated sugar
		1	teaspoon baking powder
1	egg, lightly beaten	¼	teaspoon salt
⅔	cup milk		Confectioners sugar

1. Place apricots on paper towels. Pat dry.
2. Heat 2 to 3 inches Crisco Shortening or Crisco Oil to 365°F in deep fryer or deep saucepan.
3. Combine egg and milk in large bowl. Stir in 1 tablespoon melted shortening.
4. Combine flour, granulated sugar, baking powder and salt. Add to egg mixture. Stir just until dry ingredients are moistened.
5. Dip apricots in batter. Drain off excess. Fry, a few at a time, in shortening or oil. Fry about 4 minutes or until golden brown. Turn as needed for even browning. Remove with slotted metal spoon. Drain on paper towels. Roll in confectioners sugar. Serve warm.

Tip: Be sure the apricots are well drained, as the juice will dilute the batter.

6 to 8 servings

CRISPY CORN FRITTERS

	Crisco Shortening or Crisco	½	cup milk
	Oil for deep frying	2	teaspoons Crisco Shortening,
1	cup all-purpose flour		melted
1	teaspoon baking powder	1	package (10 ounces) frozen
1	teaspoon sugar		whole kernel corn, thawed,
1	teaspoon salt		drained and chopped
2	eggs, well beaten		Syrup

1. Heat 2 to 3 inches Crisco Shortening or Crisco Oil to 365°F in deep fryer or deep saucepan.
2. Combine flour, baking powder, sugar and salt in large bowl.
3. Combine eggs, milk and 2 teaspoons melted shortening in medium bowl. Stir in corn. Add to flour mixture. Stir just until dry ingredients are moistened.
4. Drop by tablespoonfuls, a few at a time, into shortening or oil. Fry 3 or 4 minutes or until golden brown. Turn as needed for even browning. Remove with slotted metal spoon. Drain on paper towels. Serve hot with syrup.

Tip: Use one can (12 ounces) whole kernel corn, drained, in place of frozen corn.

8 servings

CLAM FRITTERS

2	egg yolks, well beaten	1	teaspoon salt
½	cup milk	½	teaspoon pepper
½	teaspoon instant minced onion	¼	teaspoon dried thyme leaves, crushed
2	cans (6½ ounces each) minced clams, drained	2	egg whites, stiffly beaten
1	cup fine dry bread crumbs		Crisco Shortening or Crisco Oil for shallow frying
1	tablespoon snipped fresh parsley		Orange or lemon slices (optional)

1. Combine egg yolks, milk and onion in large bowl. Let stand 5 minutes.
2. Stir in clams, bread crumbs, parsley, salt, pepper and thyme. Fold in egg whites.
3. Heat ¼ inch Crisco Shortening or Crisco Oil to 365°F in deep skillet.
4. Drop batter by tablespoonfuls, a few at a time, into shortening or oil. Fry until golden brown. Turn once. Garnish with orange or lemon slices, if desired.

6 servings

CHICKEN CHEESE FRITTERS

Fritters

	Crisco Shortening or Crisco	1	cup milk
	Oil for deep frying	1	can (5 ounces) boned chicken
1½	cups all-purpose flour		or
1	tablespoon baking powder	½	cup chopped cooked chicken
¾	teaspoon salt		or turkey
1	egg, beaten	¼	cup finely chopped onion

Pimiento-Cheese Sauce

3	tablespoons Crisco Shortening	½	cup (2 ounces) shredded sharp
2	tablespoons all-purpose flour		processed American cheese
½	teaspoon salt	1	jar (2 ounces) diced
1½	cups milk		pimientos, drained

1. For fritters, heat 2 to 3 inches Crisco Shortening or Crisco Oil to 365°F in deep fryer or deep saucepan.
2. Combine flour, baking powder and salt in large bowl.
3. Combine egg, milk, chicken and chopped onion. Add to dry ingredients. Stir just until dry ingredients are moistened.
4. Drop by tablespoonfuls, a few at a time, into shortening or oil. Fry 3 to 4 minutes or until golden brown. Turn once.
5. Drain on paper towels. Serve hot with Pimento-Cheese Sauce.
6. For sauce, melt Crisco in medium saucepan. Stir in flour and salt. Add milk all at once. Cook and stir on low heat until mixture is thickened and bubbly. Stir in cheese and pimientos. Stir until cheese melts.

24 fritters

AUNT EMMA'S FRIED BREAD

1	package active dry yeast
1	cup warm water (110° to 115°F)
2	tablespoons sugar
1½	teaspoons salt
2	tablespoons Crisco Shortening
2½ - 3	cups all-purpose flour, divided
	Crisco Shortening or Crisco Oil for deep frying
	Cinnamon sugar

1. Sprinkle yeast over warm water in large bowl. Add sugar, salt, 2 tablespoons Crisco and 1½ cups flour. Blend at low speed of electric mixer until dry ingredients are moistened. Increase to medium speed. Beat 3 minutes. Stir in enough remaining flour to make soft dough.
2. Turn dough onto lightly floured surface. Knead until smooth and elastic. Place dough in greased deep bowl. Turn to bring greased surface to top. Cover. Let rise in warm place until doubled (about one hour).
3. Heat 2 to 3 inches Crisco Shortening or Crisco Oil to 365°F in deep fryer or deep saucepan.
4. Cut dough into 1-inch pieces. Stretch pieces slightly. Fry 1½ minutes or until golden brown. Turn once.
5. Drain on paper towels. Shake in bag with cinnamon sugar. Serve warm.

4 dozen pieces

Breakfast Dish

In 1983 when I was 79 years old, I went to Philadelphia for the Grand Lodge Convention and remained in the city after the convention was over in order to see some of the sights. When I came down for breakfast on the morning after the convention was finished, the waiter asked if I would like something special for breakfast. I said no, but he said that since everybody else had left, he would fix me a special breakfast. He brought me two pieces of crunchy whole wheat toast each topped with an "egg nest" and garnished with lean, crisp bacon. The "nest" was fluffy egg whites that had been lightly browned on the outside with an egg yolk nestled on top. I prepare this for my husband as a special treat on the weekends to break the monotony of our usual breakfast routine.

Violet J. Brown
Bakersfield, CA

Continued on next page

Mary McLeod Bethune: Two Ingredients to a Successful Life

Once when she was asked what it took to found Bethune-Cookman College, organize the National Council of Negro Women, preside over the Negro Division of the National Youth Administration, and to do all the other remarkable things she managed to do, Mary McLeod Bethune replied by saying, "It took faith in God and faith in myself." With this response she cited what she regarded as the two basic ingredients to a successful life. Around the McLeod household in Mayesville, SC, the reality of God was accepted uncritically and Mary Jane McLeod, as she was christened, recognized by age eight the value of believing and trusting unequivocally in a sovereign power. By allying herself with such power she believed that she could invite God to become intimately involved in her history. Such a holy alliance

SUNDAY SUGARED DOUGHNUTS

⅓	cup Crisco Shortening
⅓	cup sugar
1	teaspoon salt
1	cup milk, scalded
2	eggs
2½ - 3	cups all-purpose flour, divided
1	package active dry yeast
	Crisco Shortening or Crisco Oil for deep frying
	Granulated sugar

1. Combine Crisco, sugar and salt in large bowl. Pour in scalded milk. Stir until shortening is melted. Add eggs, one at a time, beating well after each addition.
2. Combine 2 cups flour and yeast in large bowl. Add milk mixture. Beat with spoon until smooth. Stir in enough remaining flour to make soft dough.
3. Turn dough onto lightly floured surface. Knead until smooth and elastic.
4. Place dough in greased deep bowl. Turn to bring greased surface to top.
5. Cover. Let rise in warm place until doubled (about 1 hour).
6. Punch down dough. Roll to ½-inch thickness on lightly floured surface. Cut with floured 3-inch doughnut cutter. Place doughnuts and holes on baking sheet. Cover. Let rise until doubled (about 30 minutes).
7. Heat Crisco Shortening or Crisco Oil to 365°F in deep fryer or deep saucepan.
8. Fry doughnuts and holes, 4 or 5 at a time, 2 minutes or until golden brown. Turn several times.
9. Remove. Drain on paper towels.
10. Shake a few doughnuts and holes at a time with sugar in paper bag.

1½ dozen

BREAKFAST PUFFS

Crisco Shortening or Crisco Oil for frying

1½	cups all-purpose flour
½	cup confectioners sugar
1	teaspoon baking powder
1	teaspoon salt
¾	teaspoon nutmeg
½	cup milk
½	cup water
¼	cup Crisco Oil
1½	teaspoons grated lemon peel
3	eggs
	Confectioners sugar

1. Heat 2 to 3 inches Crisco Shortening or Crisco Oil to 365°F in deep fryer or deep saucepan.
2. Combine flour, ½ cup confectioners sugar, baking powder, salt and nutmeg in small bowl.
3. Combine milk, water, ¼ cup Crisco Oil and lemon peel in medium saucepan. Heat to rolling boil on medium-high heat. Add flour mixture all at once. Beat with wooden spoon until mixture pulls away from sides of pan into a ball. Remove from heat. Cool slightly. Add eggs, one at a time, beating after each addition.
4. Fill measuring tablespoon with dough for each puff. Drop into shortening or oil. Fry 3 or 4 puffs at a time, 5 to 7 minutes, or until golden brown. Turn several times. Drain on paper towels. Sprinkle top of each puff with confectioners sugar.

32 puffs

Continued
would open the way for her to rise above the fact that she was born Black, female, and poor to fulfill her destiny as a leader of her race and nation. But her faith in God was only half the story. For she also recognized early on that faith in God without faith in one's self is meaningless. Faith in one's self, she believed, is the leaven that makes faith in God meaningful in tangible ways. As she saw it, faith in one's self is faith in God in action on behalf of self and others. Mary Bethune's faith in God made it possible for her to believe in herself. Because she had faith in herself she felt empowered by her faith in God to succeed in serving the cause of humanity. By all accounts, her life was a success because it was a blend of two basic ingredients: faith in God and faith in self.

Clarence G. Newsome
Dean of the School of Divinity
Howard University
Washington, DC

23

CORNSTICKS OR MUFFINS

1¼	cups yellow cornmeal
¾	cup all-purpose flour
1	tablespoon sugar
2½	teaspoons baking powder
½	teaspoon salt
1¼	cups low-fat buttermilk
1	egg, lightly beaten
2	tablespoons Butter Flavor Crisco

1. Heat oven to 425°F. Grease well 2 cornstick pans or 12 medium (about 2½ inches) muffin cups. Place in oven to heat.
2. Combine cornmeal, flour, sugar, baking powder and salt in medium bowl.
3. Combine buttermilk, egg and Butter Flavor Crisco. Add to dry ingredients. Stir just until dry ingredients are moistened. Spoon batter into cornstick pans or muffin cups, filling almost full.
4. Bake at 425°F. Cornsticks 15 to 18 minutes. Muffins 16 to 19 minutes.

14 cornsticks (5¼ to 5½-inches) or 12 muffins

Variations:
Bacon Cornbread: Add ½ cup cooked bacon bits in step #3.

Crackling Cornbread: Add 1 cup crumbled pork cracklings in step #3.

Hot Jalapeño Cornbread: Add ½ cup finely chopped jalapeño peppers and 1 cup grated sharp cheese in step #3.

Eating Hot Jalapeño Cornbread

The first time I ate Hot Jalapeño Cornbread was when I visited my friend Edith Peck in Athens, Tennessee. Upon my arrival, and after greeting me, she said, "I have something you will love!" We sat down to dinner and the Hot Jalapeño Cornbread was delicious! I was up early the next morning before anyone else looking around the kitchen for the Hot Jalapeño Cornbread. When I found it, I warmed it in the oven, put some butter on it, and ate it. It tasted better than the day before! When Edith arose, she asked, "What are you doing up so early?" I replied, "Eating Hot Jalapeño Cornbread!"

Annie Ree Muse-Gray
Holly Springs, MS

24

CORN MUFFINS

1	cup all-purpose flour	1	teaspoon salt
1	cup yellow cornmeal	1	egg
2	tablespoons sugar	1	cup milk
1	tablespoon plus 1 teaspoon baking powder	¼	cup Crisco Oil

1. Heat oven to 425°F. Grease twelve medium (2½-inch) muffin cups.
2. Combine flour, cornmeal, sugar, baking powder and salt in large bowl.
3. Beat egg in small bowl. Add milk and Crisco Oil. Stir. Add to flour mixture. Beat just until smooth with large spoon. Fill muffin cups ¾ full.
4. Bake at 425° for 12 to 15 minutes or until lightly browned.

12 muffins

Variation:
Corn Sticks: Grease corn stick pans. Heat in oven while preparing batter. Fill pans ¾ full. Bake at 425°F for 12 to 15 minutes.

20 corn sticks

CHILI-CHEESE CORNBREAD

1	cup yellow cornmeal	1½	cups shredded Cheddar cheese (about 6 ounces)
⅔	cup all-purpose flour		
2	teaspoons baking powder	1	can (8¾ ounces) whole kernel corn, drained
½	teaspoon salt		
¾	cup dairy sour cream	1	can (4 ounces) chopped green chilies, drained
2	eggs		
¼	cup Crisco Oil		

1. Heat oven to 400°F. Grease 9-inch square pan.
2. Combine cornmeal, flour, baking powder and salt in small bowl.
3. Combine sour cream, eggs and Crisco Oil in medium bowl. Stir well. Add cornmeal mixture, Cheddar cheese, corn and chilies. Mix well. Pour into pan.
4. Bake at 400°F for 30 to 35 minutes, or until toothpick inserted in center comes out clean. Cool 10 to 15 minutes. Cut into squares. Serve warm.

One 9-inch pan

SOUL BREAD

3	cups cornmeal	1	cup cold water
1	tablespoon sugar	1	cup all-purpose flour
1½	teaspoons salt	1¼	cups molasses
2½	cups boiling water	½	teaspoon baking soda
1	small sweet potato		

1. Combine cornmeal, sugar and salt in large bowl. Pour in boiling water. Beat with electric mixer until well mixed.
2. Boil sweet potato until tender. Peel while hot. Add to meal mixture. Beat 10 minutes. Add cold water. Beat well. Add flour and molasses. Beat well.
3. Cover. Place in warm, draft-free place overnight.
4. Heat oven to 250°F. Grease and flour 10-inch Bundt pan.
5. Stir baking soda into bread mixture. Pour in pan.
6. Bake at 250°F for 3 hours.
7. Remove from oven. Cover pan tightly with foil to steam bread. Cool at least 1 hour before removing from pan.

One loaf

HERITAGE RECIPE

SAUSAGE SCRAPPLE

1	cup cornmeal	All-purpose flour
1	cup cold water	Crisco Shortening or Crisco Oil
1	teaspoon salt	
4	cups boiling water	
½	pound seasoned sausage, cooked	

1. Combine cornmeal, cold water and salt.
2. Place boiling water in top of double boiler. Add cornmeal mixture slowly. Cook and stir until thickened. Cover. Steam over hot water 15 to 20 minutes. Stir frequently. Stir in sausage.
3. Rinse inside of loaf pan with water. Fill with scrapple. Cool. Cover. Refrigerate.
4. Unmold. Cut into ¼-inch slices. Flour both sides.
5. Heat Crisco Shortening or Crisco Oil in large skillet on medium heat. Brown scrapple on both sides.

6 to 8 servings

JOHNNY CAKES

1	egg	1	teaspoon baking soda
⅓	cup sugar	1	cup all-purpose flour
¼	cup Butter Flavor Crisco,	¾	cup cornmeal
	melted, divided	1	teaspoon salt
1	cup sour milk		Maple syrup, jam or honey

1. Combine egg, sugar and 1 tablespoon plus 1 teaspoon Butter Flavor Crisco in medium bowl. Stir in sour milk and baking soda. Add flour, cornmeal and salt. Stir just until dry ingredients are moistened. Cover. Let stand in cool place for 30 minutes.
2. Pour remaining shortening on griddle or in large skillet. Heat on medium heat. Spoon tablespoonfuls of batter onto griddle. Brown on one side. Turn. Brown on other side. Serve with syrup, jam or honey.

18 Johnny Cakes

HOE CAKES

¼	cup Crisco Shortening or	1¼	cups buttermilk
	Crisco Oil	1	egg, lightly beaten
1½	cups self-rising cornmeal	1	tablespoon Crisco Shortening,
¼	teaspoon baking soda		melted

1. Heat ¼ cup Crisco Shortening or Crisco Oil to 365°F in electric skillet or on medium-high heat in heavy skillet.
2. Combine cornmeal and baking soda in medium bowl. Add buttermilk, egg and one tablespoon melted shortening. Stir just until dry ingredients are moistened.
3. Pour ¼ cup batter into skillet for each hoe cake. Fry 1 or 2 minutes or until golden brown on each side. Add additional shortening, if necessary. Drain on paper towels. Serve immediately.

6 servings

HERITAGE RECIPE

BUTTERMILK HUSH PUPPIES

Crisco Shortening or Crisco Oil for deep frying
1 cup yellow cornmeal
½ cup all-purpose flour
1½ teaspoons baking soda
½ teaspoon salt
1 cup buttermilk
1 egg, beaten
¼ cup finely chopped onion

1. Heat 2 to 3 inches Crisco Shortening or Crisco Oil to 365°F in deep fryer or deep saucepan.
2. Combine cornmeal, flour, baking soda and salt in large bowl. Stir in buttermilk, egg and onion. Mix well.
3. Drop by teaspoonfuls, a few at a time, into shortening or oil. Fry 2 minutes or until dark golden brown. Turn as needed for even browning. Remove with slotted metal spoon. Drain on paper towels. Serve immediately.

Tip: Substitute cornmeal mix for the cornmeal, salt and baking soda.

8 servings

Fried Corn Cakes

When I was a little girl, I used to make hush puppies for the whole family—only back then they were called fried corn cakes. We would have them for break-fast and dinner because they were quick and easy to make. I was only 5 when I started cooking. That's why I cooked the fried corn cakes—they were simple enough that I didn't need any help! I still love to cook, especially hush puppies. Whenever I do make them I remember when I was a little girl making them for my family.

Mrs. Lucille J. Gayle
National President
Chums, Inc.
Washington, DC

SOUPS & SALADS

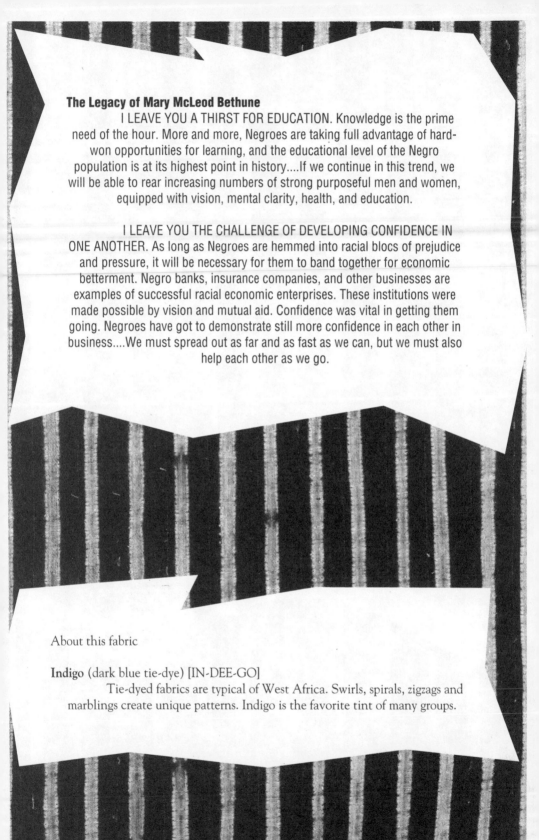

The Legacy of Mary McLeod Bethune

I LEAVE YOU A THIRST FOR EDUCATION. Knowledge is the prime need of the hour. More and more, Negroes are taking full advantage of hard-won opportunities for learning, and the educational level of the Negro population is at its highest point in history....If we continue in this trend, we will be able to rear increasing numbers of strong purposeful men and women, equipped with vision, mental clarity, health, and education.

I LEAVE YOU THE CHALLENGE OF DEVELOPING CONFIDENCE IN ONE ANOTHER. As long as Negroes are hemmed into racial blocs of prejudice and pressure, it will be necessary for them to band together for economic betterment. Negro banks, insurance companies, and other businesses are examples of successful racial economic enterprises. These institutions were made possible by vision and mutual aid. Confidence was vital in getting them going. Negroes have got to demonstrate still more confidence in each other in business....We must spread out as far and as fast as we can, but we must also help each other as we go.

About this fabric

Indigo (dark blue tie-dye) [IN-DEE-GO]
Tie-dyed fabrics are typical of West Africa. Swirls, spirals, zigzags and marblings create unique patterns. Indigo is the favorite tint of many groups.

NOVELLA'S OKRA SOUP

1	cup chopped onion	1	pound beef neck bones
10	bacon slices, cut into 1-inch pieces	¾	cup barbecue sauce
		1½	teaspoons salt
5	cups water	1¼	pounds okra, sliced
1	can (28 ounces) tomatoes		

1. Sauté onion and bacon in stockpot.
2. Add water, tomatoes, bones, barbecue sauce and salt. Bring to a boil. Cover. Simmer 1½ hours.
3. Add okra. Simmer 30 minutes.

16 servings

FRISCO SOUP

1	can (10½ ounces) condensed onion soup	1	package (10 ounces) frozen Italian vegetables in sauce
1¼	cups water	1	tablespoon butter or margarine
1	bay leaf		
1	cup cooked elbow macaroni		
1½	pounds cod, rock cod or pollock fillets, cut in 1-inch cubes		

1. Combine soup, water and bay leaf in large saucepan. Bring to a boil. Add macaroni and fish. Cover. Simmer 4 minutes. Add vegetables. Increase heat and bring to a boil. Stir. Add butter. Cover. Lower heat to simmer.
2. Cook 5 minutes or until vegetables are tender. Remove bay leaf before serving.

6 to 8 servings

Christmas Eve Nostalgia

Family get-togethers have always been a major event for my family. As a child in Louisiana, I looked forward to Sundays and major holidays. But the time I enjoyed most of all was Christmas Eve and our traditional dinner. I remember each one even better than I remember the toys and gifts I received. About dusk each Christmas Eve, my whole family, including aunts, uncles and cousins, would gather at Mama Esther and Papa Jesse's (my grandparents) home. My mother would bring cornbread; one aunt would bring bread pudding. My other aunt would bring her famous foot high cake.

After Papa Jesse sent up a prayer that was as long as any sermon and blessed everybody and everything that had anything to do with the meal, Mama Esther's piping hot gumbo was served. It had an aroma that made you want to eat for days.

Continued on next page

GENEVA'S QUICK GUMBO

1	can (14½ ounces) chicken broth
1	can (14½ ounces) tomatoes
3	cups water
1	small bay leaf
1	tablespoon dried thyme leaves
2	tablespoons butter or margarine
1	cup chopped onion
¾	cup chopped green bell pepper
1	tablespoon minced parsley
3	tablespoons filé powder (or more according to taste)
1	pound sliced chicken breast (other parts may be used)
3	hot links or Polish sausage, sliced
	Salt, pepper and garlic powder
2	cups frozen sliced okra
3	cups cooked rice
2	cups frozen baby shrimp, cooked
	Hot pepper sauce (optional)

1. Combine chicken broth, tomatoes, water, bay leaf, thyme, butter, onion, green pepper, parsley, filé powder, chicken, sausage, salt, pepper and garlic powder in stockpot or large Dutch oven. Cook 30 minutes.

2. Add okra. Cook according to time on package (8 to 10 minutes). Add rice and shrimp. Let stand 5 minutes. Remove bay leaf before serving. (If you prefer, cook rice separately and pour the gumbo over it.) Season with hot pepper sauce, if desired.

8 to 10 servings

CORN CHOWDER

8 - 10   ears of corn
1   smoked turkey wing
8   cups chicken broth
1   cup diced celery
1   cup diced carrots
1   cup diced potato
1   cup finely chopped onion
  Salt and freshly ground pepper to taste
1½ - 2   cups cream
  Chopped fresh parsley

1. Slice corn kernels into bowl. Scrape remaining part of kernels and milk from cob with the back of knife scraping downward.
2. Sauté turkey wing until done in large kettle or pot. Remove turkey wing. Remove meat from bone. Cut in small pieces.
3. Add chicken broth, corn, celery, carrots, potatoes and onions to kettle. Cover. Bring slowly to a boil. Reduce heat. Simmer slowly until vegetables are tender, about 25 to 30 minutes. Season with salt and pepper. Add cream. Reheat, but do not boil. Garnish each serving with turkey bits and chopped parsley.

6 servings

Patti LaBelle, Entertainer

Continued

After dinner, Papa Jesse would start to pick his guitar, Mama Esther would join in with her tambourine and one of my uncles would lead the singing. All the grandchildren joined in the dancing. Each year, though some of the main characters are no longer with us, we still have Christmas Eve dinner, only now I make the gumbo and my sister makes the cornbread.

Mrs. Bobbie W. Moorehead
NCNW Executive Committee-at-large
Houston, TX

33

BLACK-EYED PEA SOUP

2	smoked ham hocks	½	teaspoon salt
5	cups water	½	teaspoon pepper
1½	cups dried black-eyed peas	⅔	cup evaporated milk
1	cup chopped onion	1	tablespoon all-purpose flour
½	cup chopped celery		

1. Clean ham hocks thoroughly. Place water and ham hocks in large Dutch oven or kettle. Simmer for 45 minutes.
2. Wash and sort peas. Place in large bowl. Cover with warm water. Soak 45 minutes. Pour water off peas. Add peas, onion, celery, salt and pepper to ham hocks. Boil on medium heat 2 hours, or until meat and peas are tender. Stir occasionally.
3. Remove ham hocks. Cut meat from bone. Discard rind, fat and bone. Shred meat. Return meat to soup.
4. Combine small amount evaporated milk and flour to make paste. Stir in remaining milk gradually. Stir until well blended. Add to soup. Cook and stir until mixture comes to a boil and thickens.

6 to 8 servings

COUNTRY CHICKEN CHOWDER

2	tablespoons Butter Flavor Crisco	1	can (15 ounces) cream-style corn
1	medium onion, chopped	1	cup water
2	cans (10¾ ounces each) condensed chicken noodle soup	1	can (5 ounces) evaporated milk
		½	teaspoon white pepper
2	cups diced, cooked chicken	2	tablespoons chopped parsley

1. Melt Butter Flavor Crisco in large saucepan on medium heat. Add onion. Sauté until soft.
2. Stir in soup, chicken, corn, water, evaporated milk and pepper. Bring to a boil. Reduce heat. Simmer 10 minutes.
3. Serve sprinkled with parsley.

8 to 10 servings

SWEET POTATO SMOKED TURKEY BISQUE

3	pounds fresh sweet potatoes (4 medium to large)	4	quarts chicken stock
1	cup (2 sticks) unsalted butter, divided	1	pound smoked turkey, diced
		¼	cup garlic sauce
1	cup diced onion	4	dashes hot pepper sauce
1	cup diced celery	1	tablespoon minced fresh thyme
1	cup diced green bell pepper		Salt
3	tablespoons minced garlic		Pepper
4	ounces all-purpose flour		

1. Heat oven to 350°F.
2. Bake potatoes for 35 minutes or until tender. Cool and peel.
3. Melt ½ cup butter in medium saucepan. Add onion, celery, green pepper and garlic. Sauté until done as desired.
4. Melt remaining ½ cup butter in small saucepan or skillet. Add flour. Cook and stir until golden brown to make roux.
5. Place stock in stockpot or large Dutch oven. Bring to a boil on high heat. Add smoked turkey and sautéed vegetables. Reduce heat to medium. Cook 15 minutes.
6. Add roux. Mix until smooth. Cook 10 minutes.
7. Purée half the sweet potatoes. Add to soup along with garlic sauce, hot pepper sauce and thyme. Cook 10 minutes.
8. Dice remaining sweet potatoes. Add to soup. Season with salt and pepper.

16 to 20 servings

Joseph Randall, Chef Instructor
School of Hotel and Management
California State Polytechnic University
President, National United Culinary Association

PEANUT BUTTER BISQUE

⅓	cup Butter Flavor Crisco	½	teaspoon paprika
½	cup diced green bell pepper	½	teaspoon seasoned salt
½	cup diced celery	½	teaspoon salt
½	cup diced onion	½	teaspoon white pepper
3	tablespoons all-purpose flour	1	cup half and half
4	cups chicken broth	1	cup chopped green onions
1	cup peanut butter		

1. Melt Butter Flavor Crisco in large saucepan. Add green pepper, celery and onion. Cook on medium heat until tender.
2. Spoon cooked vegetables into blender or food processor. Liquefy. Return to saucepan. Add flour. Stir until well blended. Add broth slowly. Cook and stir on medium heat until well blended and thickened. Stir in peanut butter, paprika, seasoned salt, salt and pepper. Mix well. Reduce heat to low. Stir in half and half. Do not boil. Serve garnished with green onions.

6 servings

CODFISH GUMBO

2	tablespoons Crisco Shortening or Crisco Oil	1	can (28 ounces) tomatoes
		1½	cups frozen corn
½	pound fresh okra, sliced	¼	teaspoon black pepper
1	medium onion, sliced	⅛	teaspoon cayenne pepper
2	cloves garlic, minced	1½	pounds cod steaks
1	large zucchini, sliced		Hot cooked rice

1. Heat Crisco Shortening or Crisco Oil in large saucepan. Add okra. Sauté on medium heat 2 minutes.
2. Add onion and garlic. Sauté 5 minutes.
3. Add zucchini and undrained tomatoes. Heat on low 5 minutes.
4. Add corn, black pepper and cayenne. Lay cod steaks on top of vegetable mixture, spooning mixture over them. Cook gently 5 to 10 minutes or until the fish is done.
5. Serve immediately over rice.

4 servings

SHRIMP BISQUE

Stock

	Heads and shells from	1	rib celery with leaves
	2 pounds raw shrimp	½	lemon
8	cups water	2	cloves
½	cup dry white wine	1	sprig parsley
1	carrot, cut in thirds	1	teaspoon salt
1	onion, quartered	¼	teaspoon cayenne pepper

Soup

3	tablespoons Butter Flavor Crisco	¼	teaspoon dried thyme leaves
		2	pounds shrimp
⅔	cup finely chopped onion	2	tablespoons tomato paste
½	cup finely chopped carrot	1	cup dry white wine
½	cup finely chopped celery	6	cups shrimp stock
1	tablespoon finely chopped fresh parsley	½	cup rice
		½	cup whipping cream
½	bay leaf	¾	teaspoon salt
½	teaspoon dried tarragon leaves	¼	cup Madeira wine

1. For stock, place heads and shells of shrimp in stock pot with water, wine, carrot, onion, celery, lemon, cloves, parsley, salt and cayenne. Simmer one hour, skimming foam from top. Strain and measure 6 cups stock.
2. For soup, melt Butter Flavor Crisco in large skillet. Add onion, carrot, celery, parsley, bay leaf, tarragon and thyme. Cover. Cook 10 minutes. Stir in shrimp, tomato paste and white wine. Cover. Cook 5 minutes. Remove 10 to 12 shrimp and chop coarsely for garnish.
3. Combine stock and rice in large saucepan. Cover. Cook 20 minutes. Add shrimp mixture. Cover. Cook 10 minutes. Remove bay leaf. Purée small batches at a time in blender or food processor. Add cream, salt and Madeira wine. Heat. Garnish with shrimp.

8 servings

CREOLE CHICKEN GUMBO

Stock

3½ - 4	pounds chicken pieces	1	medium onion, quartered
3	quarts water	1	bay leaf
2	outer ribs celery, with leaves	1	teaspoon salt
1	carrot, cut in thirds		

Gumbo

⅓	cup Crisco Shortening or Crisco Oil	½	teaspoon dried marjoram leaves
½	cup all-purpose flour	½	teaspoon dried basil leaves
1	pound okra, washed and cut in ¼-inch pieces	1	can (14½ ounces) whole tomatoes
1	cup chopped onion	½	pound ham, cubed
¾	cup chopped celery	1	pound hot smoked sausage, sliced
½	cup chopped green bell pepper		
½	cup chopped green onions	1	teaspoon Worcestershire sauce
2	cloves garlic, pressed		Salt
¼	cup chopped fresh parsley		Black pepper
1	bay leaf		Cayenne pepper
¾	teaspoon dried thyme leaves		Hot pepper sauce
			Steamed rice

1. For stock, place chicken, water, celery, carrot, onion, bay leaf and salt in large Dutch oven or kettle. Bring to a boil. Simmer 25 minutes, skimming foam and fat from top. Remove meat from bones and reserve. Return bones to stock. Continue simmering.
2. For gumbo, heat Crisco Shortening or Crisco Oil in large Dutch oven or kettle. Add flour gradually. Cook and stir until medium brown. Add okra, onion, celery, green pepper. Cook and stir until okra is crisp-tender. Add green onions, garlic, parsley, bay leaf, thyme, marjoram and basil, undrained tomatoes, ham and chicken meat. Strain stock. Stir slowly into gumbo. Cook sausage. Drain well. Add to gumbo. Simmer 1½ hours, stirring occasionally. Add Worcestershire sauce, salt, pepper, cayenne and hot pepper sauce. Remove bay leaf before serving.
3. To serve, spoon desired amount of rice into individual soup bowls. Ladle gumbo over rice.

Note: Use 2 packages (10 ounces each) frozen okra if fresh is not available. Make ahead and freeze, if desired.

18 one cup servings

SHRIMP GUMBO

2	tablespoons Crisco Oil, divided
1	tablespoon plus 1½ teaspoons all-purpose flour
1	pound shrimp, shelled and deveined
1	cup chopped celery
2	onions, chopped
1½	pounds fresh okra, sliced
1	can (14½ ounces) tomatoes
4	cups water
2	bay leaves
	Salt and pepper
1	can (6 ounces) tomato paste
½	pound lobster meat
	Hot cooked rice

1. Combine 1 tablespoon plus 1½ teaspoons Crisco Oil and flour in medium skillet. Stir constantly until rich dark brown. Stir in shrimp. Cook a few minutes. Set aside.

2. Heat remaining 1½ teaspoons oil in large saucepan on medium heat. Add celery and onions. Cook until soft and transparent. Add okra. Cook until okra ceases to rope, about 30 minutes. Add undrained tomatoes, water, bay leaves, salt and pepper. Stir in shrimp mixture. Cover. Simmer 30 minutes, adding tomato paste after 15 minutes. Add lobster meat. Remove bay leaves before serving. Serve in flat bottom bowls over rice.

5 servings

Homemade Love

Growing up in Mobile, Alabama, gumbo was a part of every family gathering. We ate it in the summer. We ate it in the fall. Most of all, we enjoyed gumbo on those rare cold winter days when the combination of rich stock, tomatoes, okra, sausage and seafood served over rice would give you a feeling that can only be described as "homemade love."

Alexis Herman
National Vice President of NCNW
Washington, DC

PUMPKIN SOUP

½ - 1	pound smoked meat of your choice (pork, neckbones, turkey)
1½ - 2	quarts chicken consommé (refrigerate before using and skim off fat)
2	pounds fresh pumpkin, peeled and cut up
2 - 3	sticks celery, cut up
1	large onion, diced
2	cloves garlic, minced
½	cup chopped fresh parsley
3	carrots, thinly sliced
¾	cup green beans, cut up (or other vegetable of your choice)
1	cup small size dried pasta (shells or elbow macaroni)
1	cup shredded cabbage

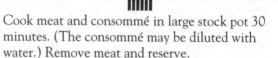

1. Cook meat and consommé in large stock pot 30 minutes. (The consommé may be diluted with water.) Remove meat and reserve.
2. Add pumpkin, celery, onion, garlic and parsley to pot. Cook 30 to 40 minutes until the pumpkin is done. Remove from heat. Cool.
3. Purée in blender. Pour purée back into pot adding more consommé if too thick.
4. Bring to a boil. Add carrots, green beans and pasta. Cook until pasta is tender.
5. Slice or cut up meat. Return to mixture. Add cabbage. Cook 10 minutes or until cabbage is done but still crunchy.

12 servings

Lower Thirteen

Once when Mrs. Bethune was travelling on a train during the dark days of segregation, she was seated in what we called "Lower 13" where any Black traveler with a first class ticket was placed. It was also a time when there were those who would not call a Black woman Missus or address her with respect. The conductor came to her and asked, "Auntie, can you make good biscuits?" Mrs. Bethune said that she looked up and replied, "I am an advisor to President Roosevelt. I am the founder of a four year accredited college. I am an organizer of women. I am the organizer and founder of the National Council of Negro Women. I am considered a leader among women. And, I make good biscuits."

Dr. Dorothy I. Height
NCNW President/CEO
Washington, DC

AMBROSIA

18 - 20   medium size navel oranges
1   can (15 ounces) pineapple chunks
1   package (7 ounces) shredded coconut
1   cup pecan pieces
       Sugar, to taste
3 - 4   bananas, sliced
½   cup cherries, pitted

1. Peel oranges with knife, removing all membrane and reserving juice. Cut oranges into small chunks over large bowl.
2. Add undrained pineapple. Stir in coconut and nuts.
3. Add sugar to taste. Add banana slices and cherries. Refrigerate overnight.

15 servings

PINK COLE SLAW

1   medium head cabbage
1   small fresh beet, peeled and finely shredded
1   small onion, finely grated (optional)
2 - 3   carrots, coarsely shredded
1   teaspoon sugar
1   teaspoon salt
¾   cup mayonnaise
¾   cup dairy sour cream
2   tablespoons lemon juice
⅛   teaspoon pepper

1. Quarter and core cabbage. Slice into thin slivers. Place in large bowl. Cover with ice water. Refrigerate one hour. Drain well.
2. Add beet, onion (if used), carrots, sugar and salt to drained cabbage. Toss.
3. Combine mayonnaise, sour cream, lemon juice and pepper in small bowl. Stir well. Pour over cabbage mixture. Toss to coat vegetables. Cover. Refrigerate several hours.

10 to 12 servings

Making Ambrosia

Cracking pecans and walnuts, grating fresh coconut, and crushing fresh pineapples for holiday ambrosia—oh what fun! The walnuts were sent to us by Grandma Frances Gurley Ross from Gurley, Alabama and the pecans that our neighbors shared with us came from Georgia. Thanksgiving and Christmas holidays were enhanced by sharing the ambrosia with everybody who visited us on those holidays. Our vegetables came from the home garden which was the pride and joy of my mother, Evangeline Ross Smith. And sharing vegetables from home gardens was a way of life in our neighborhood in Birmingham, Alabama.

Dr. Anne Smith
Cunningham
Shaker Heights, OH

OLD SOUTH CABBAGE SLAW

¾	cup sugar	1	head cabbage (about 2 pounds), shredded
¾	cup cider vinegar		
½	cup Crisco Oil	1	small red onion, peeled, halved and thinly sliced
2	teaspoons dry mustard		
1½	teaspoons celery seed, crushed	1	green bell pepper, coarsely chopped
½	teaspoon salt		
¼	teaspoon pepper		

1. Combine sugar, vinegar and Crisco Oil in small non-aluminum saucepan. Bring to a boil on medium heat, stirring occasionally. Simmer 5 minutes. Stir in dry mustard, celery seed, salt and pepper. Cool 5 minutes.

2. Place cabbage, onion and green pepper in very large glass bowl. Add dressing. Toss to coat vegetables. Cover. Refrigerate at least 4 hours, stirring occasionally. Drain before serving.

10 to 12 servings

Note: Salad can be made up to two days in advance and refrigerated, covered.

CLASSIC POTATO SALAD

6	medium red potatoes (about 2 pounds)	⅓	cup chopped celery
		⅓	cup chopped onion
3	tablespoons Crisco Oil	2	hard-cooked eggs, chopped
2	tablespoons cider vinegar	2	tablespoons snipped fresh parsley
1	teaspoon freeze-dried chives		
½	teaspoon sugar	¾	cup mayonnaise
½	teaspoon salt	2	teaspoons prepared mustard
⅛	teaspoon pepper		

1. Cook potatoes until tender. Drain. Cool slightly. Peel and slice potatoes. Place in medium serving bowl.
2. Combine Crisco Oil, vinegar, chives, sugar, salt and pepper in small bowl. Stir until blended. Pour over potatoes. Cover. Refrigerate about 2 hours.
3. Add celery, onion, eggs and parsley. Mix well.
4. Combine mayonnaise and mustard in small bowl. Stir into potato mixture. Cover. Refrigerate at least 2 hours.

6 to 8 servings

KATIE'S KRAUT SALAD

1	cup sugar
½	cup white vinegar
1	can (16 ounces) sauerkraut, well drained
½	cup chopped green onions and tops
½	cup chopped green bell pepper
1	jar (2 ounces) diced pimiento
1	tablespoon celery seed
1	tablespoon mustard seed
	Dash ground cloves
½	cup Crisco Oil

1. Combine sugar and vinegar in small non-aluminum saucepan. Bring to a boil. Cool completely.
2. Combine sauerkraut, onions, green pepper, pimiento, celery seed, mustard seed, and cloves in large glass bowl. Toss until well mixed.
3. Add Crisco Oil. Toss well.
4. Add cooled sugar-vinegar mixture. Stir well.
5. Cover tightly. Refrigerate. Marinate 12 to 24 hours.

6 to 8 servings

Note: Increase or decrease vinegar for a more tart or milder flavor.

Persistence Pays Off

I tasted Kraut Salad several times at church gatherings and covered dish suppers before I could believe that it was really made from sauerkraut. An elderly lady who never measured ingredients always brought this dish and said that she used sauerkraut as a base and added a little of this and a little of that for flavor and seasoning. Gradually I put together the basic ingredients by asking about the dish at church gatherings and covered dish suppers. The elderly lady was rather possessive of this delightful recipe and passed before I had all the details but I had enough to piece together this tasty recipe that serves easily with family dinner meals whether the entrée is meat, fish or poultry. My family expects me to carry this dish to the Kinnard and Smith Family Reunions in Middle Tennessee every year as it is a real favorite among relatives.

Katie K. White
Grand Basileus
Sigma Gamma Rho
Sorority, Inc.
Brentwood, TN

EDIBLE RAG DOLLS

	Red and yellow food color	24	white asparagus spears
3	hard cooked eggs, peeled and halved lengthwise	6	small lettuce leaves
30	whole cloves		Alfalfa spouts (optional)
2	pounds chicken salad		Carrot curls (optional)

1. Combine red and yellow food color to make warm brown color. Use to color egg halves. Turn rounded side up. Insert whole cloves across widest part of each half to form "eyes" and "mouth".
2. Shape each doll on individual dinner plate. Place egg "head" at top of plate. Shape mounds of chicken salad into upper and lower "torso". Cut tip ends of asparagus spears into twelve 2-inch and twelve 4-inch lengths for "arms" and "legs". Tint in food color mixture. (Save remaining asparagus for other uses.) Make "hair" using alfalfa sprouts or carrot curls, if desired.

6 edible dolls

Jeri Turner, Food Stylist

JESSICA'S OKRA SALAD

½	pound small fresh okra pods	8	scallions with some top, minced
	Salt		
1	head Boston lettuce, torn into bite-size pieces		Vinaigrette dressing (see recipe)

1. Wash okra. Remove tops and tails.
2. Pour water into medium saucepan. Add salt. Bring to a boil. Add okra to blanch. Drain. Refrigerate.
3. Place lettuce in salad bowl. Add okra, scallions and vinaigrette. Toss.

4 servings

HERITAGE RECIPE

CORN RELISH SALAD

¾	cup sugar	1	can (16 ounces) sauerkraut, drained and pressed to remove excess liquid
½	cup Crisco Oil		
¼	cup white vinegar		
½	teaspoon celery seed	½	cup chopped green bell pepper
¼	teaspoon whole mustard seed	⅓	cup chopped onion
1	can (17 ounces) whole kernel corn, drained	1	jar (2 ounces) diced pimiento, drained

1. Combine sugar, Crisco Oil, vinegar, celery seed and mustard seed in medium serving bowl. Stir until sugar dissolves.
2. Add corn, sauerkraut, green pepper, onion and pimiento. Mix well. Cover. Refrigerate at least 8 hours or overnight. Drain. Stir before serving.

6 to 8 servings

MEDLEY OF GREENS WITH STRAWBERRIES

3	tablespoons unsweetened orange juice	½	cup vertically sliced purple onion
1	tablespoon fresh mint	½	cup alfalfa sprouts
1	tablespoon lemon juice	¼	cup (1 ounce) finely shredded Gruyère cheese
1	teaspoon sugar		
2	cups fresh strawberry halves		
2	cups packed torn Bibb lettuce (about 2 heads)		

1. Combine orange juice, mint, lemon juice and sugar in medium bowl. Add strawberries. Toss gently.
2. Combine lettuce, onion and sprouts in large bowl. Toss gently. Add strawberry mixture. Toss gently.
3. Sprinkle with Gruyère cheese.

4 servings

The Honorable Maxine Waters, Member of the U.S. Congress

Bethune Vignette

Recalling the frequent visits Dr. Mary McLeod Bethune spent with Doctors John and Vada Watson Sommerville in their Los Angeles home, Doris Howard, the couple's daughter and now a retired educator who was a teenager at the time, remembers Dr. Bethune as an ideal house guest.

She was an early riser, prayed aloud, liked her coffee piping hot, also Cream of Wheat or oatmeal. She preferred her pancakes small, light and fluffy with generous portions of butter and pure maple syrup.

She loved food, simply prepared but good food, Howard recalls. She had her coffee in bed, arose, bathed, dressed and came downstairs for a full-course breakfast at 8:00 a.m. Breakfast consisted of the aforementioned cereal or pancakes, fresh squeezed orange juice, one slice of crisp fried bacon, and in lieu of the pancakes, one slice of wheat toast. In earlier years she "made do" with warmed-over biscuits,

Continued on next page

BETHUNE FRUIT SALAD

Fruit Mixture

1	cup cubed cantaloupe (½-inch cubes)
1	cup cubed honeydew melon (½-inch cubes)
1	cup cubed fresh pineapple (½-inch cubes)
2	peaches, sliced
½	pound grapes, whole or halved lengthwise
2	oranges, peeled and sliced
1	can mandarin oranges, drained
2	bananas, sliced

Sauce

1	carton (16 ounces) dairy sour cream
1	cup firmly packed brown sugar
	Juice of 1 orange
	Juice of ½ lemon
3	tablespoons pineapple juice
1	teaspoon cinnamon

Garnish

4 - 6 maraschino cherries (optional)

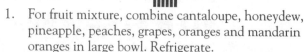

1. For fruit mixture, combine cantaloupe, honeydew, pineapple, peaches, grapes, oranges and mandarin oranges in large bowl. Refrigerate.
2. For sauce, combine sour cream, brown sugar, orange juice, lemon juice, pineapple juice and cinnamon in medium bowl. Refrigerate.
3. To serve, add bananas to fruit mixture. Spoon into individual dishes. Top with sauce. Garnish with maraschino cherries.

14 to 16 servings

Variation: May substitute mayonnaise or salad dressing for the sauce.

Delia Johnson, Caterer
Johnson's Catering

HERITAGE RECIPE

TUNA PASTA SALAD WITH HERB VINAIGRETTE

4	tablespoons Crisco Oil, divided
3	tablespoons red wine vinegar
1	clove garlic, finely minced
1	teaspoon dried basil leaves
¼	teaspoon dried oregano leaves
2½	cups uncooked small pasta shells or rotini
½	teaspoon salt
½	pound fresh green beans, trimmed, cut into 2-inch lengths
1½	cups broccoli flowerets
1	sweet red or green bell pepper, cut into thin 2-inch strips
1	can (6½ ounces) water packed white tuna, drained

1. Combine 3 tablespoons Crisco Oil, vinegar, garlic, basil and oregano in container with tight fitting lid. Shake well.
2. Cook pasta according to package directions. Drain well. Pour into large bowl. Toss with remaining 1 tablespoon oil.
3. Boil 2 quarts water in large pan. Add salt and beans. Boil 2 minutes. Add broccoli. Bring water back to boiling. Boil 3 minutes. Drain well.
4. Add beans, broccoli, green pepper and tuna to pasta. Shake dressing. Pour over salad. Toss to coat.

8 servings

Continued

molasses and/or leftovers, Bethune often confided to the Somervilles. Since she ate such a hearty breakfast, Dr. Bethune's lunch was usually a light one, consisting mainly of seasonal fruits: melons, berries, bananas, grapes and oranges. When visiting California she looked forward to having the honeydew and casaba melons, and the huge strawberries that grow profusely there. Lamb with mint jelly was Dr. Bethune's favorite entrée. Roast chicken was next and of course all kinds of seafood. She liked greens, collards, turnips, mustards and kale—cooked south-ern style—with salt pork or ham hocks; but she was exception-ally fond of carrots, string beans, rutaba-gas and asparagus. For dessert, she preferred homemade apple pie, apple Brown Betty, sweet potato pie. or assorted fruits with sour cream topping.

Libby Clark, Food Editor
The Los Angeles Sentinel
Los Angeles, CA

JASMINE'S PARTY TUNA SALAD

Salad

2	cups elbow or shell macaroni, cooked, rinsed and drained	2	cans (6½ ounces each) tuna fish
		10	hard cooked eggs, chopped

Dressing

1	cup salad dressing or mayonnaise	Garlic powder
¼	cup sweet pickle relish	Onion powder
2	tablespoons prepared mustard	Salt
2	tablespoons grated Parmesan cheese	Pepper

Garnish

¾	cup cooked bacon bits	Paprika

1. For salad, combine macaroni, tuna and eggs in large bowl.
2. For dressing, combine salad dressing, pickle relish, mustard and cheese in small bowl. Season with garlic powder, onion powder, salt and pepper. Add to salad. Toss well.
3. For garnish, sprinkle top with bacon and paprika. Refrigerate.

10 to 16 servings

CIDERED APPLE MOLD

1¾	cups apple cider or apple juice, divided	¾	cup diced, unpeeled Red Delicious apple
1	package (4 serving size) lemon flavor gelatin	¾	cup diced, unpeeled Golden Delicious apple
¼	teaspoon salt	1	can (8 ounces) pineapple tidbits, drained
¾	cup seedless white or red grapes	½	cup walnut pieces
		¼	cup finely chopped celery

1. Spray inside of 5-cup mold with cooking spray.
2. Heat 1 cup cider to boiling. Pour over gelatin and salt in medium bowl. Stir until dissolved. Stir in remaining ¾ cup cider. Refrigerate until partially set.
3. Fold in grapes, red and golden apples, pineapple, nuts and celery. Spoon into mold. Refrigerate until firm.

6 to 8 servings

CHILLED CHICKEN RICE SALAD

3½	cups cooked white, brown or wild rice, chilled	1	tablespoon sliced pimiento
2	cups diced, cooked chicken	⅔	cup Crisco Oil
⅓	cup chopped green bell pepper	2	tablespoons red wine vinegar
¼	cup finely chopped almonds	½	teaspoon salt
2	tablespoons snipped fresh parsley	¼	teaspoon pepper

1. Combine rice, chicken, green pepper, nuts, parsley and pimiento in medium serving bowl.
2. Combine Crisco Oil, vinegar, salt and pepper in small bowl. Mix well. Pour desired amount over salad mixture. Toss to coat. Refrigerate, covered, at least 2 hours. Stir before serving.

4 to 6 servings

CATFISH SALAD

2	catfish fillets, cut into 1-inch cubes	¼	cup balsamic or red wine vinegar
1	sweet red or yellow bell pepper, roasted and cut into strips	1	head Boston lettuce, torn into bite-size pieces
1	small red onion, sliced and separated into rings	2	cups arugula or romaine, torn into bite-size pieces
1	tablespoon fresh dill, chopped	4	strips bacon, cooked and crumbled
¼	cup Crisco Oil	3	ounces blue cheese, crumbled Salt and pepper

1. Place catfish cubes in skillet. Add water to cover. Simmer 5 to 7 minutes or until catfish flakes easily. Drain.
2. Combine catfish, pepper strips, onion rings, dill, Crisco Oil and vinegar in large bowl. Cover. Marinate one hour.
3. Toss with lettuce, arugula, bacon and blue cheese just before serving. Add salt and pepper to taste.

4 servings

BLUEBERRY-LEMON LAYER SALAD

Lemon Layer

½	cup boiling water	1	cup dairy sour cream
1	package (4 serving size) lemon flavor gelatin	1	can (8 ounces) crushed pineapple

Blueberry Layer

½	cup boiling water	1	cup cold water
1	package (4 serving size) strawberry flavor gelatin	1	can (16 ounces) blueberries, rinsed and drained

1. Spray inside of 6-cup gelatin mold lightly with cooking spray.
2. For lemon layer, pour boiling water over gelatin in medium bowl. Stir until dissolved. Stir in sour cream and undrained pineapple. Pour into mold. Refrigerate until almost firm (about 35 to 45 minutes).
3. For blueberry layer, pour boiling water over gelatin in medium bowl. Stir until dissolved. Stir in cold water. Refrigerate until partially set. Fold in blueberries. Spoon over lemon layer in mold. Refrigerate until firm.

8 to 10 servings

COLESLAW SOUFFLÉ

¾	cup boiling water		Dash pepper
1	package (4 serving size) lemon flavor gelatin	2	cups chopped cabbage
		¼	cup diced celery
¼	cup cold water	2	tablespoons minced green bell pepper
½	cup mayonnaise		
2	tablespoons cider vinegar	1	tablespoon minced onion
¼	teaspoon salt	¼	teaspoon celery seed

1. Spray inside of 5-cup gelatin mold lightly with cooking spray.
2. Pour boiling water over gelatin in medium bowl. Stir until dissolved. Add cold water. Stir in mayonnaise, vinegar, salt and pepper. Beat until well blended. Refrigerate until partially set.
3. Beat gelatin until fluffy. Fold in cabbage, celery, green pepper, onion and celery seed. Spoon into mold. Refrigerate until firm.

6 to 8 servings

FOUNDER'S LUNCHEON SALAD

2	tablespoons unflavored gelatin	1	cup mayonnaise
¾	cup cold water, divided	1	cup diced celery
1	can (10¾ ounces) condensed tomato soup	1	tablespoon minced onion
		1	tablespoon lemon juice
1	can (6½ ounces) tuna	1	teaspoon salt
3	packages (3 ounces each) cream cheese, diced		

1. Spray 4 to 5-cup ring mold with cooking spray.
2. Soften gelatin in ¼ cup cold water.
3. Combine soup and remaining ½ cup water in medium saucepan. Stir to combine. Heat until mixture comes to a boil.
4. Add gelatin to hot soup. Stir until dissolved. Refrigerate until thickened. Stir in tuna, cream cheese, mayonnaise, celery, onion, lemon juice and salt. Pour into 4 to 5-cup ring mold. Refrigerate until firm. Unmold. Garnish as desired.

6 to 8 servings

MYSTERY TOMATO MOLD

Mold

1	package (6 serving size) raspberry flavor gelatin	2	cans (14½ ounces) stewed tomatoes
¾	cup boiling water	1½	teaspoons lemon juice
		4	dashes hot pepper sauce

Horseradish Salad Dressing

1	cup dairy sour cream	½	teaspoon salt
1	tablespoon prepared horseradish		

1. Spray 4 to 5-cup mold with cooking spray.
2. For mold, dissolve gelatin in boiling water in medium bowl.
3. Mash undrained stewed tomatoes. Add to gelatin. Stir in lemon juice and pepper sauce. Pour into mold. Refrigerate until firm.
4. For dressing, combine sour cream, horseradish and salt. Stir until well blended.
5. Unmold gelatin. Serve with horseradish sauce.

6 to 8 servings

MOLDED CHEF'S SALAD

2	packages (4 serving size each) lemon or lime flavor gelatin	¾	cup thin Swiss or processed American cheese strips
1	teaspoon salt	¼	cup sliced scallions or chopped red onion
2	cups boiling water		
1	cup cold water	½	green bell pepper, cut in thin strips
3	tablespoons cider vinegar		
¾	cup thin cooked ham strips		

1. Spray 5-cup mold with cooking spray.
2. Dissolve gelatin and salt in boiling water in medium bowl. Add cold water and vinegar. Chill until thickened.
3. Fold ham, cheese, scallions and green pepper into gelatin. Pour into mold. Refrigerate until firm. Unmold. Garnish as desired.

5 to 6 servings

VINAIGRETTE DRESSING

¾	cup Crisco Oil	½	teaspoon salt
⅓	cup red wine vinegar	¼	teaspoon dry mustard
1	tablespoon snipped fresh parsley	¼	teaspoon pepper
1	teaspoon Worcestershire sauce	1	clove garlic, minced

1. Combine all ingredients in jar. Cover tightly and shake until blended.
2. Store, covered, in refrigerator. Shake before serving.

About 1 cup

Variations:
Italian or Herb: Eliminate Worcestershire sauce and parsley. Add ½ teaspoon dried oregano leaves, ¼ teaspoon dried basil leaves and increase dry mustard to ½ teaspoon.
Parmesan: Add ¼ cup grated Parmesan cheese to dressing.
Garlic: Heat ¼ cup Crisco Oil in small skillet. Add 6 garlic cloves, halved. Cook on low heat, stirring occasionally, about 5 minutes or until garlic is golden brown. Remove from heat. Cool. Remove and discard garlic. Transfer garlic-flavored oil to jar. Add remaining ingredients, remaining ½ cup Crisco Oil and minced garlic. Cover tightly and shake until blended. Refrigerate at least 2 hours. Shake before serving. Store covered in refrigerator.

VEGETABLES & SIDE DISHES

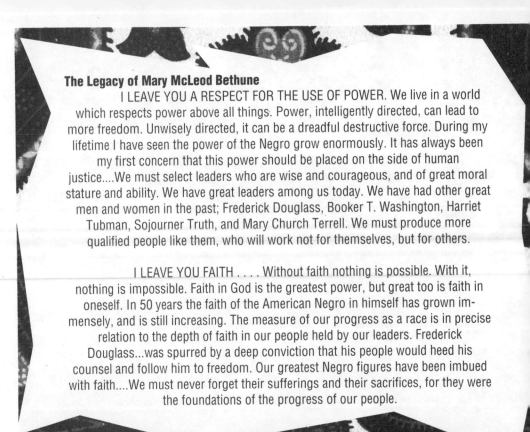

The Legacy of Mary McLeod Bethune

I LEAVE YOU A RESPECT FOR THE USE OF POWER. We live in a world which respects power above all things. Power, intelligently directed, can lead to more freedom. Unwisely directed, it can be a dreadful destructive force. During my lifetime I have seen the power of the Negro grow enormously. It has always been my first concern that this power should be placed on the side of human justice....We must select leaders who are wise and courageous, and of great moral stature and ability. We have great leaders among us today. We have had other great men and women in the past; Frederick Douglass, Booker T. Washington, Harriet Tubman, Sojourner Truth, and Mary Church Terrell. We must produce more qualified people like them, who will work not for themselves, but for others.

I LEAVE YOU FAITH . . . . Without faith nothing is possible. With it, nothing is impossible. Faith in God is the greatest power, but great too is faith in oneself. In 50 years the faith of the American Negro in himself has grown immensely, and is still increasing. The measure of our progress as a race is in precise relation to the depth of faith in our people held by our leaders. Frederick Douglass...was spurred by a deep conviction that his people would heed his counsel and follow him to freedom. Our greatest Negro figures have been imbued with faith....We must never forget their sufferings and their sacrifices, for they were the foundations of the progress of our people.

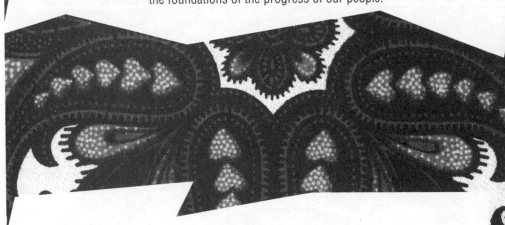

About this fabric

Dashiki Prints (green with designs) [DA-SHEE-HEE]

Brightly colored printed fabrics are typical of many countries in West and East Africa. Designs are issued for special occasions like presidential elections and papal visits and many patterns have their own names. In the 60's and 70's, these prints began being used by African-Americans as symbols of their African heritage.

HEART OF THE SOUTH FRIED OKRA

1	pound okra
1	cup cornmeal
½	cup Crisco Shortening or Crisco Oil
	Salt and freshly ground pepper

1. Rinse okra. Remove caps. Cut pods into one-half inch slices. Toss with cornmeal.
2. Heat Crisco Shortening or Crisco Oil to 365°F in electric skillet or on medium-high heat in large heavy skillet. Fry single layer of okra about 8 to 10 minutes or until golden brown on all sides. Do not overcook or okra will become too soft. Turn carefully. Drain on paper towels. Sprinkle with salt and pepper. Serve immediately.

Note: Fry smaller okra whole.

4 to 6 servings

HERITAGE RECIPE

OKRA & TOMATOES

¼	cup Butter Flavor Crisco
2	onions, chopped
2	ribs celery, chopped
2	cups peeled and chopped tomatoes
2	cups sliced young okra
1	bay leaf
	Salt and pepper

1. Melt Butter Flavor Crisco in large saucepan. Add onions and celery. Sauté until vegetables are soft.
2. Add tomatoes, okra and bay leaf. Simmer, uncovered, one hour. Season with salt and pepper. Remove bay leaf before serving.

8 servings

HERITAGE RECIPE

A New Family Favorite

My mother taught me how to cook when I was a very young girl. One Friday I was assigned to prepare a dinner which included collard greens. My mother told me to go directly to the store after school because greens went fast on Fridays. I didn't listen. I went to a basketball game instead. By the time I got to the store, there weren't enough collard greens left, so I had to get some spinach too. I decided to cook them together and, surprisingly, my whole family loved the combination! To this day, my family's favorite vegetable is my accidental spinach and collard green combination.

Mrs. Marguerite McClelland
Supreme Basileus
National Sorority of
Phi Delta Kappa
Detroit, MI

CURRIED CARROTS & RAISINS

1½	pounds carrots	1	tablespoon honey
1	tablespoon Crisco Oil	1½	teaspoons fresh lemon juice
1½	teaspoons Butter Flavor Crisco	1½	teaspoons curry powder
1	tablespoon brown sugar	1	teaspoon Dijon mustard
½	cup raisins		

1. Peel and halve carrots lengthwise. Slice diagonally into ½-inch thick pieces. Boil in water 10 minutes. Remove from heat. Drain.
2. Heat Crisco Oil and Butter Flavor Crisco in large skillet on medium heat. Add carrots. Sauté, stirring constantly, 2 minutes. Sprinkle brown sugar over carrots. Add raisins. Cook mixture 2 minutes.
3. Combine honey, lemon juice, curry powder, and mustard. Stir into skillet. Cook and stir until carrots are well glazed, about 2 or 3 minutes.

6 servings

CARROT SOUFFLÉ

3	tablespoons cornstarch	¼	cup butter, melted
1½	cups milk	1	teaspoon salt
2	cups cooked mashed carrots	¼	teaspoon honey
4	eggs, well beaten		

1. Heat oven to 400°F. Grease 1½-quart casserole or baking dish.
2. Add cornstarch to milk. Stir to dissolve. Stir into carrots. Stir in eggs, butter, salt and honey. Transfer to casserole.
3. Bake at 400°F for 45 minutes.

6 to 8 servings

Francis Williams, Actress

VEGETARIAN BLACK-EYED PEAS & RICE

1	cup dried black-eyed peas, rinsed and drained
4	cups water
3	small vegetable bouillon cubes
2	cloves garlic, crushed
1	tablespoon vegetable oil
1	tablespoon minced cilantro
1	tablespoon minced parsley
1	teaspoon salt (optional)
½	teaspoon pepper
1	large onion, chopped
2	medium scallions, chopped
1	teaspoon dried thyme leaves
1	large tomato, chopped
1	cup uncooked long-grained rice

1. Combine peas and water in large saucepan or Dutch oven. Add bouillon and garlic. Bring to a boil. Reduce heat. Stir in oil, cilantro, parsley, salt (if used) and pepper. Cover. Simmer 15 minutes.
2. Stir in onion, scallions, thyme and tomato. Cover. Simmer 15 to 20 minutes or until peas are almost soft.
3. Stir in rice. Cover. Cook until rice and peas are tender. Remove from heat. Let stand, covered, 10 minutes before serving.

4 main dish or 6 side dish servings

Susan L. Taylor, Editor-in-Chief
Essence Magazine

The Master of Black-eyed Peas

While growing up, my grandmother, Rhoda Weekes, was known among family and friends as the master of black-eyed peas and rice. You may think I'm exaggerating, but I can remember folks coming from throughout the tri-state area if they heard Mother was "cookin' up a pot."

I'd watch her throw a bit of this and a dash of that into the kettle. It still warms my spirit to remember her creating her magical dish, while I kept her company in her big, beautiful kitchen. I'm no longer a meat-eater, so the following is my vegetarian version of Rhoda Weekes's black-eyed peas and rice.

Susan L. Taylor
New York, NY

Family Tradition

Maintaining family tradition was "Flora B's" most cherished act. Born in Cameron, North Carolina, Flora B was the second oldest girl in a family of twelve children. Each child had a specific job assignment and Flora B was the designated cook; and Lord, could she cook!

She and her husband, Reverend B. F. Napier, had a virtual open house; but New Year's Day was a special family tradition. So many people came it was like a revolving door. They would start cooking a couple of days before the holiday. Rev. Napier would be in the basement preparing his specialities, and Flora B in the kitchen turning out her famous deep dish blueberry pie, succulent chicken and dumplings, spicy souse meat, baked ham, turkey stuffed with cornbread, venison, black-eyed peas, collard greens, and homemade rolls. It was a joyous and wonderful time which we miss immensely without her, but her legacy will live on forever.

Esther Napier Alli
Paterson, NJ

BLACK-EYED PEAS IN SAUCE

1	pound dried black-eyed peas
2	pounds ham hocks
2	ribs celery, chopped
2	medium onions, chopped
1	can (15 ounces) tomato purée
2	tablespoons ketchup or chili sauce
2	red pepper pods, chopped
1	clove garlic, chopped
1	bay leaf
½	teaspoon dried basil leaves

1. Soak black-eyed peas one hour.
2. Place ham in large saucepan. Cover with water. Boil 30 minutes. Add celery, onions, tomato purée, ketchup, pepper pods, garlic, bay leaf and basil. Cover. Simmer 3 to 4 hours or until peas are tender. Remove bay leaf before serving.

4 to 6 servings

HERITAGE RECIPE

CLASSIC OKRA

2	tablespoons unsalted butter
1	small onion, minced
1	pound fresh okra
¼	cup water
	Salt and freshly ground black pepper

1. Heat butter in saucepan. Add onion. Cook until translucent.
2. Cut both ends off okra. Add okra and water to onion. Cook on medium heat 10 minutes, checking to see that okra does not stick. Season with salt and freshly ground black pepper. Serve warm.

4 servings

HERITAGE RECIPE

HOPPIN' JOHN

6	cups water	1	teaspoon ground cumin
1	pound dried black-eyed peas	1	teaspoon dried thyme leaves
1	cup cubed salt pork, rinsed	1	can (6 ounces) tomato paste
1	large green bell pepper, chopped	1	teaspoon chili powder
1	large onion, chopped	2	cups uncooked rice
6	cloves garlic, minced		Salt and pepper

1. Combine water and black-eyed peas in large saucepan. Cook until almost tender, about one hour. Add more water if needed.
2. Brown salt pork in medium skillet on medium heat. Add green pepper, onion, garlic, cumin and thyme. Stir and cook until browned. Add tomato paste and chili powder. Stir. Add a little water. Stir. Pour into beans. Add rice. Stir. Add enough water to cover by 1½-inches. Cover. Bring to a boil. Reduce heat. Simmer 30 minutes. Salt and pepper to taste.

6 to 8 servings

HERITAGE RECIPE

CREOLE BLACK-EYED PEAS

2	quarts boiling water	1	dried red pepper, crushed
1	pound dried black-eyed peas	1	cup rice, cooked and drained
1	onion, diced	1½	pounds raw shrimp, shelled and deveined
½	pound lean bacon, cut into ½-inch cubes	6	scallions, trimmed and sliced
1	teaspoon salt		

1. Combine water, black-eyed peas, onion, bacon, salt and red pepper. Cook on low heat 2 hours. Add rice. Cook 20 minutes. Stir in shrimp and scallions. Cook 10 minutes.

6 to 8 servings

HERITAGE RECIPE

AKARA OR BEAN BALLS

Trouble with Cornmeal

It is difficult to write of my personal food memories without remembering my sister and brothers. Our early childhood years were spent on a farm in Pickens County, AL, where my father, the late John W. Lang, Sr., married my mother, the late Annie Lee Cole. Much of our food was grown on the farm, including corn for cornmeal and an orchard with peaches, pears, apples and berries that either subsidized the family income or were used for drying, preserving, and making jellies. My brother Bill thought cornmeal should only be used for the hogs or to make bread for the hound dogs that we used for hunting. Cornbread should never be used in place of biscuits. The rest of us basically felt the same way but not to the extreme that Bill did. One day he was sent to an Aunt's house to get cornmeal to make bread for the dogs. He thought our mother was going to

Continued on next page

Bean Balls

2	cups dried black-eyed peas or white beans
	Crisco Shortening or Crisco Oil for deep frying
1	onion
1	egg, beaten
1	teaspoon salt
	Dash cayenne pepper

Red Pepper Sauce

¼	cup Crisco Shortening or Crisco Oil
1	large onion, thinly sliced
3 or 4	medium tomatoes, fresh or 1 can (14½ ounces)
2	tablespoons tomato paste
1	teaspoon cayenne pepper, to taste
	Salt

1. For Bean Balls, soak peas or beans until outside skin loosens (a few hours or overnight). Drain off loose skins and water.
2. Heat 2 to 3 inches Crisco Shortening or Crisco Oil to 365°F in deep fryer or deep saucepan.
3. Purée beans in food processor or blender. Add water, if necessary, to achieve smooth paste.
4. Grate onion. Add to beans. Stir in egg, salt and cayenne.
5. Drop by tablespoonfuls, a few at a time, into hot shortening or oil. Fry until well browned. Remove with slotted metal spoon. Drain on paper towels. Serve hot or at room temperature with red pepper sauce.
6. For Sauce, heat Crisco Shortening or Crisco Oil in medium skillet on medium heat. Add onions. Cook until soft. Add tomatoes. Simmer until thick and well blended. Add tomato paste, cayenne and salt, to taste. Mix well. Simmer 5 to 10 minutes. Add hot water or tomato juice if mixture becomes too thick.

10 to 12 servings

HERITAGE RECIPE

ERNESTINE'S BAKED GRITS

2	tablespoons Butter Flavor Crisco
½	pound fresh mushrooms, chopped
5	cups cooked grits
4	eggs, beaten
1½	cups evaporated milk
1¾	cups grated Parmesan cheese
	Paprika to taste
2	dashes cayenne pepper

1. Heat oven to 375°F. Grease large baking dish with Butter Flavor Crisco.
2. Melt Butter Flavor Crisco in large skillet. Add mushrooms. Sauté until mushrooms give up their liquid, about 5 minutes.
3. Place grits in large bowl. Mash if they are leftovers. Add mushrooms, eggs, evaporated milk, cheese, paprika and cayenne. Stir gently to mix. Pour into casserole.
4. Bake at 375°F for 25 to 30 minutes.

8 servings

HERITAGE RECIPE

Continued

make cornbread for dinner; so, he conveniently forgot that he was sent for cornmeal and asked for flour. The Aunt knew better since she was in town when Mama had bought flour. So the cornmeal was sent along with Bill, but it never arrived at our house because he planted a row of cornmeal all the way from our Aunt's house to our house. Bill arrived home with an empty pail. Needless to say, you probably know what happened! Bill got a whipping, not because he planted the cornmeal, but because he didn't tell the truth. It was at this point that Mama realized she had to do something to get us to like cornbread; so, she began making cornbread almost like pound cake with sugar, butter and eggs. To this day, we all "love" cornbread but only cooked Mama's way.

Lula L. Lang-Jeter
National Vice President
NCCW
Arlington, VA

"The Goodie"

Every spoonful of those baked beans tasted so indescribably good that I closed my eyes to savor the flavor. Oh, but no clever phrase could capture the rapture that was mine as I let my tongue press against each bean; one-by-one, and extract the tastes of pungent garlic, scorched, diced onions, rich brown sugar and smoked, thick and meaty bacon. They blended on my palate like the smooth inseparable sound of the MJQ. Reluctantly, I drifted out of my Modern Jazz Quartet trance to scheme with my sister about how we could repeat our pleasure before mother shooed us away like annoying house flies from her "company only" baked beans deluxe. It was that Saturday night that we learned what to look for in life. Edging her spoon along the baking dish, Janet whispered, "Here, Sonia, Do you want some more of the goodie?" I answered with my traditional first child belligerence, "No, I want another serving. What's the goodie anyhow?" "Taste it", she offered with

Continued on next page

OLD-FASHIONED BAKED LIMA BEANS

3	cups large dried lima beans
2	quarts boiling water
1	bay leaf
2	sprigs celery leaves
5	sprigs parsley
¾	pound salt pork, sliced
⅓	cup sorghum molasses
¼	cup firmly packed brown sugar
2	teaspoons dry mustard
2	teaspoons salt
⅛	teaspoon pepper
1	medium onion, chopped
½	cup sherry wine

1. Rinse lima beans. Add to boiling water in large saucepan. Boil 2 minutes. Cover. Let stand one hour.
2. Tie together bay leaf, celery leaves and parsley. Add to lima beans. Boil one hour. Drain lima beans, reserving 1½ cups liquid.
3. Heat oven to 250°F.
4. Arrange drained lima beans and sliced pork in layers in 2-quart baking dish with slices of pork on top.
3. Combine molasses, brown sugar, dry mustard, salt, pepper and onion with 1½ cups liquid from lima beans. Pour over lima beans. Cover.
4. Bake at 250°F for 2½ hours. Remove cover. Pour sherry over lima beans. Bake one hour.

8 servings

NAVY BEANS & PIG TAILS

Continued

2	pounds pig tails, salt pork or neckbones
2	cups dried navy beans
1	small onion
	Salt and pepper

1. Place meat in large saucepan. Cover with water. Simmer until meat is tender. Remove meat from broth.
2. Add navy beans, whole onion, salt and pepper. Simmer until beans are tender. Add additional water as needed.
3. Remove meat from bones. Stir into beans. Simmer on low heat until beans mash easily with fork and broth has thickened.

6 servings

HERITAGE RECIPE

GRITS SPOONBREAD

⅓	cup quick-cooking grits
1	teaspoon sugar
½	teaspoon salt
2	cups milk, scalded
3	eggs, separated
3	tablespoons Butter Flavor Crisco
	Red-eye gravy

1. Combine grits, sugar and salt. Stir into milk. Bring to a boil. Reduce heat to low. Cook and stir 4 to 5 minutes or until very thick. Cool.
2. Heat oven to 375°F.
3. Beat egg yolks. Stir into grits.
4. Beat egg whites until stiff peaks form. Fold into grits mixture.
5. Melt Butter Flavor Crisco in 1½-quart casserole. Spoon in grits.
6. Bake at 375°F for 35 to 40 minutes or until lightly browned. Serve immediately with red-eye gravy.

6 servings

HERITAGE RECIPE

patient coaxing. UHM! UHM! Why would anyone ever want to eat the baked beans again if you could just have that rim of the blended flavors bordering the cooking vessel? Needless to say, we trimmed that rim with spoons and fingers until we were caught. But that was only the beginning, because once we discovered "the goodie" we kept an eye or two open for it in kitchens everywhere. We found it in the syrup-soaked, flaky crust tucked in the corner of cobbler pans. We found it in the crusty, cheesy, buttered corners of pans holding macaroni and cheese. We found it where the grill takes over when the Bar-B-Que sauce stops. We found it around the edges of legs of lamb bathed with garlic, rosemary, lemon slices and lamb flavor. Here are some helpful hints for goodie seekers. Look at "marginal stuff" . . . just on the edge of being no good . . . that's where you'll really find "the goodie".

Sonia Walker, Regional Coordinator NCNW Black Family Reunion Celebration Memphis, TN

63

OLD-FASHIONED COUNTRY BEANS

½	pound bacon ends, cut in chunks	2	teaspoons salt
2	pounds green beans, cut in halves	1	teaspoon sugar
		¼	teaspoon cayenne pepper
2	onions, quartered	1	pound new potatoes, scraped

1. Place bacon in large saucepan. Cover with water. Boil 20 minutes.
2. Add green beans, onions, salt, sugar and cayenne. Boil 15 minutes.
3. Add potatoes. Boil until potatoes are tender.

6 to 8 servings

HERITAGE RECIPE

SAVORY BAKED LIMA BEANS

2	pounds dried baby lima beans	1	cup tomato ketchup
½	cup chopped onion	½	cup dark molasses
1	teaspoon salt	1	pound well seasoned pork sausage
½	teaspoon dry mustard		

1. Cover lima beans with water. Soak overnight.
2. Simmer lima beans until they are beginning to soften. Drain off water until they are just covered. Transfer to shallow baking dish.
3. Heat oven to 375°F.
4. Combine onion, salt, dry mustard, ketchup and molasses. Stir into beans.
5. Form sausage into 6 patties. Place on top of lima beans.
6. Bake at 375°F for 1 hour 30 minutes or until sauce bubbles and sausage is slightly brown.

6 servings

DIPPO'S SUCCOTASH

1	pound dried baby lima beans	1	tablespoon pepper
1	ham bone or 3 ham hocks*	1	can (28 ounces) tomatoes
2	onions, quartered	1	can (17 ounces) whole kernel corn**
3	hot peppers		
2	quarts water or stock	8	flour tortillas (6 to 7-inch), cut into 3-inch strips
1	tablespoon sugar		
1	tablespoon salt	2	cups diced ham

1. Soak beans several hours or overnight in warm water. Drain. Combine beans, ham bone, onions, hot peppers, water, sugar, salt and pepper in Dutch oven or kettle. Cook on low heat 3 hours.
2. Add tomatoes and corn. Cool 30 minutes. Add tortillas. Cook 30 minutes.
3. Remove ham bone from mixture. Pull or cut meat from bone. Dice enough to make 2 cups. (Use additional leftover ham, if needed.) Return diced ham to bean mixture. Reheat, if necessary.

8 to 10 servings

* Precook ham hocks one hour before adding to beans.
** Substitute fresh corn cut from cob for canned corn, if desired.

Katherine Stewart
Stewart's Catering School

RED BEANS WITH TOMATO SAUCE

1	pound dried red beans	2	red pepper pods
	Ham ends, skin, bone or bacon	1	clove garlic, chopped
		1	bay leaf
2	quarts water		Several cumin seeds
1	can (8 ounces) tomato sauce		Salt and pepper
1	small onion, chopped		

1. Soak beans 2 to 3 hours. Drain.
2. Chop ham or bacon finely. Place in large saucepan. Add water. Cover. Boil 10 minutes. Add beans, tomato sauce, onion, pepper pods, garlic, bay leaf, cumin seeds and salt and pepper to taste. Cover. Simmer 3 hours or until beans are tender. Stir often. Add more water or tomato sauce, as needed. Remove bay leaf before serving.

4 to 6 servings

HERITAGE RECIPE

Family Reunion
My father's family has gathered in North Carolina each year for a reunion on the second Sunday in August for more than 40 years. The purpose of this get together is to promote fellowship, socialize, celebrate achievements, exchange information, discuss family and world issues, and allow each new generation of children to get to know each other. We usually have 100-150 people attend, including extended family, and hosting the reunion has always rotated among my dad's seven siblings, five of whom survive. Traditionally the host family provides the basic meal and those who attend bring something extra. Everybody looked forward to eating specialties such as: Aunt Lillian's fried corn, Aunt DeDe's deviled crab cakes, Aunt Marion's cakes and pies, Aunt BeBe's homemade rolls and macaroni and cheese, Aunt Josephine's cornbread, and Cousin
Continued on next page

NDIWO ZA MPIRU WOTENDERA (MUSTARD GREENS WITH PEANUT SAUCE)

2	bunches fresh mustard greens or spinach
	Water
1/4	teaspoon salt
1	bunch green onions, chopped
1/2	pound cherry tomatoes
1/8	teaspoon crushed black pepper
1/2	cup peanut butter
1/4	cup water
	Hot cooked rice

1. Wash greens carefully. Trim off any tough stems. Hold three or four leaves together and tear into small, even pieces.
2. Bring small amount water to a boil. Add salt and greens. Cook until greens are tender.
3. Turn greens over in pan and add chopped onions, whole cherry tomatoes and pepper. Cook until slightly limp.
4. Form creamy paste with peanut butter and water. Pour paste over entire surface of greens. Cook slowly 10 minutes, stirring continually to blend. Continue to cook until moist, not runny. Serve with rice.

Lena Nozizwe, Television Star

HERITAGE RECIPE

MARION GRACE'S SMOTHERED CABBAGE

4 or 5	slices bacon or salt pork
1	head cabbage, chopped
1	tablespoon cider vinegar
1	tablespoon sugar
⅛	teaspoon freshly ground black pepper

1. Fry bacon in large skillet on medium heat until crisp. Remove. Drain. Crumble.
2. Add cabbage to skillet a little at a time. Allow to wilt after each addition. Add vinegar, sugar and pepper. Cover. Cook about 20 minutes or until soft. Stir in bacon just before serving.

4 to 6 servings

BAKED EGGPLANT

2	large eggplants
½	teaspoon salt
¼	cup Butter Flavor Crisco
2	eggs, lightly beaten
½	cup regular or skim evaporated milk
	Salt and pepper
1	cup shredded American cheese
½	cup shredded Cheddar cheese
1	cup bread crumbs
	Paprika

1. Heat oven to 350°F. Grease 13 X 9 X 2-inch baking pan with Butter Flavor Crisco.
2. Peel and dice eggplant into 1½-inch pieces. Place in large saucepan. Cover with water. Add salt. Cook until soft. Mash eggplant. Stir in Butter Flavor Crisco, eggs, evaporated milk. Season with salt and pepper.
3. Layer half each of eggplant mixture, cheese and crumbs in baking pan. Repeat. Sprinkle with paprika.
4. Bake at 350°F for 30 to 35 minutes or until set. Garnish with paprika.

10 to 12 servings

Continued

Hattie's greens. The annual reunions were originally organized by my aunt, Lucille Daniels Albright, who was active in NCNW and worked with Mary McLeod Bethune and Dorothy Height. She cooked gourmet dishes such as oyster casserole, pheasant, and duck with orange sauce. One of Aunt Lucille's famous breakfasts was chitterlings, battered and fried and served with grits, eggs, hot homemade bread, and her own jam. She made everything from scratch from fresh products raised on their farm. She was a creative, effortless cook who set a beautiful table with elegant china, colorful tablecloths, and an array of silver for each of the different courses.

Mrs. Donna L. Rice
Columbia, MD

AUNT ETHEL'S BAKED SQUASH

3	pounds summer squash, sliced		1	tablespoon sugar
3	eggs, beaten		1	teaspoon salt (optional)
½	cup chopped onions		½	teaspoon pepper
½	cup butter or margarine, divided		½	cup Italian bread crumbs

1. Heat oven to 375°F. Grease 1½-quart casserole.
2. Place squash in large saucepan. Cover with water. Cook until tender. Drain thoroughly. Mash.
3. Add eggs, onions, ¼ cup butter, sugar, salt, if used, and pepper to squash. Mix well. Pour in baking dish.
4. Melt remaining ¼ cup butter. Pour over squash. Sprinkle with bread crumbs.
5. Bake at 375°F for approximately one hour or until top is browned.

6 servings

SUMMER SQUASH CASSEROLE

2	pounds zucchini or yellow squash, about 6 cups sliced		1	cup dairy sour cream
			1	cup shredded carrots
¼	cup chopped onion		1	package (8 ounces) herb seasoned stuffing mix
	Salt (optional)			
1	can (10¾ ounces) condensed cream of chicken soup		½	cup melted butter or margarine

1. Heat oven to 350°F.
2. Combine squash and onion in large saucepan. Cover with water. Season with salt, if desired. Cook 5 minutes. Drain.
3. Combine soup and sour cream in large bowl. Stir in carrots. Fold in squash and onions.
4. Combine stuffing mix and butter. Spread half into bottom of 12 X 7½ X 2-inch baking dish. Spoon in vegetable mixture. Sprinkle with remaining stuffing.
5. Bake at 350°F for 30 minutes or until heated thoroughly.

8 servings

COUVE À MINEIRA—COLLARD GREENS & OKRA, BAHIA STYLE

3	bunches collard greens
1	pound fresh okra
1	large red onion, sliced
5	cloves garlic, crushed
2	tablespoons soy or other vegetable oil
2	tablespoons palm oil (optional)
1	tablespoon ground coriander
½	teaspoon cayenne pepper
½	cup coarsely chopped cilantro leaves

1. Wash collard leaves individually on both sides with rubbing motion. Stack approximately 15 leaves evenly. Roll from long side in cigar fashion. Cut into ⅛-inch ribbons. Continue until all leaves are cut. Drop into boiling salted water just to cover. Blanch 4 minutes only. Drain. Set aside. Reserve one cup cooking liquid.
2. Wash okra. Cut off tops. Slice diagonally into about 4 to 5 slices per stem. Sauté onion, okra and garlic in soy oil and palm oil (if used) 8 minutes.
3. Add drained collards, coriander and cayenne. Stir-fry on medium-high heat 5 minutes. Serve immediately with cilantro as garnish. Add a little pot likker, if desired.

6 to 8 servings

Magie Laini Raine, Art Cuisinist
Founder/CEO Africa House of Los Angeles

HERITAGE RECIPE

We've Gotta Have Our Greens!

I remember my great grandmother, Evie Raine picking and washing collards from her garden, then stacking, rolling and cutting them into strips and cooking them with salt pork or ham pieces (from a hog that Papa Frank had raised, killed and cured). Mama Evie then cooked these greens, with her other seasonings, all day long…and they were wonderful. The aroma of fresh greens and ham permeated the air like an "air appetizer" and when we sat down to eat, everyone wanted the greens first.

While researching cuisines of the African diaspora, one of the wonderful dishes I discovered was Couve à Mineira. It's served daily at Africa House. Guests order collards only and caterers order them by the case. We gotta have our greens!

Magie Laini Raine
Los Angeles, CA

My Mother's Greens

We have a huge and very close family so we rotate our traditional holiday gatherings among the various homes. My mother, Anna Tidmore, always makes the greens, cornbread dressing and sweet potato pie; those three dishes and chitlins are required at every holiday dinner. New dishes may be added, but if they displace these family icons, it's not a proper holiday meal.

My mother would prepare her greens by cleaning a mix of collard, mustard and turnip greens. Then she would boil a smoked pig knuckle (I once offered to replace the pig knuckle with smoked turkey, but she would have none of it), pour off the juice, and then add fresh water and the greens. She seasoned to taste using onion, garlic, sage and "her seasonings" and simmered until the greens were limp. Then all you needed was some cornbread.

Marjorie Bradford
Regional Coordinator
NCNW Black Family
Reunion Celebration
Cincinnati, OH

COLLARD GREENS WITH NECKBONES

1	pound pork neckbones
2	bunches collard greens
1	tablespoon bacon drippings
	Dash red pepper sauce
	Salt and pepper

1. Parboil neckbones in large saucepan. Remove from broth.
2. Add greens. Cook on low heat until tender.
3. Add bacon drippings, red pepper sauce. Season with salt and pepper.

4 to 6 servings

HERITAGE RECIPE

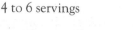

CORN PUDDING

¼	cup butter or margarine, melted and divided
4	cups cream-style corn
4	eggs, beaten
¾	cup all-purpose flour
½	cup evaporated milk
2	tablespoons firmly packed brown sugar
½	teaspoon nutmeg
½	teaspoon cinnamon
	Salt and pepper
	Bread crumbs
2	tablespoons butter or margarine

1. Heat oven to 350°F. Grease 10-inch baking dish, 2½-inches deep, with 2 tablespoons melted butter.
2. Combine corn, eggs, flour, evaporated milk, 2 tablespoons melted butter, brown sugar, nutmeg, cinnamon, salt and pepper. Pour mixture into baking dish. Sprinkle top with bread crumbs. Dot with remaining 2 tablespoons butter.
3. Bake at 350°F for 40 to 60 minutes or until knife inserted in the center comes out clean. Serve hot.

8 servings

Joyce B. Dinkins, Wife of Mayor of New York City

CORN PUPPY CASSEROLE

½	cup Butter Flavor Crisco
1	cup finely chopped onions
2	tablespoons all-purpose flour
2	tablespoons sugar
1	teaspoon salt
1	teaspoon pepper
½	teaspoon garlic powder
¼	teaspoon dry mustard
½	cup milk
1	cup cornmeal
1	can (8¾ ounces) whole kernel corn, drained
1	can (15 ounces) cream-style corn
3	eggs, lightly beaten
½	cup cracker crumbs
1	tablespoon Butter Flavor Crisco, melted

1. Heat oven to 350°F.
2. Melt Butter Flavor Crisco in large saucepan. Add onions. Cook and stir until tender. Remove from heat. Stir in flour, sugar, salt, pepper, garlic powder and dry mustard. Cook on low heat until bubbly. Add milk gradually, stirring constantly. Cook until slightly thickened. Stir in cornmeal, whole kernel corn, cream-style corn and eggs. Pour into ungreased 1½ to 2-quart casserole.
3. Toss cracker crumbs with melted Butter Flavor Crisco. Sprinkle over casserole.
4. Bake at 350°F for 30 to 40 minutes or just until center is set.

6 to 8 servings

Aunt Isabelle's Table

I remember Aunt Isabelle as warm, cheerful, and blessed with humorous aphorisms. I also remember some of the food she cooked, in particular, the "corn puppy.'" Corn puppies were prepared during the winter months whenever unexpected company arrived. We would all gather at the round table and sit down to a meal of crisp, golden fried chicken, thick slices of tender cured ham, fresh collard greens and string beans, seasoned black-eyed peas, crisp green salad, and piping hot biscuits and corn puppies with butter melting all over them. As long as we sat, different desserts would be put on the table ranging from pound cake to a tangy and potent homemade peach brandy.

Mary Melson Alexander Laurelton, NY

CORN OYSTERS

2	eggs, separated
1½	cups crushed corn (1 cup if using fresh corn)
1	tablespoon lowfat milk
¼	cup all-purpose flour
1	teaspoon sugar
¼	teaspoon coarsely ground pepper
2	tablespoons Crisco Shortening or Crisco Oil

1. Beat egg yolks in large bowl. Add corn and milk. Stir in flour, sugar and pepper.
2. Beat egg whites until stiff peaks form. Fold into corn batter.
3. Heat Crisco Shortening or Crisco Oil in large skillet on medium heat. Drop batter by tablespoonfuls into skillet. Cook about 1½ minutes per side, until golden brown and puffy. Add more shortening or oil to skillet, if needed. Serve hot.

4 servings

TOMATO PUDDING

1	can (28 ounces) tomatoes*
3 - 4	slices stale (dry) bread
⅔	cup sugar
¼	cup butter, melted
1	teaspoon freshly grated black pepper
	Pinch of salt

1. Heat oven to 350°F.
2. Combine tomatoes, bread, sugar, butter, pepper and salt. Mix well with your hands, breaking up the tomatoes. Transfer to 1-quart casserole or baking dish.
3. Bake at 350°F for about 45 minutes.

* Don't try to get fancy and use fresh tomatoes in this recipe. It doesn't work with the kind of tomatoes you get in the market today.

4 to 6 servings

Barbara Bond, Restaurateur
Barbara's Bounty

Vegetable or Dessert?

This recipe is from Gold Point, North Carolina. It was given to my mother by my father's mother. There is an on-going "discussion" about how this "pudding" is served—as a vegetable or as a dessert. My father claims my grandmother served it as a dessert—she probably did. However, my mother always served it as a vegetable. Give it a try!

Barbara Bond
Cincinnati, OH

TOMATO GRAVY

2	tablespoons Crisco Oil
1	onion, coarsely chopped
1	clove garlic, crushed or chopped
½	green bell pepper, coarsely chopped
2	cups tomatoes, fresh or canned
1	tablespoon all-purpose flour
1	teaspoon sugar
1 - 2	green chile peppers (optional)
3 - 5	slices bologna or salami, quartered (optional)
	Salt and pepper
	Hot cooked rice or grits

1. Heat Crisco Oil in skillet. Sauté onion, garlic and green pepper until onions are soft.
2. Add tomatoes, flour, sugar, chile peppers and bologna. Cover. Simmer 15 to 20 minutes. Season with salt and pepper.
3. Serve over rice at dinner or grits at breakfast.

Stephanie Honeywood
Black Lifestyles

SUMMER GREEN TOMATO CRISPS

4	very firm green tomatoes
½	cup yellow cornmeal
1¼	teaspoons salt
½	teaspoon sugar
⅛	teaspoon pepper
¼	cup Crisco Shortening or Crisco Oil

1. Cut out stem ends of tomatoes. Slice ½-inch thick.
2. Combine cornmeal, salt, sugar and pepper on waxed paper. Coat both sides of tomato slices with mixture.
3. Heat Crisco Shortening or Crisco Oil to 365°F in electric skillet or on medium-high heat in large heavy skillet. Place single layer of tomato slices in skillet. Brown each side lightly. Cook only until tender. Serve immediately.

HERITAGE RECIPE

4 servings

Loosening the Joints

Tomato Gravy brings back memories of breakfast at Grandma's, in the country. Each morning Grandma made biscuits—tender, golden, flaky, fluffy biscuits—enough to fill her whole family. That included five or six grown children and their spouses and children.

All the men who came to help that day would join us for breakfast. Family visits were a time for work and repair. In the country, something was being built or fixed each day—the plumbing, the pump, the car, the fan or the tractor needed repair. Peas or cotton needed picking. A shed or a new room needed to be built. There were always men working at break of day. Everyone needed a good hot breakfast to start the day off right. My uncles used to say that nothing was better at "loosening the glue in their joints" than piping hot Tomato Gravy and grits!

Stephanie Honeywood
Los Angeles, CA

MACARONI & CHEESE DELUXE

1	package (8 ounces) elbow macaroni, cooked
2	cups cream-style cottage cheese
2	cups shredded sharp Cheddar cheese
1	carton (8 ounces) sour cream
1	egg, lightly beaten
¾	teaspoon salt
	Paprika

1. Heat oven to 350°F. Grease 2-quart casserole or baking dish.
2. Cook macaroni following package directions. Drain.
3. Combine cottage cheese, cheese, sour cream, egg and salt. Fold in macaroni. Spoon into casserole. Sprinkle with paprika.
4. Bake at 350°F for 45 minutes.

6 to 8 servings

Kitchen Reflections

Often I visited my mother in San Diego. It's never long before the kitchen is full of the spicy smells of good home cooking from Malawi, South Africa. There is a rich and satisfying variety in African food with available ingredients, and the recipes are not difficult to make.

Lena Nozizwe
Los Angeles, CA

(*Publisher's note*: Nozizwe's mother, Princess Alice Msuba Siwundhia, is the daughter of a tribal chief in Malawi.)

NDIWOA ZA MANDANDA (EGG DISH)

¾	cup peanut oil
6	medium size firm, ripe tomatoes, cubed
4	medium onions, chopped
6	hard-cooked eggs, shelled and pierced all over with toothpick
1	tablespoon Indian curry powder
1	teaspoon salt
¼	teaspoon cayenne pepper or chili powder
½	cup boiling water
	Hot cooked rice

1. Heat oil in deep frying pan. Add tomatoes and onions. Mix well.
2. Add curry powder, salt and cayenne.
3. Immerse the eggs in mixture.
4. Add boiling water. Cover. Cook slowly 12 minutes.
5. Serve on fluffy rice.

Lena Nozizwe, Television Star

HERITAGE RECIPE

MACARONI, PEANUTS & CHEESE

1	cup elbow macaroni
3	tablespoons Butter Flavor Crisco, divided
2	tablespoons all-purpose flour
½	teaspoon salt
	Dash cayenne pepper
1	cup milk
2	cups (8 ounces) shredded American cheese
1	cup coarsely ground peanuts
¼	cup unseasoned dry bread crumbs

1. Heat oven to 350°F. Grease 1-quart casserole or baking dish with Butter Flavor Crisco.
2. Cook macaroni following package directions. Drain.
3. Melt 2 tablespoons Butter Flavor Crisco in medium saucepan on medium heat. Stir in flour, salt and cayenne. Add milk all at once. Cook and stir until thickened and bubbly. Add cheese. Stir until melted. Stir in peanuts.
4. Layer macaroni and sauce in casserole.
5. Melt remaining 1 tablespoon Butter Flavor Crisco. Add crumbs. Stir to blend. Sprinkle over casserole.
6. Bake at 350°F for 25 to 30 minutes or until bubbly and crumbs are browned.

4 servings

Practice Makes Perfect

As a young girl, born and reared on the outskirts of a small, sparsely populated town in Jones, Oklahoma, I constantly read all kinds of magazines and books, including cookbooks. My mother was a teacher who did not care a lot about cooking. I constantly tried to get her to try the new recipes I read about, but with 9 boys and 2 girls, I can now understand why she did it her way! Macaroni and cheese was my favorite dish. Mother could never make enough. When I was 12 years old, I was allowed to try cooking and made many attempts to improve that macaroni and cheese dish. I thank my mother for giving me the opportunity to cook at an early age because those trial runs were excellent training.

Hazel Isaiah-Ransom
Chair, Life Members
Guild of Southern
California
Los Angeles, CA
NCNW

Macaroni and Cheese

My favorite dish is macaroni and cheese as prepared by my mother. Hers is a thick, golden mixture that is moist, but firm. While I was growing up, we only had macaroni and cheese on special occasions. When I'm cooking (something I find to be therapeutic probably because I don't do it everyday) and want to make macaroni and cheese, I'll call Mom for the recipe. If she isn't home, then I call my older sister, Kelley, in Bethlehem, Pennsylvania whose macaroni and cheese almost rivals Mom's. And my younger sister, Allyson, who's a vegetarian, has found macaroni and cheese to be a good staple for her diet. For holidays my sisters and I return to Milwaukee to visit our parents, Ruth and Erskine Tucker, for a festive meal of greens, stringbeans, turkey and stuffing, and my favorite, macaroni and cheese.

Buddy Tucker
Cincinnati, OH

MACARONI & CHEESE WITH WHITE SAUCE

1	cup (4 ounces) elbow macaroni
4	tablespoons butter or margarine, divided
1	small onion, minced
3	tablespoons all-purpose flour
2	cups milk
	Salt and pepper
1½	cups shredded sharp cheese

1. Heat oven to 325°F.
2. Cook macaroni in boiling water until tender. Rinse and drain.
3. Heat 1 tablespoon butter in skillet. Sauté onion until tender.
4. Combine flour, remaining 3 tablespoons butter, milk, salt and pepper in saucepan. Cook and stir on medium heat until smooth and creamy. Add onion, stir to mix.
4. Layer half of macaroni in baking dish, add one-third of cheese. Repeat layers. Pour on white sauce. Top with remaining cheese. Bake at 325°F for 30 minutes. Serve hot.

4 to 6 servings

Nancy Wilson, Entertainer

MARLA'S HASH BROWN SURPRISE

1	bag (32 ounces) frozen chopped hash brown potatoes, thawed	1	can (10¾ ounces) cream of chicken soup
1	container (16 ounces) dairy sour cream	1	cup chopped onions
2	cups Cheddar cheese	¼	cup butter or margarine, melted

1. Heat oven to 375°F.
2. Combine potatoes, sour cream, cheese, chicken soup, onions and butter in large bowl. Stir until well blended. Transfer to 13 X 9-inch baking pan.
3. Bake at 375°F for one hour or until brown.

12 to 16 servings

Marla Gibbs, Actress

DEEP-FRIED MASHED POTATO BALLS

	Crisco Shortening or Crisco Oil for deep frying	⅛	teaspoon pepper
¼	cup water	¼	cup all-purpose flour
2	tablespoons Crisco Shortening	1	egg
¾	teaspoon salt	2	cups mashed potatoes (about 3 medium potatoes)

1. Heat 2 to 3 inches Crisco Shortening or Crisco Oil to 365°F in deep fryer or deep saucepan.
2. Combine water, 2 tablespoons shortening, salt and pepper in medium saucepan. Bring to a boil. Stir in flour. Cook and stir until mixture forms ball. Cool slightly, about 2 minutes.
3. Beat in egg. (Dough will be very thick.) Add potatoes. Mix well.
4. Drop by rounded tablespoonfuls, a few at a time, into shortening or oil. Fry 3 to 5 minutes or until golden brown. Turn as needed for even browning. Remove with slotted metal spoon. Drain on paper towels. Serve immediately.

Tip: Shape mashed potato mixture into balls ahead of time. Fry as above.

4 to 6 servings

GLAZED SWEET POTATOES & TURNIPS

4	medium sweet potatoes or yams, peeled and cut into chunks	½	cup orange juice
		¼	cup butter or margarine, melted
4	medium turnips, peeled and cut into chunks	½	teaspoon mace
		½	teaspoon salt
⅔	cup firmly packed brown sugar	2	oranges, peeled and sliced

1. Heat oven to 400°F.
2. Boil sweet potatoes and turnips until partially cooked. Place vegetables in shallow baking dish.
3. Combine brown sugar, orange juice, butter, mace and salt. Pour over vegetables.
4. Bake uncovered at 400°F for about 30 minutes. Baste often with pan juices. Vegetables are done when pan juices are reduced and vegetables are glazed. Garnish with orange slices.

8 servings

SWEET POTATO BONBONS

3	pounds sweet potatoes, cooked and peeled	¼	teaspoon nutmeg
		2	tablespoons rum, light or dark
¼	cup Butter Flavor Crisco	6	marshmallows, halved
½	cup firmly packed brown sugar	½	cup melted Butter Flavor Crisco
1	teaspoon salt		
1	teaspoon grated orange peel	4	cups cornflakes, crushed
½	teaspoon cinnamon	12	pecan halves

1. Mash sweet potatoes until light and fluffy. Beat in ¼ cup Butter Flavor Crisco, brown sugar, salt, orange peel, cinnamon, nutmeg and rum. Let cool.
2. Heat oven to 450°F. Grease baking sheet with Butter Flavor Crisco.
3. Divide potatoes into 12 equal portions. Work each potato portion around marshmallow half. Coat with Butter Flavor Crisco. Roll in cornflakes. Top with nut half. Place on baking sheet.
4. Bake at 450°F for 8 to 10 minutes. Serve immediately.

12 Bonbons

SWEETATER FINGERS

6	medium sweet potatoes or yams, cooked and peeled	½	cup firmly packed brown sugar
¼	cup all-purpose flour	1	teaspoon salt
¼	cup Crisco Shortening or Crisco Oil	½	teaspoon nutmeg

1. Cut sweet potatoes into fingers or strips. Coat each with flour.
2. Heat Crisco Shortening or Crisco Oil to 365°F in electric skillet or on medium-high heat in large skillet. Fry potato fingers 4 to 5 minutes or until golden brown.
3. Combine brown sugar, salt and nutmeg. Sprinkle over sweet potatoes. Toss lightly until sugar mixture melts. Serve immediately.

6 servings

SWEET POTATO PANCAKES

2	medium sweet potatoes or yams, peeled and grated	2	eggs, lightly beaten
⅓	cup finely chopped onion	¾	teaspoon salt
2	tablespoons all-purpose flour	¼	cup plus 2 tablespoons Crisco Shortening or Crisco Oil, divided
1	tablespoon milk		

1. Heat oven to 300°F.
2. Combine potatoes, onion, flour, milk, eggs and salt. Mix well.
3. Heat ¼ cup Crisco Shortening or Crisco Oil in large skillet on low to medium heat. Place about 2 tablespoons potato mixture in skillet. Press flat with spatula to about 4 inches in diameter. Repeat. Cook each pancake 5 minutes on each side until brown and crisp. Add remaining 2 tablespoons shortening or oil as needed.
4. Drain on paper towels. Remove to large baking pan. Keep warm in 300°F oven.

6 servings

WILLETTE'S YAM CASSEROLE

.6 to 8	medium yams or sweet potatoes	1	teaspoon cinnamon
½	cup Butter Flavor Crisco	½	teaspoon nutmeg
½	cup sugar	½	cup raisins
2	eggs	½	cup miniature marshmallows
1	can (12 ounces) frozen orange juice concentrate, thawed or fresh orange juice		

1. Heat oven to 350°F. Grease 1½ or 2-quart casserole or baking dish with Butter Flavor Crisco.
2. Boil yams in skins until tender. Peel. Mash.
3. Combine yams, Butter Flavor Crisco, sugar and eggs in large bowl. Beat with hand mixer to blend, adding as much orange juice concentrate as needed for good consistency. Stir in cinnamon and nutmeg. Beat 2 minutes. Stir in raisins. Transfer to casserole. Sprinkle marshmallows over top.
4. Bake at 350°F for 30 minutes.

Note: Can be baked covered or uncovered. A light crust will form if uncovered.

6 to 8 servings

APPLE MALLOW YAMBAKE

2	apples, cored and sliced	2	cans (16 or 18 ounces each) yams or sweet potatoes, drained
½	cup firmly packed brown sugar		
⅓	cup chopped pecans		
½	teaspoon cinnamon	¼	cup butter or margarine
		2	cups miniature marshmallows

1. Heat oven to 350°F.
2. Toss apples, brown sugar, nuts and cinnamon. Alternate layers of apples and yams in 9-inch square baking pan. Dot with butter.
3. Bake at 350°F for 35 to 40 minutes.
4. Sprinkle marshmallows over yams and apples. Broil until lightly browned.

6 to 8 servings

PRESIDENT'S POTATO PUDDING

4	medium yams or sweet potatoes, unpeeled
2	cups water, divided
3	eggs, well beaten
2	cups sugar
½	cup cane syrup
⅓	cup butter, melted
½	cup evaporated milk
⅓	cup all-purpose flour
¼	cup margarine, melted
	Salt
1	cup milk
1	teaspoon nutmeg
¼	teaspoon cloves
¼	teaspoon cinnamon

1. Heat oven to 350°F. Grease 2-quart baking dish or casserole.
2. Wash potatoes. Cut out undesirable spots. Grate potatoes coarsely. Rinse grater with 1 cup water over grated potatoes. Add eggs, sugar, syrup, butter, evaporated milk, flour, margarine and season with salt. Mix well. Stir in milk, remaining 1 cup water, nutmeg, cloves and cinnamon. Pour into baking dish.
3. Bake at 350°F for 45 minutes to one hour or until browned. Stir every 15 minutes during baking.

6 to 8 servings

Mary O. Ross, President
Woman's Convention Auxiliary
National Baptist Convention

A Prayer
I know these things
must always be

To keep our nation
strong and free.

One is good health
from food nourishing
and dear,

Eating elegantly with
loved ones far and
near.

One is ready heart and
hand

To love, and serve, and
keep a peaceful land.

One is the Word and
following His Way
Where people, daily,
eat, work, witness and
pray.

So long as these are
kept alive,
Nation and people will
happily survive.

Mary O. Ross
Detroit, MI

BANANA YAM CASSEROLE

4	large or 6 medium yams or sweet potatoes, cooked and mashed	½	teaspoon cinnamon
		½	teaspoon salt
		¼	teaspoon nutmeg
⅓	cup Crisco Shortening or Crisco Oil	¼	teaspoon ground cloves
		2	medium firm-ripe bananas, peeled and cut in ½-inch slices
⅓	cup chopped onion		
½	cup orange juice		
2	tablespoons firmly packed brown sugar	⅓	cup chopped pecans

1. Heat oven to 350°F. Grease 2-quart casserole or baking dish.
2. Heat Crisco Shortening or Crisco Oil in large skillet. Add onion. Sauté about 5 minutes or until tender.
3. Add yams, orange juice, brown sugar, cinnamon, salt, nutmeg and cloves. Mix well.
4. Turn half of mixture into casserole. Layer bananas over yam mixture. Top with remaining yams. Sprinkle with nuts.
5. Bake at 350°F for 30 to 35 minutes or until heated thoroughly.

8 to 10 servings

SAUTÉED BANANAS

2	tablespoons Crisco Shortening	2	tablespoons confectioners sugar
2	tablespoons orange juice		
4	firm ripe bananas		

1. Melt Crisco in large skillet on medium heat. Stir in orange juice.
2. Peel bananas. Cut in half crosswise and then lengthwise. Place in skillet. Cook 5 minutes, turning once.
3. Arrange bananas in serving dish. Sprinkle with confectioners sugar. Serve hot for dessert or as an accompaniment to veal, ham or poultry.

4 servings

MEDITERRANEAN SPINACH PIE

1	bunch green scallions, chopped
1	cup plus 2 tablespoons butter
2	pounds fresh spinach, or 2 packages (8 ounces) frozen spinach, chopped
6	eggs, lightly beaten
½	pound feta cheese, crumbled
8	ounces cottage cheese
2	tablespoons farina
½	cup fresh dill
1	teaspoon salt
½	teaspoon pepper
½	pound phyllo pastry leaves

1. Heat oven to 375°F.
2. Sauté scallions in 2 tablespoons butter.
3. Place spinach in small amount of boiling water in large saucepan. Cover. Cook until wilted. Drain.
3. Mix together scallions, eggs, feta cheese, cottage cheese, farina, dill, spinach, salt and pepper. Blend well.
4. Melt 1 cup butter. Unwrap pastry leaves. Cover leaves with damp towel. Cover sides of spring tube pan with pastry leaves, brush with butter, and let sides of leaves hang over the top of pan.
5. Pour filling into pan and spread evenly. Fold over the sides of pastry leaves to cover filling and place two leaves, brushed with butter, over the top. Place on cookie sheet.
6. Reduce oven to 350°F. Bake for 1 hour 15 minutes or until golden brown and puffed. Remove from oven. Let stand 15 minutes. Unmold. Serve on platter.

The Pastry Chef

My childhood recollections of Spinach Pie are very vivid and glowing. Back then, prepared pastry leaves were not available at the supermarket, and making the dough was a detailed and delicate process. My cousin, though, was quite a pastry chef. While he made the pastry, he would placate me by giving me my own small clump of dough, which I was permitted to roll with my miniature rolling pin. I mimicked his gestures and when the operation was completed, my contribution was added to the main recipe. The finished product was delicious and a small child was delightfully entertained and occupied for an hour. I am most grateful for these pleasant memories.

Dr. Marie H. Stellos
National President
Top Ladies of
Distinction, Inc.
St. Louis, MO

A Gift of Liberian Soul Food

In 1955, following the World YWCA Convention at Royal Holloway College in England, I went to Liberia with the wife of the Minister of Defense. Ms. Jones was so gracious to me during my stay that I quickly said yes when she asked me to take a gift to her son, who was studying at Yale University. Little did I realize that I would be given a big, round package, which she brought to the airport. When I came through customs at Kennedy Airport, the customs officer asked about the package. When I said it was a gift, he wanted to know its value. I was suddenly embarrassed when I couldn't answer his questions about what it was, its value and the like. Finally in desperation, he tore back the covering and out came the strange odor of foo foo, which was such a shock to him that he almost threw it back in my arms. He said, "Move out." Embarrassed

Continued on next page

HOT SPAGHETTI VEGETABLE SALAD

1	pound box spaghetti
½	cup mayonnaise
⅓	cup plus 2 teaspoons Crisco Oil
¼	teaspoon salt
¼	teaspoon pepper
6	medium tomatoes, cut in wedges
1½	pounds mozzarella cheese
1½	pounds watercress
1	box (10 ounces) frozen green peas, thawed
1	box (6 ounces) frozen pea pods, thawed, or 1 cup fresh
½	cup freshly grated Parmesan cheese

1. Heat oven to 350°F. Grease 13 X 9 X 2-inch baking dish.
2. Cook spaghetti following package directions. Drain.
3. Combine mayonnaise, Crisco Oil, salt and pepper in small bowl.
4. Layer half spaghetti, ⅓ tomatoes, ⅓ mozzarella, ½ watercress, green peas, pea pods and Parmesan in baking dish. Spoon small amount of mayonnaise mixture over each layer. Repeat. Arrange remaining tomatoes and mozzarella on top.
5. Bake at 350°F for 20 to 25 minutes or until hot and bubbly or until tomatoes and cheese brown lightly.

12 servings

PEPPERS STUFFED WITH VEGETABLES & RICE

3	medium green bell peppers, halved lengthwise and seeded
2	tablespoons Butter Flavor Crisco
⅓	cup chopped green onions and tops (3 or 4 onions)
⅓	cup finely chopped celery
1½	cups cooked rice
1	medium tomato, finely chopped
1	teaspoon chili powder
¾	teaspoon salt
¼	cup ketchup
12	thin slices Monterey Jack cheese (each about 3 X 1½ X ⅛-inch)
¼	cup water

1. Heat oven to 350°F.
2. Boil enough water to cover peppers in large saucepan. Add peppers. Boil 4 minutes. Drain. Rinse with cold water.
3. Melt Butter Flavor Crisco in small skillet on medium heat. Add onions and celery. Sauté until crisp-tender. Transfer to mixing bowl. Stir in rice, tomato, chili powder and salt. Fill pepper halves generously with rice mixture. Place in ungreased 9-inch square pan. Spoon ketchup over top of each filled pepper. Top each with 2 cheese slices. Pour water into bottom of pan.
4. Bake, uncovered, at 350°F for 25 to 30 minutes, or until heated through.

6 servings

Variation : Replace rice with 1½ cups corn kernels, fresh, frozen (thawed) or canned.

Continued

again, I moved on. As I walked through the door, someone pointed me out to the young man who had been waiting for the plane to arrive. As he came towards me, I handed him the open pan. The very smell of foo foo made him happy. With tears rolling down his cheeks, he said, "My mother knows how I love foo foo." And , his joy in receiving his own soul food took away my uneasy feeling and made me glad that I was the carrier of his favorite food.

Dr. Dorothy I. Height
NCNW President/CEO
Washington, DC

SOUTHERN RICE CAKES

3	tablespoons butter or margarine	1	egg	
¼	cup chopped onion	3	tablespoons all-purpose flour	
¼	cup chopped green bell pepper	3	tablespoons cornstarch	
¼	cup chopped red bell pepper	3	tablespoons cream	
1	tablespoon fresh thyme or 1 teaspoon dried		Pinch of cayenne pepper	
2	cups overcooked rice		Salt and black pepper	
			Clarified butter or margarine	

1. Heat butter in medium skillet. Add onion, green pepper, red pepper and thyme. Sauté lightly.
2. Remove from heat. Pour into mixing bowl. Add rice and egg. Stir in flour and cornstarch. Add cream, cayenne, season with salt and pepper. Add more cream if necessary to make a smooth batter.
3. Heat clarified butter in skillet. Add scoops of rice cake mixture. Press down with spatula. Cook until browned on both sides.

4 to 6 servings

Clayton Sherrod, President
Chef Clayton's Food Systems, Inc.

PERFECT RICE

3½	cups water	1	tablespoon butter or margarine
1½	cups uncooked long grain rice		
1	teaspoon salt		

1. Bring water to a boil in large saucepan on medium heat. Stir in rice, salt and butter.
2. Cover. Lower heat to simmer. Cook about 20 minutes.
3. Remove saucepan from heat. Let stand 5 minutes or until remaining water is absorbed. Fluff with fork. Serve.

6 to 8 servings

MAIN MEAL DISHES

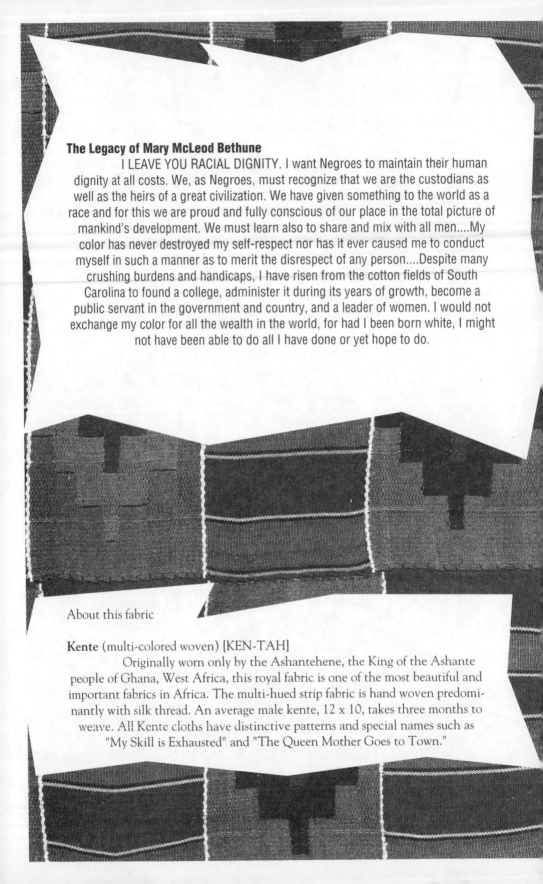

The Legacy of Mary McLeod Bethune

I LEAVE YOU RACIAL DIGNITY. I want Negroes to maintain their human dignity at all costs. We, as Negroes, must recognize that we are the custodians as well as the heirs of a great civilization. We have given something to the world as a race and for this we are proud and fully conscious of our place in the total picture of mankind's development. We must learn also to share and mix with all men....My color has never destroyed my self-respect nor has it ever caused me to conduct myself in such a manner as to merit the disrespect of any person....Despite many crushing burdens and handicaps, I have risen from the cotton fields of South Carolina to found a college, administer it during its years of growth, become a public servant in the government and country, and a leader of women. I would not exchange my color for all the wealth in the world, for had I been born white, I might not have been able to do all I have done or yet hope to do.

About this fabric

Kente (multi-colored woven) [KEN-TAH]

Originally worn only by the Ashantehene, the King of the Ashante people of Ghana, West Africa, this royal fabric is one of the most beautiful and important fabrics in Africa. The multi-hued strip fabric is hand woven predominantly with silk thread. An average male kente, 12 x 10, takes three months to weave. All Kente cloths have distinctive patterns and special names such as "My Skill is Exhausted" and "The Queen Mother Goes to Town."

MARINATED FLANK STEAK WITH GINGER SOY SAUCE

2	cups Worcestershire sauce	1	tablespoon firmly packed
1	cup soy sauce		brown sugar
½	cup red wine	½	teaspoon cracked black pepper
1	tablespoon chopped onion		Flank Steak
½	teaspoon minced garlic	2	pinches ginger
1	bay leaf		

Sauce

6	teaspoons water	Remaining marinade
2	teaspoons corn starch	

1. Combine Worcestershire, soy sauce, wine, onions and garlic. Add bay leaf, brown sugar, pepper and ginger. Mix thoroughly.
2. Pierce flank steak with fork several times. Place in plastic container. Cover with marinade. Marinate overnight in refrigerator. Remove meat. Reserve marinade.
3. Grill meat over charcoal or mesquite grill until desired doneness. Slice on bias.
4. For sauce, combine water and corn starch in small bowl. Bring marinade to low boil. Add cornstarch mixture, stirring until thickened. Serve over flank steak immediately.

6 servings

Steven Leake, Executive Chef
Hook's Catering

PEPPERONCINI ROAST

3 - 4	pound rump or 7-bone pot roast	Seasoned salt
	Pepperoncini peppers	Seasoned pepper
1	packet (1 ounce) dry onion soup mix	Garlic powder
		Onion powder

1. Heat oven to 325°F.
2. Place large sheet heavy duty foil in baking pan. Place roast in center of foil. Pull up sides of foil. Pour undrained peppers over roast. Add onion soup mix. Season with seasoned salt, pepper, garlic powder and onion powder.. Wrap in aluminum foil.
3. Bake at 325°F for 6 hours.

12 to 16 servings

Memories of Fannie Lou Hamer

It was dinnertime in Raleigh, NC, in 1968, and my mother, Lee, who had inherited extraordinary culinary skills from Marf, her mother, was the chef. We were at my grandmother Marf's table in my childhood home. My husband Paul, our new daughter, Camarf, and I were the beneficiaries of a wondrous feast. A meal fit for a queen—and the honored guest was royalty indeed. Fannie Lou Hamer was coming to dinner! Whenever Fannie Lou visited, dinner conversations were always exciting. She shared her love for her husband "Pap", and her children, the awesome experiences of her involvement with the Student Non-Violent Coordinating Committee, all the intimate details of her challenging the segregated Mississippi Freedom Democratic Party in 1964, her warm regard for Harry and Julie Belafonte, her gratitude for the 'royal' treatment from the then New York

Continued on next page

MOUI NAGDEN (RICE IN BEEF STEW)

3	pounds stewing beef, cubed
1	teaspoon curry powder
1	teaspoon white pepper
	Salt
	Crushed red pepper
1	bay leaf
½	cup vegetable oil
1	medium onion, sliced
1	large ripe tomato, quartered
1	large green bell pepper, diced
1	cup cooked red kidney beans (optional)
6	cups water
1½	cups uncooked long-grained rice

1. Season beef with curry powder, white pepper, salt and crushed red pepper. Place in Dutch oven. Add bay leaf and small amount of water. Cook on low heat until meat is tender. Reserve stock.
2. Heat oil in skillet. Add meat. Brown on all sides. Remove meat. Strain oil. Wash and dry skillet.
3. Return oil to same skillet. Add onion. Cook 5 minutes. Add tomato, green pepper and kidney beans (if used). Cook 10 minutes. Add meat.
4. Stir in reserved stock and water. Add rice. Cover tightly. Bring to a boil on high heat. Reduce heat to medium. Cook, stirring once or twice, until rice is cooked as desired. Remove bay leaf before serving.

4 to 6 servings

JoAnn Eusery Simpson, Executive Chef
Hook's Catering

HERITAGE RECIPE

ANGELS' STANDING RIB ROAST

1	jar (8 ounces) Dijon mustard
1	large onion, minced
3	cloves garlic, minced
1	tablespoon seasoned salt
1	tablespoon coarse ground black pepper
½	teaspoon salt
8 - 10	pound beef rib roast

1. Heat oven to 500°F.
2. Combine mustard, onion, garlic, seasoned salt, pepper and salt in small bowl. Apply generously to meat. Place in roasting pan.
3. Roast at 500°F for 10 minutes. Reduce oven temperature to 350°F. Roast 2 hours for rare, 3 hours for well done. Baste occasionally. Serve warm.

Note: Use drippings from meat to make Yorkshire pudding or as gravy spooned lightly over meat slices or mashed potatoes.

8 to 10 servings

Jack Britton, Executive Chef
Gene Autry/California Angels

Continued

Commissioner, Eleanor Homes Norton, her meeting with the Kennedy Women, her admiration of Marian Wright Edelman, and her high regard for Dorothy Height—so many shared memories of her wonderful and meaningful life at our table.

But what I remember most were the hilarious times that we shared while we stuffed ourselves and split our sides with uncontrollable laughter at Fannie Lou's great stories and reminiscences. Here was this great freedom fighter finding humor in the most painful and oppressive experiences of her life. She was so witty and so funny.

This blend of eating, fellowship and nourishment by Fannie Lou's wisdom, indomitable spirit, philosophy of life and incredible humor was food for the body and soul.

Betty Walker, Esquire
Paul Walker, Esquire
Columbia, MD

COUNTRY POT ROAST

⅓	cup all-purpose flour
2	teaspoons salt
⅛	teaspoon pepper
3 - 4	pound chuck pot roast
3	tablespoons Crisco Shortening or Crisco Oil
2	cups water
1	bay leaf, crushed
8	small onions, peeled
8	small potatoes, peeled
8	small carrots
2	medium turnips, peeled and quartered
¼	cup chopped green bell pepper
1	clove garlic, minced
½	cup cold water
¼	cup all-purpose flour

❖

1. Combine ⅓ cup flour, salt and pepper. Coat meat evenly.
2. Heat Crisco Shortening or Crisco Oil in Dutch oven on medium heat. Brown meat well on all sides. Add 2 cups water and bay leaf. Cover. Simmer for 2 hours. Do not boil. Add water during cooking, if needed.
3. Add onions, potatoes, carrots, turnips, green pepper and garlic to Dutch oven. Cover. Simmer for one hour or until meat and vegetables are tender.
4. Remove meat and vegetables. Arrange on heated platter. Keep warm. Strain liquid. Add water, if necessary, to make 1½ cups liquid. Return to Dutch oven.
5. Blend ½ cup cold water and ¼ cup flour until smooth. Slowly stir into pot roast liquid. Cook and stir until gravy thickens and comes to a boil. Cook and stir for one minute. Serve with meat.

8 servings

❖

Big Mama's Cookin'
My grandmother, Claudia Mae Bowen, always had holiday dinners at her home in Olive Branch, Mississippi. The food was great and the family always looked forward to "Big Mama's Cookin'. Oh, she was famous for a lot of good things, but most of all for her cooking. If you went to her house, even if it was for the first time, you just had to stay for dinner. I can remember her waking me up before daylight rattling pans to start Sunday dinners.

Tracy Archie Hogan
Memphis, TN

SKILLET BEEF & MACARONI

1½	pounds ground beef	1	cup water
2	cups uncooked elbow macaroni	1	teaspoon salt
		¼	teaspoon pepper
½	cup minced onion	1 - 1½	tablespoons Worcestershire sauce
½	cup chopped green bell pepper		
2	cans (8 ounces) tomato sauce		

1. Cook beef in large skillet until it loses its redness.
2. Remove beef from skillet. Add macaroni, onion and green pepper to meat drippings. Cook until macaroni turns yellow.
3. Return meat to skillet. Add tomato sauce, water, salt, pepper and Worcestershire. Cover. Simmer 25 minutes.

6 servings

HAMBURGER, NOODLE, & CREAM CHEESE CASSEROLE

8	ounces noodles	1	cup cottage cheese
1	tablespoon Butter Flavor Crisco	1	package (8 ounces) cream cheese, softened
2	pounds ground beef	¼	cup dairy sour cream
1	can (8 ounces) tomato sauce	⅓	cup green onions, chopped

1. Heat oven to 350°F. Grease large casserole or baking dish with Butter Flavor Crisco.
2. Cook noodles following package directions. Drain.
3. Melt Butter Flavor Crisco in large skillet on medium heat. Brown ground beef. Stir in tomato sauce. Remove from heat. Combine cottage cheese, cream cheese, sour cream and green onions. Stir until well blended.
4. Layer half noodles, cheese mixture and meat. Repeat.
5. Bake at 350°F for 30 minutes.

8 servings

BLACK SKILLET BEEF WITH CABBAGE & RED POTATOES

6	cups water	1	tablespoon chopped garlic
1	pound beef, cut in thin pieces		Salt and pepper
8	red-skin potatoes, cut in half	½	head small cabbage
1	onion, chopped	2	large carrots, cut in thirds

1. Place large black skillet on high heat. Add water, beef, potatoes, onion, garlic, salt and pepper. Cook until half liquid is reduced.
2. Add cabbage and carrots. Cook 35 minutes or until cabbage and carrots are tender. Serve hot.

4 to 6 servings

Johnny Rivers, Executive Chef
Walt Disneyworld Resorts

SHEPHERD'S PIE

8	white potatoes, peeled	1	can (16 ounces) carrots, drained
3	pounds chopped beef		
	Salt and pepper	1	can (15 ounces) peas, drained
1	can (17 ounces) corn, drained		Seasoned salt

1. Heat oven to 375°F.
2. Boil potatoes until tender. Cool. Mash very fine.
3. Place meat in large skillet on medium heat. Season with salt and pepper. Sauté and stir until meat is cooked.
4. Place meat, corn, carrots and peas in 13 X 9 X 2-inch baking pan. Stir until blended. Sprinkle with seasoned salt. Cover with potatoes.
5. Bake at 375°F until potatoes are brown.

6 to 8 servings

MACARONI BEEF PIE

¼	cup packaged bread crumbs, divided
1½	pounds ground beef
1	medium onion, chopped
2	cloves garlic, minced
2	teaspoons salt, divided
1⅔	cups extra thick spaghetti sauce
2	cups uncooked elbow macaroni
¼	cup Butter Flavor Crisco
¼	cup all-purpose flour
2	cups milk
2	eggs
1	cup grated Parmesan cheese

1. Heat oven to 375°F. Grease 9-inch pie plate well with Butter Flavor Crisco. Sprinkle sides and bottom with 2 tablespoons bread crumbs.
2. Cook beef, onion, garlic and 1½ teaspoon salt in large skillet on medium heat until beef is well browned, stirring occasionally. Drain off any excess drippings. Stir in spaghetti sauce. Cook and stir until mixture is thick enough to hold its shape. Cool.
3. Cook macaroni following package directions. Drain. Melt Butter Flavor Crisco in same pan. Stir in flour and remaining ½ teaspoon salt. Cook and stir one minute. Add milk gradually. Cook and stir until mixture thickens and bubbles.
4. Beat eggs in small bowl. Pour half the white sauce into eggs, beating constantly until well mixed. Return mixture to sauce remaining in pan. Cook one minute. Remove from heat. Stir in cheese and cooked macaroni. Spoon ⅔ of the macaroni mixture into pie plate. Spread into even layer to line bottom and up side to rim. Spoon meat mixture into center. Cover with remaining macaroni mixture. Sprinkle top with remaining bread crumbs.
5. Bake at 375°F for 30 minutes or until lightly browned on top. Let stand 15 minutes before serving. Cut into wedges to serve.

8 servings

United Civil Rights Leadership

What many have never known and what I cannot forget is a "food memory" with Stephen Currier, who had an almost Biblical sense of the importance of breaking bread together. In February 1963, Mr. Currier, President of Taconic Foundation in New York, brought together Roy Wilkins, NAACP; Whitney M. Young, Jr., National Urban League; James Farmer, CORE; Jack Greenburg, NAACP Legal Defense Fund; C. Eric Lincoln, who had written about the Black Muslims; Martin Luther King, Jr., Southern Christian Leadership Conference; James Foreman, Student Non-Violent Coordinating Committee and me. We came together with a kind of contract that we would work jointly with the officers of the Foundation, as they studied how philanthropy could be more effective in improving conditions of African-Americans.
Each of us agreed to come regularly and send no substitutes. This we did, except of course, when Dr. King was in the

Continued on next page

JR'S CHILI

2	tablespoons Crisco Shortening or Crisco Oil
1	large onion, chopped
1	clove garlic, crushed
1½	pounds chopped chuck
1	pound hot Italian sausage
1	can (14½ ounces) stewed tomatoes
1	can (8 ounces) tomato sauce
1	can (6 ounces) tomato paste
1	hot cherry pepper, sliced
¼	cup firmly packed dark brown sugar
1	tablespoon chili powder, or to taste
¼	teaspoon cayenne pepper
2	cans (16 ounces) red beans or kidney beans
	Salt and pepper
	Hot cooked rice (optional)
	Cheddar cheese (optional)

1. Heat Crisco Shortening or Crisco Oil in stockpot on medium heat. Add onions and garlic. Cook until transparent. Add chuck.
2. Remove sausage from casing and add to pot. Cook and stir until meat browns. Stir in tomatoes,, tomato sauce, tomato paste, cherry pepper, brown sugar, chili powder, cayenne and undrained beans. Season with salt and pepper. Stir well.
3. Cook on low heat for 45 minutes. Serve plain or over rice. Sprinkle with Cheddar cheese, if desired.

10 to 12 servings

CARIBBEAN MEAT PIE

Filling

1	pound ground beef
½	cup tomatoes
1	medium onion, chopped
2	tablespoons Crisco Shortening
1	tablespoon cider vinegar
1	tablespoon minced fresh parsley
1	tablespoon chopped olives
1	tablespoon chopped green bell pepper
2	teaspoons salt
1	teaspoon dried thyme leaves
1	clove garlic, minced
	Dash pepper
1	cup water
1	tablespoon all-purpose flour
1	tablespoon sherry wine
	Pinch dry mustard

Crust

Dough for 9-inch Classic Crisco Single Crust

1. For filling, combine beef, tomatoes, onion, Crisco Shortening, vinegar, parsley, olives, green pepper, salt, thyme, garlic and pepper in large skillet or dutch oven. Cover. Simmer on low heat until tender.
2. Heat oven to 425°F.
3. Combine water and flour. Stir until smooth. Add to skillet. Cook and stir until thickened. Add sherry and mustard. Remove from heat. Pour into shallow baking dish or 9-inch pie plate.
4. For crust, roll dough large enough to cover baking dish. Cover filling with crust. Flute edge. Cut slits for escape of steam.
5. Bake at 425°F for 30 to 40 minutes or until crust is golden brown.

6 to 8 servings

HERITAGE RECIPE

Continued

Birmingham jail. Each, augmented by others in different fields, was to study and report on an area such as housing, employment, education, health, etc. The dinner or luncheon meetings were always held in a beautiful setting like the Taconic offices or the Carlyle Hotel. There were high moments of camaraderie in the face of deep concerns. I always took away a few of the delicious macadamia nuts. Month after month our relationship with each other grew deeper. There was a sense of unity, however diverse the tactics of the different groups. Around the dinner table with Lloyd Garrison, John Simon and Jane Lee Eddy, we discussed issues and problems facing African-Americans. It was as if it were the hand of God that we had become so cohesive a group by June 12, 1963, when Medgar Evers was assassinated. We quickly gathered around the tragedy. Stephen Currier decided to invite one hundred potential supporters to

Continued on next page

PAPA'S OXTAIL STEW

Continued

breakfast at the Carlyle. Each of us agreed to speak to the critical and worsening conditions. Roy Wilkins spoke and had to leave to attend Evers' burial at Arlington Cemetery. Whitney Young made it clear that all of the civil rights organizations were hurting and knew more about what was needed than we were able to do. The outpouring of support, in both tax exempt and taxable funds, was unprecedented in the civil rights struggle. From that point, we moved beyond the original agenda agreement. We formalized the strong bonds among the group and organized for strategic planning and action for equality and justice, and incorporated under the name of the "United Civil Rights Leadership." When the "March on Washington" developed, A. Philip Randolph was represented by Bayard Rustin. The meal table was pivotal for what the press began to call the "Big Six."

Dr. Dorothy I. Height
NCNW President/CEO

2	pounds lean oxtails, washed and drained
	Salt and pepper
2	cups sliced cabbage (slice leaves into bite-size pieces by rolling several leaves together and slicing in 1/4-inch strips)
1	can (14½ ounces) tomatoes
1	medium onion, coarsely chopped or diced
1	medium green bell pepper, coarsely chopped or diced
½	cup instant rice
	All-purpose seasoning
	Red pepper flakes
2	bouillon cubes
1	cup diced, peeled potatoes
6 - 8	okra pods, cut in ½-inch chunks
1	cup frozen peas

1. Place oxtails in stockpot. Cover with cold water. Add pinch of salt and pepper. Bring to a boil. Reduce heat. Simmer until tender, about 3 hours.
2. Add cabbage, tomatoes, onion, green pepper, rice, seasonings, bouillon cubes and potatoes. Simmer until vegetables are tender.
3. Add okra and peas. Simmer no more than 5 minutes.

8 servings

Note: The fat may be skimmed off the oxtail liquid before adding the vegetables for a heart healthy stew.

HERITAGE RECIPE

TEXAS TONGUE

1	medium beef tongue	1	cup raisins
1	bay leaf	3	cups cooked tomatoes
⅓	cup Crisco Oil	½	cup sliced olives
1½	cups chopped onion	⅓	cup chopped green bell pepper
1	clove garlic, minced		Salt

1. Wash tongue. Place in large saucepan. Add bay leaf. Cover with water. Bring to a boil. Simmer until tender. Remove tongue. Plunge into cold water for 5 minutes. Remove skin and roots.
2. Heat oven to 350°F.
3. Heat Crisco Oil in large skillet. Add onions and garlic. Sauté until browned. Add raisins. Cook and stir 5 minutes. Add tomatoes, olives, green pepper and salt to taste. Simmer 5 minutes.
4. Place tongue in roasting pan. Pour sauce over tongue. Cover.
5. Bake at 350°F for one hour. Baste occasionally.

HERITAGE RECIPE

6 to 8 servings

OLD STYLE LIVER & ONIONS

½	cup all-purpose flour	1	large onion, thinly sliced and separated into rings
1	teaspoon ground sage		
¾	teaspoon salt	⅛	teaspoon instant minced garlic
½	teaspoon paprika	2	tablespoons snipped fresh parsley
⅛	teaspoon cayenne pepper		
1	pound beef liver, membrane removed, cut into 4 X 1 X ¼-inch strips	¼	cup white wine or chicken broth
¼	cup Crisco Shortening or Crisco Oil	1	tablespoon lemon juice

1. Combine flour, sage, salt, paprika and cayenne in large plastic bag. Add liver. Shake to coat. Remove liver from bag. Set aside.
2. Heat Crisco Shortening or Crisco Oil in medium skillet on medium heat. Add onion and garlic. Sauté until onion is tender. Push to one side of skillet. Add liver. Fry 6 to 8 minutes, or until no longer pink, turning over 1 or 2 times.
3. Stir together liver and onions. Sprinkle with parsley. Add wine and lemon juice. Cook, stirring constantly, 1 to 2 minutes.

4 servings

ROAST TENDERLOIN OF PORK WITH HERB TOMATO MARINADE

2	pork tenderloins (about ¾ pound each)	2	tablespoons fresh oregano or 2 teaspoons dried
1½	cups olive oil	2	tablespoons fresh thyme or 2 teaspoons dried
¾	cup apple juice		
1	small apple, diced	1	tablespoon cracked black pepper
½	cup chopped canned tomatoes		
2	tablespoons fresh basil or 2 teaspoons dried	1	cup white wine
			Fresh herb sprigs (optional)

1. Place pork in large non-metal container.
2. Combine olive oil, apple juice, apple, tomatoes, basil, oregano, thyme and pepper. Pour over pork. Marinate overnight in refrigerator.
3. Heat oven to 350°F.
4. Remove pork from marinade. Sear in oven-proof skillet. Add marinade and wine to skillet. Cover loosely with foil.
5. Bake at 350°F for 30 minutes, basting occasionally. Remove foil. Bake 15 to 20 minutes or until meat thermometer registers 170°F. Remove from oven. Let stand 5 minutes before slicing.
6. Add more white wine to skillet, if necessary. Reduce to one-half. Strain through cheesecloth. Pour over meat. Garnish with sprigs of fresh herbs, if desired.

4 to 6 servings

Clayton Sherrod, President
Chef Clayton's Food Systems, Inc.

BAKED HAM
À LA MOMMA PAN

8 - 10	pound sugar cured ham
1	liter ginger ale
1½	cups firmly packed brown sugar
½	teaspoon ground cloves

1. Place ham in large deep pan. Cover with water. Bring to a boil. Reduce heat. Simmer 20 minutes per pound, adding more water, as needed, to keep ham covered.
2. Combine ginger ale, brown sugar and cloves in small saucepan. Bring to a boil. Cook 10 minutes.
3. Heat oven to 350°F when ham is done.
4. Remove ham from liquid. Trim off most of fat. Score with knife. Place on rack in roasting pan. Pour ginger ale mixture over ham.
5. Bake at 350°F for 30 to 40 minutes, basting often.

16 to 20 servings

Joseph Randall, Chef Instructor
School of Hotel & Restaurant Management
California State Polytechnic University
President, National United Culinary Association

Thanks, Momma

Momma Pan did all the cooking, but Pansy, my sister, and I got to help. I tell people often that I learned how to eat long before I learned how to cook. Momma Pan taught us how to eat fresh vegetables from the Broad Street Market and fresh meats from Foster's Store. Getting to lick the spoon of a hand beaten pound cake was the joy of my youth. Momma would always bake a small test Bundt cake, just for me—melt in your mouth good! Thanks, Momma.

Joseph Randall,
Los Angeles, CA

BILLY'S RIBS

Ribs

10	pounds pork ribs (small ends)	1	tablespoon pepper
2	quarts water	1	teaspoon onion salt
2	medium onions, chopped	1	clove garlic, sliced
¼	cup liquid hickory smoke		Paprika
2	tablespoons salt		

Sauce

8	cups assorted bottled barbecue sauces	2	hot pepper pods
		1	tablespoon brown sugar
1	bottle ketchup	1	clove garlic, sliced
1	bottle (12 ounces) beer	1	teaspoon seasoned salt
1	onion, chopped		

1. For ribs, remove all fat and tissue from ribs.
2. Combine water, onions, liquid smoke, salt, pepper, onion salt, garlic and paprika in stockpot. Add ribs. Marinate overnight in refrigerator.
3. For sauce, combine barbecue sauces, ketchup, beer, onion, pepper pods, brown sugar, garlic, and seasoned salt in large pan. Simmer on low heat for one hour.
4. Prepare grill for cooking. Heat or build fire.
5. Remove ribs from marinade. Brush thoroughly with sauce. Place on grill. Turn ribs and baste with sauce until done, about 1 to 1½ hours.

6 to 8 servings

*Marilyn McCoo-Davis, **Entertainer***

CARTER HILL BARBECUE RIBS

4	pounds fresh spareribs, cracked
1	quart cider vinegar
1	cup firmly packed dark brown sugar
1	tablespoon coarsely ground black pepper
½	teaspoon salt
¼	teaspoon cayenne pepper
¼	teaspoon paprika
2	large cloves garlic, crushed

1. Cut ribs into 3 or 4-inch pieces. Rinse in cold water. Drain. Pour vinegar into large glass dish. Add brown sugar, pepper, salt, cayenne, paprika and garlic. Mix well. Place ribs in mixture to marinate overnight in refrigerator.
2. Heat oven to 450°F.
3. Place ribs in baking pan. Pour 1 cup marinade over top. Bake at 450°F. Baste occasionally with the sauce. Brown ribs on both sides. Reduce heat to 350°F after 30 minutes. Continue to baste while cooking another 1½ hours or until done.

Robert A. Hall, NCNW Associate Life Member

The Big Meeting

Carter Hill is the name of the Baptist Church in Walton County, Georgia. It was the center for the Big Meeting my family attended every Third Sunday in August. People gathered from miles around. Every family brought food and there was plenty to eat. Everyone shared the food from a long table stretched across the church yard. The Big Meeting was the kick off for the week's revival. As children we looked forward to the happy times with lots of good food and new friends. My grand-mother always made her special barbecue which became a favorite. Grandma kept her recipe to herself. Years later my Aunty Lou passed it on to me with fond memo-ries of the good eating at the Big Meeting.

Robert A. Hall
New York, NY

SPICED SPARERIBS

4 - 5	pounds spareribs, cracked through center	1	tablespoon beef stock base
2	teaspoons salt, divided	2	teaspoons brown sugar
2	cups boiling water	3	whole allspice
2	tablespoons ketchup	1	teaspoon cayenne pepper
2	tablespoons Worcestershire sauce	½	teaspoon grated lemon peel
2	tablespoons red wine vinegar	¼	teaspoon caraway seed
		2	teaspoons arrowroot
		1	tablespoon cold water

1. Heat oven to 350°F.
2. Trim excess fat from ribs. Cut into serving size pieces. Sprinkle with 1 teaspoon salt. Arrange in large flat baking dish.
3. Bake at 350°F for 1 to 1½ hours, turning several times.
4. Remove from oven. Drain off drippings. Sprinkle with remaining 1 teaspoon salt.
5. Combine boiling water, ketchup, Worcestershire sauce, vinegar, stock base, brown sugar, allspice, cayenne, lemon peel and caraway seed. Pour over ribs.
6. Bake at 350°F for one hour, turning frequently. Arrange ribs on platter. Skim off fat from liquid in pan.
7. Combine arrowroot and cold water. Stir into liquid in pan. Cook and stir until sauce is thickened. Pour over ribs.

6 servings

Linda Hopkins, Broadway Star

YAM PORK CHOP SKILLET

1	tablespoon Crisco Shortening or Crisco Oil	1	medium green bell pepper, cut into rings
4	pork shoulder chops	¼	teaspoon dried thyme leaves
4	medium yams or sweet potatoes, peeled and thinly sliced	¼	teaspoon dried marjoram leaves
			Salt and pepper to taste
1	large onion, thinly sliced	1	can (14½ ounces) tomatoes

1. Heat Crisco Shortening or Crisco Oil in large skillet on medium heat. Brown pork chops.
2. Arrange yam slices, onion slices and green pepper rings over pork chops. Sprinkle with thyme, marjoram, salt and pepper. Top with tomatoes. Cover. Cook on low heat one hour or until tender.

4 servings

CREOLE PORK CHOPS & CORNBREAD CASSEROLE

4	tablespoons Butter Flavor Crisco, divided	1	can (14½ ounces) whole tomatoes, undrained, cut up
8	pork chops, ½-inch thick	1	can (8 ounces) tomato sauce
⅓	cup chopped onion	1	teaspoon brown sugar
⅓	cup chopped celery	½	teaspoon chili powder
¼	cup chopped green bell pepper	¼	teaspoon salt
1	large clove garlic, minced	⅛	teaspoon black pepper
2	cups crumbled cornbread	⅛	teaspoon cayenne pepper
1	egg, lightly beaten	1	bay leaf

1. Heat oven to 350°F. Melt 2 tablespoons Butter Flavor Crisco in large skillet on medium heat. Add 4 chops. Brown both sides. Repeat with remaining chops. Remove from skillet. Set aside. Add remaining 2 tablespoons Butter Flavor Crisco, onion, celery, green pepper and garlic to skillet. Cook and stir until tender. Remove from heat.
2. Combine cornbread, egg and half of onion mixture in medium bowl. Set aside.
3. Add tomatoes, tomato sauce, brown sugar, chili powder, salt, pepper, cayenne and bay leaf to remaining mixture in skillet. Simmer about 10 minutes. Remove from heat. Remove bay leaf.
4. Place 4 pork chops in 3-quart casserole. Spread cornbread mixture over chops. Arrange remaining chops on top. Pour sauce over chops. Cover.
5. Bake at 350°F for 45 to 55 minutes, or until chops are tender.

8 servings

Leah Chase, Chef/Co-Owner
Dooky Chase Restaurant

OVERNIGHT BREAKFAST SAUSAGE CASSEROLE

1	pound bulk sausage, browned and drained
1	cup grated sharp Cheddar cheese
6	eggs, lightly beaten
2	cups milk
½	cup butter or margarine, melted
½	teaspoon dry mustard
½	teaspoon salt

1. Layer sausage in bottom of 12 X 8 X 2-inch baking dish. Sprinkle with cheese.
2. Combine eggs, milk, butter, dry mustard and salt. Pour over sausage and cheese. Refrigerate overnight.
3. Heat oven to 350°F. Bake casserole for 35 minutes or until set.

4 servings

❖

SOUTHERN PORK CHOP CASSEROLE

2	tablespoons Crisco Shortening or Crisco Oil
6 - 8	pork chops
1	cup uncooked long-grain rice
1	envelope (1 ounce) dry onion soup mix
1	can (10¾ ounces) mushroom soup
	Water

1. Heat oven to 375°F.
2. Heat Crisco Shortening or Crisco Oil in large skillet on medium heat. Brown pork chops.
3. Sprinkle uncooked rice in bottom of large baking dish. Sprinkle dry soup mix over rice. Place pork chops on top. Pour undiluted mushroom soup over chops. Add enough water to cover.
4. Bake uncovered at 375°F for one hour.

6 to 8 servings

Benny Stewart, Executive Chef-Instructor
Food Management/Culinary Arts

Going Home
All of my parents' children: my brother Robert, my sisters Caryliss and Constance, and myself live in cities away from their home in St. Louis. Coming together has special meaning to us. We know we're at home when we have our big traditional Saturday breakfast. We feast and commune over homemade biscuits, salmon croquettes, cheese eggs, bacon, herbal teas, chicken wings and rice. Being at home is truly beautiful.

Dr. Vanessa J. Weaver
First National Chair
NCNW Black Family
Reunion Celebration
Los Angeles, CA

106

SAUSAGE LIMA BEAN SKILLET

1	package (10 ounces) frozen lima beans	⅛	teaspoon dried marjoram leaves
¼	teaspoon salt	2	tablespoons cold water
1	tablespoon Crisco Shortening or Crisco Oil	1	tablespoon all-purpose flour
¼	cup finely chopped onion	½	cup sliced pitted ripe olives
1	pound bulk pork sausage	1	cup dairy sour cream
¼	cup water		Toasted cornbread or French bread slices
¼	teaspoon nutmeg		

1. Cook lima beans following package directions. Drain. Season with salt.
2. Heat Crisco Shortening or Crisco Oil in large skillet on medium heat. Add onion. Cook until crisp-tender, stirring occasionally. Separate sausage into small pieces. Add to skillet. Pour in ¼ cup water. Bring to a boil. Cover. Simmer 15 minutes.
3. Drain off drippings. Stir in nutmeg and marjoram. Stir in a blend of 2 tablespoons cold water and flour. Cook and stir for one minute.
4. Mix in lima beans and olives. Blend in sour cream, a small amount at a time. Heat thoroughly (do not boil).
5. Serve at once with slices of cornbread.

4 to 6 servings

HOG HEAD SOUSE

1	large hog head	4	red peppers
4	pig's feet	1	teaspoon salt
4	pig's ears	½	teaspoon sage
1	cup cider vinegar		Crackers

1. Split hog head. Clean thoroughly, removing eyes and brains. Scald. Scrape clean.
2. Place hog head, feet and ears in large stockpot. Simmer about 4 hours or until tender.
3. Remove meat from bone. Place meat in large bowl. Mash. Drain off any fat. Add vinegar, peppers, salt and sage. Stir to combine. Transfer to bowl or dish. Refrigerate 24 hours. Slice. Serve with crackers.

18 to 24 servings

HERITAGE RECIPE

SAUSAGE & EGG QUICHE

Crust

Unbaked 9-inch Classic
Crisco Single Crust

Filling

8	ounces bulk pork sausage	1	cup (4 ounces) shredded Cheddar cheese
4	hard-cooked eggs, shelled and chopped		
		3	eggs, beaten
1	cup (4 ounces) shredded Swiss cheese	1¼	cups coffee cream or milk
		¾	teaspoon salt
		⅛	teaspoon pepper

1. Heat oven to 350°F.
2. For crust, bake pie shell at 350°F for 7 minutes.
3. For filling, cook sausage in skillet. Drain well. Sprinkle hard-cooked egg in bottom of partially baked pie shell. Top with sausage, Swiss and Cheddar cheeses.
4. Combine eggs, cream, salt and pepper. Pour over cheese. Bake at 350°F for 30 to 35 minutes or until set. Let stand 5 minutes before serving.

6 servings

STUFFED FRESH PORK OR HAM SHANK

6 - 8	pounds fresh pork or ham shank, bone removed	3	bunches collard greens, cooked
1	tablespoon salt	1	clove garlic, sliced
1	teaspoon coarsely ground black pepper	1	onion, sliced

1. Heat oven to 325°F.
2. Rub roast with salt and pepper. Fill bone cavity with collards. Skewer or sew up cavity. Make tiny slits in meat. Insert garlic slices into slits. Place in roasting pan. Place onions on top of meat.
3. Bake at 325°F for 2½ to 3 hours or until meat is done. Cool slightly. Slice.

10 to 12 servings

METROPOLITAN A.M.E. FAVORITE SAUSAGE RICE CASSEROLE

1	pound sausage	1	can (10¾ ounces) cream of chicken soup
1	cup uncooked long grain rice		
1	can (10¾ ounces) cream of mushroom soup	1	can (10¾ ounces) cream of celery soup
		1	can water

1. Heat oven to 350°F.
2. Crumble sausage into medium skillet. Brown on medium heat. Drain. Spoon into 2-quart casserole. Add rice, mushroom soup, chicken soup, celery soup and water. Stir well.
3. Bake at 350°F for 30 to 35 minutes, stirring after 25 minutes. Bake until rice is tender.

4 to 6 servings

HERITAGE RECIPE

HAM HOCKS & RED BEANS

1	pound dried red beans	1	red pepper pod
2	quarts water	1	clove garlic, minced
1	pound ham hocks		Salt and pepper
1	onion, minced		

1. Soak beans 2 to 3 hours or overnight. Drain.
2. Place beans in large saucepan. Cover with water. Bring to a boil. Add hocks, onion, red pepper, garlic, salt and pepper to season. Reduce heat. Simmer 2 hours or until tender.

4 to 6 servings

HERITAGE RECIPE

NEW ORLEANS RED BEANS & RICE

1	pound dried red beans
8 - 10	cups water
2	tablespoons Crisco Shortening or Crisco Oil
1	large onion, chopped
¼	cup chopped celery
2	cloves garlic, chopped
1	ham bone with ham (about ½ pound)
2	tablespoons chopped parsley
1	teaspoon salt
1	bay leaf
½	teaspoon hot pepper sauce
¼	teaspoon dried thyme leaves
5	cups hot cooked rice

1. Place beans in large saucepan. Cover with water. Let beans soak until they float to top.
2. Heat Crisco Shortening or Crisco Oil in large skillet. Add onions, celery and garlic. Saute until tender. Add to beans. Add ham bone, parsley, salt, bay leaf, hot pepper sauce and thyme. Simmer about 1 hour and 30 minutes or until tender. Remove bay leaf before serving. Serve over rice.

8 to 10 servings

HERITAGE RECIPE

The Rhythm Section

If you understand jazz music, you can appreciate this: My cooking roots are from Cajun country. Years ago my husband noticed that most of my recipes begin with onions, bell peppers, celery, tomato sauce, stewed tomatoes and seasonings. From this combination, one can branch out into so many different dishes. And so, my husband named the beginning of my recipes "The Rhythm Section." Now, when I am trying to decide what to cook, my husband says, "Let's at least get "The Rhythm Section" going!"

Gloria Price Bryant
San Antonio, TX

CHITLINS À LA CALIFORNIA

10	pounds chitterlings
1	cup diced onion
1	cup diced celery
6	small hot peppers
3	cloves garlic, minced
2	tablespoons salt
1	tablespoon black pepper
1	cup cider vinegar
1	tablespoon sugar

1. Soak chitterlings in warm salt water 30 minutes. Cut each into 12-inch pieces. Slit open. Remove all fat particles and debris. Wash in warm to hot water 3 to 5 times. Place in large Dutch oven or kettle. Add onion, celery, peppers, garlic salt and pepper. Bring to a boil. Reduce heat. Cook on medium-low heat 4 hours.
2. Add vinegar and sugar. Cook on low heat one hour.

6 servings

Delia Johnson, Caterer
Johnson's Catering

HERITAGE RECIPE

I Didn't Inherit Mom's Cooking Skills

My mother, Flora Spearman Shy, was a tremendous cook and none of her skill was passed on to me. She lived until she was 80 years old and continued to cook all of the holiday meals for my sister and me and our families. She loved to cook and cooked everything from "scratch." One year when she was not feeling up to cooking the holiday meal, she gave us directions and we managed to do almost as well as she did. She instructed me on preparing chitlins: how to wash each piece and take off some, but not all of the fat, to add a bit of vinegar to the water, cook on high heat at first, then cook very slowly until tender, adding peppers, salt and other seasonings at the half-done stage. Those chitlins were wonderful, but when I tried the same thing later at home, it didn't turn out right at all. I definitely did not inherit Mom's ability to cook!

Mary Shy Scott
Supreme Basileus
Alpha Kappa Alpha
Sorority, Inc.
Atlanta, GA

SPICED PIG'S FEET

6	young pig's feet, split	1	teaspoon whole cloves
2	cups wine or tarragon vinegar	1	teaspoon dry mustard
2	onions	1	teaspoon celery seed
2	bay leaves		Pinch marjoram
1	tablespoon paprika		Salt and pepper
1	red pepper pod		

1. Wash pig's feet well. Cover with cold salted water. Soak. Drain. Place in stockpot. Cover with cold water. Simmer one hour.
2. Add vinegar, onion, bay leaves, paprika, red pepper, cloves, dry mustard, celery seed, marjoram, salt and pepper to season. Simmer until tender.

6 to 8 servings

HERITAGE RECIPE

PIG'S FEET IN TOMATO SAUCE

6	medium pig's feet, split	2	red pepper pods
	Lemon juice	2	bay leaves
3	large onions, chopped	1	clove garlic
3	ribs celery and tops, chopped		Salt, pepper and paprika
1	green bell pepper, chopped	1	can (15 ounces) tomato purée
½	cup cider vinegar		

1. Wash pig's feet. Rub with lemon juice. Place in stockpot. Cover with water. Simmer 30 minutes.
2. Add onions, celery, green pepper, vinegar, red pepper, bay leaves, garlic, salt, pepper and paprika to season. Bring to a boil.
3. Add tomato purée. Simmer until tender.

6 to 8 servings

HERITAGE RECIPE

112

SOUTHERN STYLE BARBECUED PIG'S FEET

Pig's feet

10	pounds pig's feet, split

Barbecue sauce

4	cups cider vinegar	1	tablespoon Crisco Oil
½	cup red wine	1	tablespoon paprika
1	can (6 ounces) tomato paste	2	teaspoons crushed bay leaves
4	hot green peppers	2	teaspoons dry mustard
1	tablespoon plus 1 teaspoon salt	½	teaspoon minced garlic

1. For feet, wash. Place in stockpot. Cover with cold water. Simmer one hour.
2. For sauce, combine vinegar, wine, tomato paste, hot peppers, salt, Crisco Oil, paprika, bay leaves, dry mustard and garlic in large bowl. Stir well.
3. Heat oven to 250°F. Grease large casserole or baking dish.
4. Drain pig's feet. Arrange in casserole. Pour sauce over feet.
5. Bake at 250°F for one hour or until tender.

20 servings

HERITAGE RECIPE

PIG'S FEET NORTHERN STYLE

6	pig's feet, halved lengthwise	2	tablespoons salt
1	cup diced celery	1	tablespoon black pepper
1	cup diced onion	1	bottle (14 ounces) ketchup
6	small hot peppers or 1 teaspoon cayenne pepper	1	cup cider vinegar
2	cloves garlic, minced	1	tablespoon sugar

1. Clean pig feet thoroughly, scraping to remove excess hair and particles around toes. Wash in warm salt water 3 times.
2. Combine pig feet, celery, onion, hot peppers, garlic, salt and black pepper in large Dutch oven or kettle. Add water to cover well. Cook on low heat 3 hours.
3. Add ketchup, vinegar and sugar. Cook on low heat one hour.

6 servings

Florence Cassell, Herb-Spice Producer

HERITAGE RECIPE

PARTY PIG'S FEET

4 - 6	pig's feet
2 - 3	white potatoes
2	onions
1	rib celery
2	tablespoons cider vinegar
2	cloves garlic, crushed
1	teaspoon salt
2	tablespoons pickling spice
2	hot red pepper pods
1	teaspoon black peppercorns
1	bay leaf
½	teaspoon mustard seed
	Cheese cloth

1. Wash feet. Place in stockpot. Cover with water. Parboil 8 minutes. Remove feet. Rinse. Pour out water. Return feet to pan. Cover with water. Repeat parboil procedure.
2. Place feet in stockpot. Cover with fresh water. Add potatoes, onions, celery, vinegar, garlic and salt.
3. Make spice bag by placing pickling spice, red peppers, peppercorns, bay leaf and mustard seed on piece of cheese cloth. Pull up sides to form pouch. Secure at top with thread. Add to stockpot. Bring to a boil. Reduce temperature. Simmer 2 hours or until tender.

4 to 6 servings

HERITAGE RECIPE

They Ate Everything but the Spice Bag

I enjoy cooking special meals for the Christmas and New Year's holidays. One year I made my Party Pig's Feet to serve over the New Year's weekend at a party to celebrate my husband's birthday. Our guests liked them so well they ate everything but the spice bag.
During Christmas holidays I entertain several friends for lunch. I make it special and use my china and crystal.

Marian Grace
Cincinnati, OH

STEWED KIDNEYS

2   beef, veal or pork kidneys, cut in ½-inch squares

6   onions, minced (about 2 cups)

Salt

Cayenne pepper

Black pepper

Butter or margarine

All-purpose flour

1. Place kidneys and onion in large saucepan. Cover with water. Simmer 2 hours. Cool. Add salt, cayenne and black pepper to season. Simmer one hour.
2. Make gravy with stock. Use 3 tablespoons butter and 2 tablespoons flour for each cup of liquid. Melt butter. Stir in flour. Add liquid. Cook and stir until mixture comes to a boil and thickens.

4 to 6 servings

Variation: Add carrots, celery, green pepper and tomato during last hour of cooking.

HERITAGE RECIPE

PIG'S LIVER & LIGHTS (LUNG)

1   pig's liver and lights, sliced

2 - 3 potatoes

6 or 7 slices bacon

2   onions

Bunch of parsley, chopped

2   sage leaves, crumbled

Salt and pepper

1. Heat oven to 350°F.
2. Wash liver and lights.
3. Parboil potatoes.
4. Place meat, potatoes, bacon and onions in alternate layers in deep casserole or baking dish. Sprinkle parsley, sage, salt and pepper over each layer. Add a little water.
5. Bake at 350°F for 2 hours.

4 to 6 servings

HERITAGE RECIPE

SWEETBREADS OR BRAINS

	Sweetbreads or brains	Salt
2	tablespoons lemon juice	

1. Remove membrane and arteries from sweetbreads.
2. Place in large saucepan. Cover with 4 cups water. Add lemon juice and salt to season. Simmer 20 minutes. Remove. Plunge in cold water. Drain. Reserve stock.

6 to 8 servings

Serving suggestions:

Creamed Sweetbreads : Prepare a basic white sauce. Cut meat into small cubes. Add to sauce along with cooked mushrooms, chicken, oysters, celery or peas. Serve in patty shells or on toast.

Scrambled Eggs and Brains : Break brain apart into small pieces. Melt 1 tablespoon Butter Flavor Crisco in large skillet. Combine 4 eggs and 4 tablespoons milk. Add brains and eggs to skillet. Cook and stir until set. Season with salt and pepper.

Fried Brains or Sweetbreads : Cut brains or sweetbreads into 1-inch pieces. Dip in egg and crumbs. Pan or deep fry until golden brown. Serve with lemon slices, tomato sauce or ketchup.

HERITAGE RECIPE

NECKBONES

4	pounds pork neckbones	3	tablespoons Crisco Shortening or Crisco Oil	
1	tablespoon salt			
1	teaspoon pepper	1	medium onion, sliced	
¼	teaspoon sage		All-purpose flour (optional)	

1. Wash neckbones in warm water. Drain. Dry.
2. Combine salt, pepper and sage. Season neckbones.
3. Heat Crisco Shortening or Crisco Oil in large skillet on medium heat. Brown neckbones. Remove to Dutch oven or kettle. Cover with water. Add any remaining seasoning. Cover. Simmer one hour or until meat is almost done. Add onion. Simmer 20 to 30 minutes. Thicken broth with flour, if desired.

4 to 6 servings

HERITAGE RECIPE

SAUTÉED BREAST OF CHICKEN WITH JALAPEÑO BUTTER

Jalapeño Butter

½-inch	cube fresh ginger	5	parsley sprigs
1	large clove garlic	½	cup butter, softened
1	large jalapeño pepper, seeded		Salt to taste

Chicken

4	boneless chicken breasts (4 ounces each)		Southern Rice Cakes (see page 86)
	Seasoning salt		Red, yellow and green bell peppers (optional)
	Freshly ground pepper		
1	cup Crisco Puritan Oil		

1. For butter, drop ginger in spinning blade of a food processor or blender, followed by garlic and jalapeño pepper. Stop machine. Scrape down bowl.
2. Turn machine on, add parsley, then butter and salt. Thoroughly blend all ingredients.
3. Shape butter into log. Wrap in parchment paper. Freeze until needed.
4. For chicken, season with salt and pepper.
5. Heat Crisco Puritan Oil in large skillet. Sauté chicken on both sides until golden brown and cooked through.
6. Serve on Southern Rice Cakes, topped with pat of Jalapeño Butter.
7. Garnish with red, yellow and green bell peppers, if desired.

4 servings

Clayton Sherrod, President
Chef Clayton's Food Systems, Inc.

LEMON BASIL GRILLED CHICKEN

½	cup Crisco Oil	2	cloves garlic, minced
¼	cup lemon juice	½	teaspoon salt
2	tablespoons white wine vinegar	¼	teaspoon freshly ground black pepper
1	tablespoon dried basil leaves	4	boneless, skinless chicken
1	teaspoon grated lemon peel		breast halves (about 1 pound)

1. Combine Crisco Oil, lemon juice, vinegar, basil, lemon peel, garlic, salt and pepper in shallow baking dish. Add chicken, turning once to coat both sides. Refrigerate 30 to 45 minutes, turning once.
2. Prepare charcoal for grilling, or heat broiler. Grill or broil chicken 4 inches from heat, turning once, 3 to 5 minutes per side or until just cooked through.

4 servings

SWEET & SPICY BARBECUED GRILLED CHICKEN

1	frying chicken (2½ to 3 pounds) cut into 8 pieces	2	tablespoons firmly packed brown sugar
2	tablespoons Butter Flavor Crisco	1	tablespoon Worcestershire sauce
2	cloves garlic, minced	½	teaspoon salt
1	cup chopped onion	½	teaspoon chili powder
1	can (8 ounces) tomato sauce	¼	teaspoon pepper
¼	cup chili sauce		

1. Prepare outdoor grill for cooking. Place chicken, skin-side down, on grill about 6 inches from medium-hot coals. Grill chicken 20 minutes, turning once.
2. Melt Butter Flavor Crisco in small saucepan on medium heat. Add garlic and onion. Cook and stir until onion is tender. Stir in tomato sauce, chili sauce, brown sugar, Worcestershire sauce, salt, chili powder and pepper. Simmer 5 minutes longer to blend flavors.
3. Brush chicken with sauce. Grill 15 to 20 minutes, turning several times. Brush often with sauce.

4 servings

POULET YASSA

5	tablespoons peanut oil, divided		Salt and freshly ground black pepper
	Juice of 6 lemons	2½-3½	pounds frying chicken pieces
3	large onions, sliced	½	cup water
6	fresh hot red chilies, cut in small pieces		Hot cooked rice

1. Combine 4 tablespoons oil, lemon juice, onions, chilies, salt and pepper in glass baking dish. Place chicken in marinade. Turn to coat well. Marinate 2 hours in refrigerator.
2. Heat broiler. Place chicken on broiler pan. Reserve marinade. Broil until lightly browned.
3. Place remaining oil in a large skillet on medium heat. Remove onions from marinade. Add to skillet. Sauté until tender. Add marinade. Bring to a boil. Add chicken pieces and water. Simmer on low heat for 20 minutes or until done. Serve with rice.

6 servings

LA MARDI GRAS CHICKEN BREAST

5 - 6	boneless chicken breasts	½	onion, julienned
2	cups Italian low-calorie dressing (oil based)	2	tablespoons butter, margarine or oil
3	tablespoons Cajun seasoning		Hot cooked rice
½	green, yellow and red peppers, julienned		

1. Wash chicken breasts and pat dry. Place in dish.
2. Mix Italian dressing and Cajun seasoning. Pour over chicken. Cover. Refrigerate. Marinate 3 to 6 hours.
3. Remove chicken from marinade. Grill or cook in blackened skillet until done.
4. Sauté peppers and onion in butter in skillet while chicken is cooking.
5. Top chicken with peppers and onions. Serve over rice.

Bobby Black, Executive Chef
Heritage Place

Playtime Pranks
When I was a child, all of the play activities were centered around the church. My house was right across the street from it, so most of the children in the neighborhood came to my house for water. On the days when my mother cooked fried chicken, we could smell it while we were playing. Most of us knew that mama would put the chicken on top of the stove in a bowl with a cloth cover when she was done. On fried chicken days, everyone took turns going for water and came out with a piece of chicken in one hand and water in the other. We thought we were fooling my mother. Although she never accused us of taking the chicken, at dinner time she would look at the bowl (still mysteriously full) and say, "I know I cooked more chicken than this." When I was older, she told me she knew we were taking it, but that she always had extra hidden in the oven.

Barbara Van Blake,
National Treasurer
NCCW
Washington, DC

CLASSIC SKILLET FRIED CHICKEN

¾	cup all-purpose flour
1	teaspoon salt
¼	teaspoon pepper
1	frying chicken (2½ to 3 pounds), cut up or use chicken pieces
½	cup Crisco Shortening or Crisco Oil

1. Combine flour, salt and pepper in paper or plastic bag. Add a few pieces of chicken at a time. Shake to coat.
2. Heat Crisco Shortening or Crisco Oil to 365°F in electric skillet or on medium-high heat in large heavy skillet. Fry chicken 30 to 40 minutes without lowering heat. Turn once for even browning. Drain on paper towels.

4 servings

Note: For thicker crust, increase flour to 1½ cups. Shake damp chicken in seasoned flour. Place on waxed paper. Let sit for 5 to 20 minutes before frying.

Variation:
Spicy Fried Chicken   : Increase pepper to ½ teaspoon. Combine pepper with ½ teaspoon poultry seasonings, ½ teaspoon paprika, ½ teaspoon cayenne pepper and ¼ teaspoon dry mustard. Rub on chicken before step 1. Substitute 2¼ teaspoons garlic salt, ¼ teaspoon salt and ¼ teaspoon celery salt for 1 teaspoon salt. Combine with flour in step 1 and proceed as before.

CRISP & SPICY DRUMSTICKS

12	fryer drumsticks
1	cup all-purpose flour
2	teaspoons garlic powder
1	tablespoon seasoning salt
1	tablespoon black pepper
1	tablespoon cayenne pepper
2	cups Crisco Oil

1. Wash drumsticks, shake off excess water. Place in very large bowl. Place flour in large plastic bag.
2. Pour garlic powder, seasoning salt, black pepper and cayenne over chicken. Mix well with hands until all chicken pieces are coated with spice mixture.
3. Place 3 drumsticks at a time in flour. Shake gently. Remove excess flour from drumsticks as you are removing them from bag. Place on waxed paper or paper towels, making sure pieces don't touch. Let stand for about 20 minutes, or until flour coating looks moist.
4. Heat Crisco Oil in large skillet on high heat. Add drumsticks, making sure they do not touch. Cook on one side 15 seconds, then turn. Cover with lid. Lower heat to medium high. Brown on both sides. Remove. Place on cooling rack lined with triple layer of paper towels. Let stand 5 minutes, then serve.

6 servings

Aunt Berdie's House

My Aunt Berdie always had Sunday dinner at her house. She lived just a few houses away from the church and the family went there right after morning worship. It was so much fun. We could hardly wait to run down the street to the piping hot food and the lingering odors of Southern fried chicken and yeast rolls. I really miss it.

Crystal Ann Cruse
Cincinnati, OH

CHICKEN & CABBAGE SKILLET

¼	cup Crisco Shortening or Crisco Oil	1½	teaspoons salt, divided
1	frying chicken (2½ pounds), cut up or use chicken pieces	1	teaspoon caraway seed
		1	cup cider vinegar
½	cup all-purpose flour	1	cup water
1	pound cabbage, coarsely chopped (about 8 cups)	3	medium tart red apples, cored and cut in ½-inch rings
2	tablespoons all-purpose flour	3	tablespoons brown sugar

1. Heat Crisco Shortening or Crisco Oil in large heavy skillet on medium heat. Coat chicken evenly with ½ cup flour. Add chicken pieces. Brown evenly on all sides. Cook until done. Remove from skillet. Drain on paper towels. Pour off drippings.
2. Put cabbage in skillet. Combine 2 tablespoons flour, ½ teaspoon salt, and caraway seed. Sprinkle over cabbage. Stir in vinegar and water.
3. Arrange apple rings over cabbage. Sprinkle with brown sugar.
4. Arrange chicken pieces over apple rings and cabbage. Sprinkle with remaining 1 teaspoon salt.
5. Cover and cook 10 minutes on medium heat. Uncover. Cook 5 minutes or until cabbage and chicken are tender.

4 to 6 servings

JAMBALAYA L'ACADIEN

1	tablespoon Crisco Shortening	½	medium green bell pepper, chopped
1	tablespoon all-purpose flour		
1	cup or more raw duck, chicken or turkey giblets, ground	½	clove garlic, minced
		1	teaspoon salt
1½	cups hot water	½	teaspoon cayenne pepper
2	white onions, chopped	3	cups cooked rice
2	ribs celery, chopped		

1. Melt Crisco in large skillet. Add flour. Cook and stir on low heat until dark red-brown.
2. Add giblets, water, onions, celery, green pepper, garlic, salt and cayenne. Cook on low heat one hour. Combine with rice.

4 servings

DEVILED CHICKEN WINGS

24	chicken wings
¼	cup ketchup
¼	cup Crisco Oil
2	tablespoons lemon juice
1	tablespoon chili powder
1	teaspoon lemon pepper seasoning
½	teaspoon ground oregano
½	teaspoon onion powder
⅛	teaspoon cayenne pepper

1. Prepare outdoor grill for cooking.
2. Cut off wing tips. Discard or save for another use. Rinse and dry. Place on grill about 6 inches from medium-hot coals. Grill 15 minutes.
3. Combine ketchup, Crisco Oil, lemon juice, chili powder, lemon pepper, oregano, onion powder, and cayenne. Brush on wings. Brush often with sauce. Grill until tender.

Note: Wings can be baked or broiled. Brush often with sauce. Cook until tender.

6 to 8 servings

My Weakness

My husband said shortly after we were married, "I didn't know that chickens had so many wings until I met you." Chicken wings prepared any way at all are my weakness.

Jacqui Gates
National President
National Association
of Negro Business and
Professional Women's
Clubs, Inc.
Palisades Park, NJ

123

FAMILY FAMOUS CHICKEN & DUMPLINGS

1	stewing chicken (5 to 6 pounds), cut up or 2 frying chickens, cut up
2	sprigs parsley
4	ribs celery with leaves
1	carrot, sliced
1	small onion, cut up
2½	teaspoons salt, divided
¼	teaspoon pepper
1	bay leaf
1½	cups all-purpose flour, divided
2	teaspoons baking powder
½	cup milk
2	tablespoons Crisco Shortening, melted
2	tablespoons chopped fresh parsley
1	cup cold water

1. Place chicken in stockpot. Add enough water to cover. Add parsley, celery, carrot, onion, 2 teaspoons salt, pepper and bay leaf. Cover. Bring to a boil. Simmer 2½ hours.
2. Combine 1 cup flour, baking powder and remaining ½ teaspoon salt in medium bowl. Combine milk and Crisco. Add with chopped parsley to dry ingredients. Stir just until dry ingredients are moistened. Drop by tablespoonfuls directly onto chicken in boiling broth. Cover tightly. Return to boiling. Reduce heat (don't lift cover). Simmer 12 to 15 minutes.
3. Strain chicken broth. Measure 4 cups into saucepan. Bring to a boil. Combine remaining ½ cup flour and 1 cup cold water. Add gradually to broth. Mix well. Cook and stir until thickened.

6 to 8 servings

We Knew We Were Home

My family could not afford summer camp, so we were sent away to New Jersey to visit relatives. We enjoyed the visits, but their food was different from what we were accustomed to. The Sunday we were brought home by our father, we knew we were home when he opened the door and we smelled the stewed chicken.

Lucille F. Finigan
Brooklyn, NY

KWANZAA JOLLOF RICE

2	tablespoons plus 1½ teaspoons Crisco Oil, divided
1	frying chicken, cut in small pieces
3	medium onions, chopped
2	small green bell peppers, chopped
½	pound raw shrimp, shelled and deveined
6	cups water
¾	cup chopped carrots
¾	cup cut green beans
¾	cup peas
3	medium tomatoes, cut up
1	teaspoon salt
½	teaspoon black pepper
½	teaspoon cayenne pepper
1	sprig thyme, crushed, or 1 teaspoon dried
1½	cups uncooked long-grain rice
¼	cup tomato paste

1. Heat 2 tablespoons Crisco Oil in stockpot or kettle. Brown chicken. Add onions and green peppers. Cook on medium heat 5 to 10 minutes.
2. Sauté shrimp in remaining 1½ teaspoons oil in small skillet.
3. Bring 6 cups water to a boil in large saucepan. Add carrots, green beans and peas. Cook about 5 minutes.
4. Drain vegetables, reserving 3 cups cooking liquid. Add to chicken in stockpot along with shrimp, tomatoes, salt, black pepper, cayenne and thyme. Reduce heat to low. Simmer 5 minutes.
4. Combine rice and tomato paste in bowl. Stir until rice is coated. Stir into stockpot. Add small amounts of water as needed to prevent sticking. Cook about 20 minutes or until chicken, vegetables and rice are tender.

6 servings

HERITAGE RECIPE

Kwanzaa

In 1977 my two best friends and I received grants to travel to Nigeria; our first trip to Africa! We learned first hand about Nigerian foods, art and traditions. During the first holiday season after our return, we had a wonderful Kwanzaa celebration encompassing our three families and a host of friends. My family enjoyed it so much that we've continued the celebrations for the past thirteen years. Our family is quite extended; it included five generations until my grandmother, "Mama Pride" died last year, and of course my two best friends and their families are always invited. The younger children have known Kwanzaa for their entire lives and eagerly look forward to it. Our menu is truly African and American including a variety of dishes from an English wassail beverage to the jollof rice recipe included here.

Helen E. Baker
Indianapolis, IN

GROUNDNUT STEW

1	chicken, cut into pieces	⅔	cup peanut butter
1	inch piece ginger	2	teaspoons salt
½	medium onion plus 1 cup chopped	2	hot chilies, crushed or 1 teaspoon cayenne pepper
2	cups water*	1	medium eggplant, peeled and cubed
2	tablespoons tomato paste		
1	tablespoon peanut oil	2	cups fresh or frozen okra, thawed
1	cup chopped tomato		

1. Combine chicken, ginger, onion half and water in large saucepan. Heat to a boil. Reduce heat. Simmer until chicken is partially cooked.
2. Combine tomato paste and peanut oil in large Dutch oven. Cook on low heat 5 minutes. Add chopped onion and tomato. Cook and stir until onion is clear.
3. Remove partially cooked chicken from saucepan. Add to onion-tomato paste mixture. Add about half of broth. Stir in peanut butter, salt and chilies. Cook 5 minutes on medium heat.
4. Stir in eggplant and okra. Cook until chicken and vegetables are tender. Add more broth, if needed, to maintain stew-like consistency.

* To serve as soup, increase water to 6 cups.

4 to 6 servings

Melvin Hooks, Executive Chef
Hook's Catering

HERITAGE RECIPE

CHICKEN & SAUSAGE JAMBALAYA

6	bacon slices, chopped	1½	cups water
1½	cups sliced celery	½	cup garlic flavored barbecue sauce
1	cup uncooked long-grain rice		
1	cup chopped onion	1	teaspoon salt
1	cup chopped green bell pepper	¼	teaspoon cayenne pepper
1	can (14½ ounces) tomatoes	1½	cups diced cooked chicken
½	pound cooked smoked sausage, cut into ½-inch pieces		

1. Fry bacon until crisp in 3-quart Dutch oven or large deep skillet.
2. Stir in celery, rice, onion and green pepper. Cook and stir 5 minutes.
3. Add undrained tomatoes, sausage, water, barbecue sauce, salt and cayenne. Stir. Bring to a boil. Cover. Simmer 20 minutes, stirring occasionally.
3. Add chicken.

4 servings

BISCUIT-TOPPED DEEP DISH CHICKEN BAKE

Chicken Mixture

1	tablespoon Butter Flavor Crisco
1½	cups fresh green beans
2	medium carrots, cut into julienne strips
1	medium onion, chopped
½	cup thinly sliced celery
½	cup water
¼	cup all-purpose flour

1½	teaspoons instant chicken bouillon granules
1	tablespoon snipped fresh parsley or 1 teaspoon dried
½	teaspoon poultry seasoning
¼	teaspoon salt
¼	teaspoon pepper
2	cups milk
2	cups cut-up cooked chicken or turkey

Biscuits

1	cup all-purpose flour
1½	teaspoons baking powder
¼	teaspoon salt
1	tablespoon snipped fresh parsley or 1 teaspoon dried

2	tablespoons Butter Flavor Crisco
½	cup milk

1. Heat oven to 375°F. Grease 2-quart casserole.
2. For chicken mixture, melt Butter Flavor Crisco in large saucepan. Add green beans, carrots, onions and celery. Cook and stir on medium heat until onion is tender. Add water. Bring to a boil. Reduce heat. Cover. Simmer about 12 minutes or until carrots are tender.
3. Stir flour, parsley, poultry seasoning, salt and pepper into milk Add bouillon granules to vegetables. Cook and stir on medium heat until mixture thickens and comes to a boil. Remove from heat. Stir in chicken. Pour into casserole.
4. For Biscuits, combine flour, baking powder, salt and parsley in small bowl. Cut in Butter Flavor Crisco using pastry blender or 2 knives until coarse crumbs form. Stir in milk. Drop by tablespoonfuls on top of casserole to form 8 biscuits. Bake at 375°F for 35 to 40 minutes or until bubbly and biscuits are browned.

4 to 6 servings

CHICKEN FEET STEW

2	pounds chicken feet	1	cup green beans
5	potatoes, cut in eighths	3	bay leaves
4	onions, quartered	1	clove garlic, minced
3	carrots, sliced		Salt and pepper

1. Cut nails. Wash feet. Place in stockpot. Cover with water.
2. Add potatoes, onions, carrots, green beans, bay leaf, garlic, salt and pepper to season. Simmer until tender. Remove bay leaf before serving.

6 to 8 servings

HERITAGE RECIPE

CAJUN CHICKEN "DIRTY" RICE

¼	cup Butter Flavor Crisco	2	cloves garlic, minced
1	pound chicken gizzards, finely chopped	2	teaspoons salt
1	pound chicken livers, finely chopped	1	teaspoon black pepper
1½	cups diced onions	⅛	teaspoon cayenne pepper
½	cup diced celery	3	cups hot cooked rice
½	cup diced green bell pepper	½	cup chopped parsley (optional)

1. Heat Butter Flavor Crisco in large skillet on medium heat. Add gizzards and livers. Brown.
2. Add onion, celery, green pepper, garlic, salt, black pepper and cayenne. Mix well. Cover. Cook on medium heat, stirring occasionally, until vegetables are tender. Add rice and parsley. Mix lightly. Garnish with parsley, if desired. Serve hot.

8 servings

ROAST TURKEY IN PEANUT BUTTER

10 - 12	pound turkey	1	teaspoon celery salt
½	cup peanut butter	1	teaspoon pepper
1	tablespoon all-purpose flour	⅓	cup milk or cream
1	tablespoon paprika	1	cup water
1	tablespoon salt		

1. Heat oven to 325°F.
2. Prepare turkey for roasting.
3. Combine peanut butter, flour, paprika, salt, celery salt and pepper. Stir until blended, adding enough milk to make medium paste.
4. Spread paste over entire turkey, covering well. Place on rack in roasting pan. Add 1 cup water to pan.
5. Bake at 325°F for 3 or 4 hours or until meat thermometer registers 180° to 185°F. Baste every 30 minutes with pan juices.

Note: Stuffed turkey requires 30 to 45 minutes more roasting time.

WEEKNIGHT CROQUETTES

2	tablespoons Crisco Shortening or Crisco Oil	1	tablespoon chopped parsley
2	tablespoons finely chopped onion	½	teaspoon salt
2	tablespoons all-purpose flour	⅛	teaspoon pepper
½	cup chicken broth	1	egg, lightly beaten
1	egg, lightly beaten	¾	cup dry bread crumbs
2	cups very finely chopped or ground cooked turkey or chicken		Crisco Shortening or Crisco Oil for deep frying
			White or cheese sauce

1. Heat 2 tablespoons Crisco Shortening or Crisco Oil in skillet. Add onion. Cook on medium heat 2 minutes or until tender. Stir in flour. Add chicken broth gradually, stirring until sauce is thick and smooth.
2. Remove skillet from heat. Mix in one egg. Add turkey, parsley, salt and pepper. Stir until well blended.
3. Spread mixture on plate. Refrigerate at least 2 hours.
4. Shape mixture into 6 balls. Roll in remaining egg, then in bread crumbs.
5. Heat Crisco Shortening or Crisco Oil to 365°F in a deep fryer or deep saucepan. Fry turkey croquettes 5 to 6 minutes. Drain on paper towels. Serve with a basic white or cheese sauce.

6 Croquettes

TURKEY WINGS & MUSHROOMS MARENGO

6	slices bacon, cut in 1-inch pieces	½	pound mushrooms, sliced
		1	can (28 ounces) tomatoes
10	turkey wings, tips removed	2	cups water
	Salt and pepper	2	chicken bouillon cubes
	All-purpose flour	¼	cup chopped parsley
1	large onion, chopped	3 - 4	drops hot pepper sauce
1	clove garlic, minced		Croutons
½	cup all-purpose flour		Parsley

1. Heat oven to 350°F.
2. Fry bacon until almost crisp in large skillet on medium heat. Remove. Drain on paper towels.
3. Rinse turkey wings. Pat dry. Sprinkle with salt and pepper. Dust with flour. Brown lightly in bacon drippings. Remove. Arrange in large roasting pan.
4. Sauté onion and garlic in drippings remaining in skillet. Stir in ½ cup flour and brown. Add mushrooms. Cook and stir 2 minutes. Add tomatoes, water and bouillon cubes. Cook 5 minutes. Stir in parsley and hot pepper sauce. Spoon over wings. Cover. Bake at 350°F for 2 hours. Remove cover. Sprinkle bacon pieces over top. Return to oven. Bake until bacon is crisp (about 20 minutes). Garnish with croutons and parsley.

8 to 10 servings

QUICK TURKEY HASH

¼	cup Crisco Shortening or Crisco Oil	2	cups diced cooked potatoes
1	cup sliced mushrooms	1	tablespoon snipped parsley
½	cup finely chopped onion	1	teaspoon salt
2	cups diced cooked turkey	⅛	teaspoon pepper
		⅔	cup evaporated milk

1. Heat Crisco Shortening or Crisco Oil in large saucepan on medium heat. Add mushrooms and onion. Sauté about 5 minutes.
2. Remove from heat. Stir in turkey, potatoes, parsley, salt and pepper. Add evaporated milk gradually, stirring gently. Heat mixture thoroughly (about 5 minutes).

Variation:
Hash Cakes : Prepare hash (finely chopping mushrooms, turkey and potatoes and reducing evaporated milk to ⅓ cup). Cool. Shape hash into 6 patties and coat well with ¼ cup all-purpose flour. Heat 2 tablespoons Crisco Shortening or Crisco Oil in large skillet. Add hash cakes. Brown on both sides.

6 servings

STEWED TURKEY NECKS

½	cup all-purpose flour	1	rib celery, chopped
¾	teaspoon salt	4	cloves garlic, minced
¼	teaspoon freshly ground black pepper	1	bay leaf
		2	cups water
3	pounds turkey necks	4	chicken bouillon cubes
2	tablespoons Crisco Shortening or Crisco Oil	2	teaspoons celery seed
		¼	teaspoon red pepper flakes
1	cup chopped onion		Salt and pepper

1. Combine flour, salt and pepper in paper or plastic bag. Add a few necks at a time. Shake to coat.
2. Heat Crisco Shortening or Crisco Oil in stockpot on medium heat. Brown necks on all sides. Add onion, celery, garlic and bay leaf. Sauté 3 minutes. Add water, bouillon cubes, celery seed and red pepper flakes. Cover. Cook on medium-low heat 2 hours or until meat is very tender. Add additional salt and pepper to taste, if needed.

4 servings

HERITAGE RECIPE

OLD FASHIONED ROAST TURKEY WITH TWO STUFFINGS

Turkey

10 - 12 pound turkey
Oil

Salt
Pepper

Bread Stuffing

½ cup (1 stick) butter or margarine
2 cups diced celery
1 cup diced onion
1 small container oysters (optional)
4 cups seasoned bread crumb stuffing mix

2 green hot pepper pods, finely diced (optional)
1 tablespoon poultry seasoning
1 teaspoon sugar
1 teaspoon salt
Black pepper

Cornbread Stuffing

½ cup (1 stick) butter or margarine
2 cups diced celery
1 cup diced onion
4 cups cornbread stuffing crumbs
2 green hot pepper pods, finely diced (optional)

1 tablespoon poultry seasoning
1 teaspoon sugar
1 teaspoon salt
Black pepper
1 cup sliced water chestnuts (optional)
½ cup slivered almonds (optional)

1. For turkey, rinse and dry turkey thoroughly. Rub or brush with oil. Sprinkle with salt and pepper. Prepare one of the following stuffings.
2. For bread stuffing, melt butter in large skillet. Add celery and onion. Sauté 3 minutes on medium heat. If using oysters, cut in one-inch pieces. Sauté one minute. Add to celery-onion mixture. Stir in stuffing crumbs, diced hot pepper (if desired), poultry seasoning, sugar, salt and black pepper. Toss lightly to mix. Cool.
3. For cornbread stuffing, melt butter in large skillet. Add celery and onion. Sauté 3 minutes on medium heat. Add cornbread stuffing crumbs, diced hot pepper (if desired), poultry seasoning, sugar, salt and black pepper. Toss lightly to mix. Cool. Add water chestnuts and almonds (if desired).
4. Heat oven to 500°F.
5. Stuff and truss turkey. Place on rack in roasting pan.
6. Roast at 500° for 15 minutes. Reduce heat to 350°F. Roast 4 hours or until meat thermometer reaches 180° to 185°F, basting occasionally.

10 to 12 servings

Robert O. Love, Executive Chef-Instructor-RT
Los Angeles Trade and Technical College

NANA'S SWEET POTATO DRESSING

1	pound sweet potatoes (about 3 medium), peeled and cut into 2-inch chunks
1	teaspoon salt, divided
¼	cup plus 2 tablespoons Butter Flavor Crisco, divided
1	cup chopped celery
¼	cup chopped onion
¼	teaspoon poultry seasoning
¼	teaspoon pepper
½	pound ground seasoned pork sausage
3	cups seasoned croutons
1	medium apple, cored and chopped
¼	cup raisins
1	egg, lightly beaten
½	teaspoon instant chicken bouillon granules
⅓	cup hot water

1. Place sweet potatoes in large saucepan. Add ½ teaspoon salt and enough water to cover. Heat to boiling. Cover. Simmer 20 to 25 minutes or until fork tender. Drain. Cool.
2. Heat oven to 350°F. Grease 2-quart casserole or baking dish with Butter Flavor Crisco.
3. Melt 2 tablespoons Butter Flavor Crisco in medium skillet on medium heat. Add celery and onion. Cook and stir until tender. Stir in remaining ½ teaspoon salt, poultry seasoning and pepper. Transfer to large mixing bowl.
4. Brown sausage in large skillet, stirring to break apart. Drain if necessary. Add to celery and onion. Stir in croutons, apple and raisins. Mix in egg.
5. Melt remaining ¼ cup Butter Flavor Crisco. Dissolve bouillon granules in hot water. Add melted Butter Flavor Crisco and bouillon to sausage mixture. Cut sweet potatoes into ½-inch cubes. Add to mixing bowl. Mix well. Transfer to casserole. Bake, uncovered, at 350°F for 35 to 40 minutes, or until golden brown.

8 to 10 servings

Unforgettable Memories

Growing up as one of the Cole children was really memorable. Christmas was a very special time in our household. The food was always delicious and satisfying— everything from turkey and dressing to sweet potato pie.
Now that I have my own family, I try to give them the same things that my family gave me: Tender Loving Care and Affection.

Natalie Cole,
Entertainer and
Recording Artist
Los Angeles, CA

OYSTER STUFFING

4	cups finely diced celery
1	cup diced onion
2	cups water
1	cup Butter Flavor Crisco or butter
3	cups oysters, cut in pieces (reserve liquid)
8	cups dry bread crumbs
1	tablespoon poultry seasoning
1	tablespoon salt
1	teaspoon pepper

1. Combine celery, onion and water in medium saucepan. Simmer until tender. Drain, reserving 1 cup liquid.
2. Melt Butter Flavor Crisco in large skillet. Add celery and onion. Sauté. Add oysters.
3. Combine bread crumbs, poultry seasoning, salt and pepper in large bowl. Add celery mixture. Toss to mix. Moisten with reserved cooking and oyster liquid.

Stuffing for 12 to 15 pound turkey

HOLIDAY RICE STUFFING

¼	cup Butter Flavor Crisco
1	cup chopped green onions
1	cup chopped celery
1	cup chopped parsley
1	cup grated carrots
2	cups cooked long grain rice
6	cups giblet broth
	Salt and pepper

1. Melt Butter Flavor Crisco in large saucepan. Cook onions, celery, parsley and carrots 10 minutes, stirring frequently. Add rice. Stir until well mixed.
2. Add giblet broth. Season with salt and pepper. Cover. Cook 25 minutes. Serve with poultry.

6 to 8 servings

Undercover Oysters

My mother, Sallie Palmer, was a master food camouflager. She and Daddy would not allow my brother, my sister or me to say we didn't like something without tasting it. Once we identified the disliked food for her, she would become very creative and "doctor up" recipes so that we would eat things like spinach, squash, okra, liver and oysters—just to name a few.

Oysters presented the greatest challenge for her; my brother vowed never to eat oysters under any circumstance. One year the stuffing for Thanksgiving dinner was extraordinarily delicious. My brother ate more than anyone else, not realizing it was Oyster Stuffing. We ate it for years before she told the secret.

Juetta Coleman
President, Section of the Oranges
South Orange, NJ

TRIPLE CORN STUFFING

½	pound bacon (8 to 10 slices)
1½	cups chopped celery
½	cup chopped onion
4	cups coarse cornbread crumbs
4	cups toasted bread crumbs
2	teaspoons poultry seasoning
½	teaspoon salt
1	can (17 ounces) cream-style corn
1	can (17 ounces) whole kernel corn

1. Cook bacon in large skillet on medium heat until crisp. Drain. Reserve ½ cup drippings in skillet. Crumble bacon. Set aside. Add celery and onion to skillet. Cook until tender but not brown.
2. Combine bacon, celery mixture, cornbread, bread crumbs, poultry seasoning, salt and cream-style corn in large bowl. Drain whole kernel corn, reserving liquid. Add corn to stuffing with some of the liquid for moist stuffing. Toss well.

Stuffing for 12 to 15 pound turkey

Jennifer Thomas, Vice President
Los Angeles Sentinel

My Favorite Meal

My grandmother always made special dinners for family gatherings, especially on Sundays. My uncles, aunts, cousins and I looked forward to going to her house to see what was for dinner. These meals were a joy and filled with lots of laughter. We would have contests to see who could eat the most of our favorite meals. Even though I was one of the youngest children, I was always the winner when grandmother made chicken and dressing. To me this was the most delicious and even today, it is still my favorite meal. The chicken would be golden brown with the most delicious cornbread dressing and a rich giblet gravy. I can't forget the special cranberry relish that grandmother made with fresh cranberries and oranges. This meal was ***soooo gooood*** that I would pass up dessert for more chicken and dressing.

Wilhelmina D. Goff
Deputy Executive Director
Delta Sigma Theta Sorority, Inc.
Washington, DC

No "Queen of the Kitchen"

Mary McLeod Bethune was able to elevate the simple, but distinctive, culinary art of the women who came to help in the early years at Daytona Beach. At her request, they would make fish sandwiches (usually mullet) and sweet potato pies, which Mrs. Bethune sold to the workers who laid the historic Flagler Railroad tracks. These tracks lie some six blocks east of Bethune-Cookman College—The Child of Her Heart. On Founder's Day, the college dining facility serves the traditional fish and sweet potato pies.

No "Queen of the Kitchen," Mrs. Bethune simply did not include cooking in her busy agenda, but she did carefully inform others around her—family members, relatives, chefs, hostesses, and friends— of her tastes and food preferences. High on her list of favorites were chicken and rice (especially rice); string beans and asparagus (among the

Continued on next page

FRIED MEALED CATFISH

2 - 3	cups Crisco Shortening
1	cup corn meal
½	cup all-purpose flour
2	teaspoons salt
1	teaspoon pepper
½	teaspoon garlic salt
½	teaspoon onion salt
1	pound boneless catfish
	Lemon wedges (optional)

1. Heat Crisco to 365°F in deep fryer or deep saucepan.
2. Combine corn meal, flour, salt, pepper, garlic salt and onion salt in paper or plastic bag.
3. Put 3 or 4 pieces of fish in bag. Shake until well coated. Fry fish until brown and tender. Garnish with lemon wedges, if desired.

4 to 6 servings

HERITAGE RECIPE

CODFISH CAKES

1	pound dried cod fish
2	eggs, well beaten
1	pound all-purpose flour
1	pound green bell peppers, finely chopped
1	pound onions, finely chopped
1	pound scallions, finely chopped
2	tablespoons hot peppers, chopped
1	teaspoon crushed garlic
1	cup milk
	Crisco Oil

1. Soak cod fish in water to remove excess salt. Flake fish into small pieces
2. Combine eggs, flour, fish, green peppers, onions, scallions, hot pepper, garlic and milk. Mix well.
3. Heat Crisco Oil in large skillet on medium heat. Drop batter by small spoonfuls into skillet. Fry until brown on all sides. Remove and place on paper towels to drain. Serve hot or cold.

10 to 12 servings

Continued

relatively few vegetables that she liked—she called green vegetables "medicine"); brown sugar cookies (one before bedtime); Jello (preferably lemon-flavored); pound cake; tapioca pudding; lemonade and strong black tea.

The ex-Director of the College Dining Room, Mr. Charles Francis, baked fruit cakes from an original recipe. Mrs. Bethune enjoyed them and transformed them into a delicious commercial product sold seasonally by the college. Some still have the colorful maroon and gold tins in which the fruit cakes were sold, including me. I keep it among my memories, my "food memories," that is, of the past.

Cleo S. Higgins, Ph. D.
Distinguished Professor, Emeritus, Bethune-Cookman College
Daytona Beach, FL

CATFISH STEW & RICE

3	cups water	2	large tomatoes, chopped
2	medium potatoes, diced		Salt and pepper
1	large onion, chopped	4	fresh boneless catfish fillets, halved
1	tablespoon chopped garlic		
½	head small cabbage, chopped		Hot cooked rice

1. Combine water, potatoes, onion, and garlic in large pot. Cook on high heat 15 minutes. Lower heat.
2. Add cabbage, tomatoes, salt and pepper. Cook 10 minutes.
3. Add catfish. Cook 15 minutes. Remove from heat. Serve over rice.

4 to 6 servings

Johnny Rivers, Executive Chef
Walt Disneyworld Resorts

SHRIMP CURRY

1	pound large shrimp, washed and deveined	½	green bell pepper, chopped
2	tablespoons lemon juice	2	tablespoons curry powder
¼	teaspoon garlic powder	½	cup water
¼	teaspoon onion salt	2	cups hot cooked rice
2	tablespoons vegetable oil		Raisins
1	medium onion, chopped		Shredded coconut

1. Place shrimp in non-metal container. Combine lemon juice, garlic powder and onion salt. Pour over shrimp. Let stand 10 minutes.
2. Heat oil in large skillet. Add onion and green pepper. Sauté. Stir in curry powder. Add water slowly. Simmer 15 minutes. Add shrimp. Cook 15 minutes.
3. Serve over rice. Garnish with raisins and coconut. Serve hot.

4 servings

Anna Maria Horsford, Television Star

BAKED STUFFED FLOUNDER

8	pieces flounder filet
1	pound crab meat
½	teaspoon cayenne pepper
½	cup chopped green bell pepper
3	tablespoons mayonnaise
1	egg, beaten
4	slices butter or margarine
2	tablespoons lemon juice

1. Heat oven to 450°. Grease shallow roasting pan.
2. Wash fish. Pat dry.
3. Combine crab meat, cayenne, green pepper, mayonnaise and egg.
4. Place 4 pieces of fish in roasting pan. Place 2 heaping tablespoons of crab mixture on each piece of fish. Top with remaining fish. Place slice of butter on each fish. Sprinkle with lemon juice.
5. Bake 30 minutes. Baste. Broil 5 minutes. Baste. Broil 5 more minutes.

4 servings

Family Favorite

Seafood is our family's favorite food. I remember my father preparing baked shad for the family. This was always an exciting time. So whenever I serve stuffed flounder, I have fond memories of days past.

Alberta O. Johnson
President
NCNW Section
Washington, DC

139

AUNTIE LATER'S SHRIMP ÉTOUFFÉ

¼	cup chopped onion
¼	cup chopped celery
¼	cup chopped green bell pepper
3	tablespoons butter or margarine
3	tablespoons vegetable oil
2	pounds shrimp (16 to 20 per pound)
1	tablespoon garlic powder
1	tablespoon cayenne pepper
2	tablespoons seasoned salt
2	tablespoons paprika
¾	cup all-purpose flour
3	cups seafood stock
½	cup medium quality cream sherry

1. Sauté onions, celery and green pepper in butter and oil in large skillet until onion is translucent. Add shrimp. Sauté 2 minutes. Add garlic powder, cayenne, seasoned salt and paprika. Sauté 30 seconds.
2. Stir in flour. Cook 4 minutes. Add seafood stock. Simmer 15 minutes. Add cream sherry. Simmer 30 minutes.

8 servings

*Eric L. Roberson, Sr., Executive Chef/Restaurateur
Aunt Gussye's Place*

Auntie Later

In my grandma's family, there were 14 children. When the last was born, 8 years after the others, they named her "Later." She grew up to be a very strong Black woman who owned a chain of hair salons that serviced both Blacks and whites in the segregated Los Angeles of the 1950's. Auntie Later was also a good cook. Every Sunday, we would have a family meal that consisted of fried chicken, a bowl of étouffé and a host of other homemade delicacies. Auntie even made the cream sherry that she added to her étouffé.

Eric L. Roberson, Sr.
Pasadena, CA

WILMA RUDOLPH'S SHRIMP SUPREME

¼	cup corn oil	1	can (14½ ounces) whole
1	pound shrimp, shelled and		tomatoes
	deveined	¼	pound mushrooms, quartered
1	green bell pepper, cut in 1-	¼	cup dry vermouth
	inch squares	⅛	teaspoon hot pepper sauce
1	medium onion, coarsely	2	tablespoons chopped cilantro
	chopped		or parsley
2	cloves garlic, minced	1	tablespoon lime juice
1	tablespoon chili powder		Hot cooked rice

1. Heat corn oil in large skillet on medium heat. Add shrimp. Sauté until shrimp turns pink. Remove shrimp. Add green pepper, onion, garlic and chili powder. Sauté 5 minutes. Add undrained tomatoes. Crush tomatoes. Stir in mushrooms, vermouth and hot pepper sauce. Bring to a boil. Reduce heat. Simmer, stirring occasionally, 15 minutes. Stir in shrimp, cilantro and lime juice. Serve over rice.

4 to 6 servings

Wilma Rudolph, Athlete

SHRIMP SOUTH LOUISIANA

¼	cup plus 1 tablespoon Crisco	1	can (about 10 ounces) hot and
	Shortening		spicy tomatoes
¼	cup all-purpose flour	1	can (8 ounces) tomato sauce
1	large onion, chopped		Salt and pepper
6	green onions, chopped	1	tablespoon Worcestershire
¼	cup chopped green bell pepper		sauce
½	cup chopped celery	2	pounds shrimp, peeled and
1	teaspoon minced garlic		deveined
			Hot cooked rice

1. Combine Crisco Shortening and flour in large saucepan. Cook and stir until dark brown.
2. Add onions, green onions, green pepper, celery and garlic. Add tomatoes and tomato sauce. Season with salt, pepper, and Worcestershire sauce. Simmer 30 minutes.
3. Add shrimp. Cook 20 minutes. Serve over rice.

6 servings

Everyday Crab

To this day, seafood, especially any dish prepared with crabmeat, takes me back to my childhood. Crab was not a luxury item then—it was included in everyday meals. We would often go to Southern Fish and Oyster Company, down the bay in Mobile, Alabama, to buy our crabs for gumbo, omelettes, casseroles and salad. As a child, I was fascinated by the way crabs pinched and pulled at each other as they were lifted out of the barrel and tossed into a sack for us to take home. Cleaning the crabs and picking out the meat made for an all-day activity. We were a large family who enjoyed crabmeat nearly every way our mother prepared it. Others may think of pot roast, chicken soup or apple pie, but for me, crab dishes say "home."

Yvonne Kennedy, Ph.D.
National President
Delta Sigma Theta
Sorority, Inc.
Mobile, AL

DEEP FRIED MARYLAND CRAB CAKES

Crab Cakes

¼	cup (½ stick) butter or margarine
4	ounces finely chopped onion
8	slices white bread
4	egg yolks
1½	teaspoons dry mustard
1½	teaspoons monosodium glutamate (MSG)
¾	teaspoon salt
¾	teaspoon white pepper
½	cup mayonnaise
1	tablespoon Worcestershire sauce
3	dashes hot pepper sauce
3	pounds crabmeat
	Shortening or oil for deep frying

Breading

2	eggs, beaten
1	cup milk
1	cup all-purpose flour
1	cup bread crumbs

1. For crab cakes, melt butter in small saucepan. Add onion. Sauté until tender, but not brown.
2. Trim crusts from bread. Flatten slices and dice.
3. Combine bread, onion and egg yolks in large bowl. Add dry mustard, MSG, salt, pepper, mayonnaise, Worcestershire sauce and hot pepper sauce. Stir to mix. Add crabmeat. Form into 2-ounce cakes.
4. Heat shortening or oil to 350°F.
5. For breading, combine eggs and milk in small bowl. Dip cakes in flour and then in egg mixture. Roll in crumbs.
6. Deep fry 5 minutes or until golden brown.

4 to 4½ dozen cakes

Joseph Randall, Chef Instructor,
School of Hotel & Restaurant Management
California State Polytechnic University
President, National United Culinary Association

RIO'S CURRY GOAT

3	pounds goat meat, cut in 2-inch squares	1	tablespoon dried thyme leaves
1½	onions, divided	2	teaspoons pepper
3	tablespoons curry powder	1	teaspoon salt
		¼	cup Crisco Oil

1. Place meat in glass baking dish. Season with 1 chopped onion, curry, thyme, pepper and salt. Cover. Refrigerate overnight.
2. Remove meat from refrigerator next day. Place meat in large saucepan. Cover with water. Add oil. Simmer 1 hour 30 minutes. Add remaining half chopped onion. Simmer 15 minutes.

6 servings

RABBIT

Rabbit

½	cup all-purpose flour	1	4-pound rabbit, cleaned and cut into 6 to 8 pieces
1	teaspoon each of salt, pepper, paprika	1	large onion, sliced
	Cooking oil	1	green bell pepper, seeded and sliced

Gravy

¼	cup drippings from pan		Salt and pepper
¼	cup all-purpose flour		Hot cooked rice or mashed potatoes
2	cups water		

1. For rabbit, combine flour, salt, pepper and paprika in bag. Shake well.
2. Place rabbit, one piece at a time, in bag. Shake to coat well.
3. Heat small amount of oil in 12-inch skillet on medium heat. Sauté onion and bell pepper. Remove from skillet.
4. Add rabbit. Brown each piece well, don't crowd. Remove as each piece browns.
5. For gravy, add flour to drippings. Stir until brown. Stir in water. Bring to a boil. Reduce heat to simmer.
6. Add rabbit and sautéed vegetables. Season with salt and pepper. Cover pan. Simmer until rabbit is tender. Serve over rice or mashed potatoes.

6 to 8 servings

Nancy Wilson, Entertainer

GEORGINE'S LEG OF LAMB

1	tablespoon rosemary
½	teaspoon freshly ground black pepper
1	tablespoon salt
4	drops hot pepper sauce
1	tablespoon thyme
3	large cloves garlic, finely chopped
½	teaspoon ginger
½	teaspoon peppercorns
	Juice of 1 lemon
5 - 6	pound leg of lamb
2	large onions, sliced

1. Combine rosemary, pepper, salt, hot pepper sauce, thyme, garlic, ginger, peppercorns and lemon juice.
2. Make 3 scores on each side of leg. Fill each scored pocket with herb mixture. Rub leg well with it. Place onion slices over the leg. Place in plastic bag along with any remaining herb mixture. Close bag. Refrigerate one day.
3. Heat oven to 350°F. Remove lamb from bag. Place in shallow roasting pan. Add one cup water.
4. Roast at 350°F. Baste often. Roast until meat thermometer reaches 140°F for rare, 160°F for medium or 170°F for well done.

6 to 8 servings

Georgine Carter, Chef of Jeannette Rockefeller

Her Own Touch

Georgine Carter's background as a cook is unique. As a little girl, she learned to cook by watching her mother. When she moved to New York, she learned Jewish food culture from a Jewish family who employed her. Then she picked up all sorts of ethnic recipes as well as the favorite dishes of her subsequent employers.

Of all her wonderful dishes, her leg of lamb was my favorite. Along the way she learned how to present each dish so beautifully that you hated to disturb it, but when the dish was leg of lamb, I couldn't stand to wait too long to taste it.

Everything Georgine cooked had her own touch, and everything she cooked was absolutely marvelous.

Jeannette Rockefeller
Palm Springs, CA

FAMILY DESSERTS

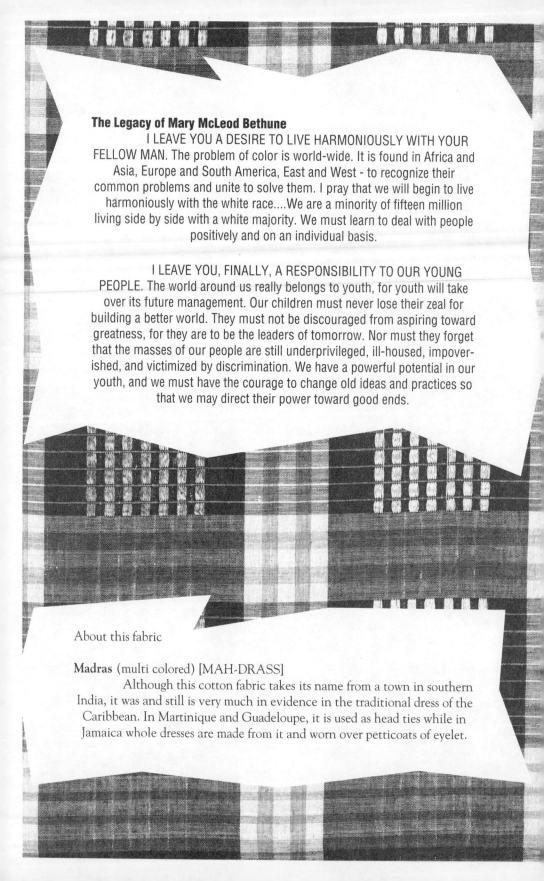

The Legacy of Mary McLeod Bethune
I LEAVE YOU A DESIRE TO LIVE HARMONIOUSLY WITH YOUR FELLOW MAN. The problem of color is world-wide. It is found in Africa and Asia, Europe and South America, East and West - to recognize their common problems and unite to solve them. I pray that we will begin to live harmoniously with the white race....We are a minority of fifteen million living side by side with a white majority. We must learn to deal with people positively and on an individual basis.

I LEAVE YOU, FINALLY, A RESPONSIBILITY TO OUR YOUNG PEOPLE. The world around us really belongs to youth, for youth will take over its future management. Our children must never lose their zeal for building a better world. They must not be discouraged from aspiring toward greatness, for they are to be the leaders of tomorrow. Nor must they forget that the masses of our people are still underprivileged, ill-housed, impoverished, and victimized by discrimination. We have a powerful potential in our youth, and we must have the courage to change old ideas and practices so that we may direct their power toward good ends.

About this fabric

Madras (multi colored) [MAH-DRASS]
Although this cotton fabric takes its name from a town in southern India, it was and still is very much in evidence in the traditional dress of the Caribbean. In Martinique and Guadeloupe, it is used as head ties while in Jamaica whole dresses are made from it and worn over petticoats of eyelet.

*When our founder, Mary McLeod Bethune, needed money in 1904 to keep
the school doors open she baked and sold Sweet Potato Pies. This is her
recipe.* **Dr. Dorothy I. Height**

MARY MCLEOD BETHUNE'S SWEET POTATO PIE

Filling

9	medium sweet potatoes or yams (about 4 pounds)
1	cup (2 sticks) butter or margarine, softened
½	cup granulated sugar
½	cup firmly packed brown sugar
½	teaspoon salt
¼	teaspoon nutmeg
3	eggs, well beaten
2	cups milk
1	tablespoon vanilla

Crust

3	unbaked 9-inch Classic Crisco Single Crusts

1. For filling, boil sweet potatoes until tender. Peel and mash.
2. Heat oven to 350°F.
3. Combine butter, granulated sugar, brown sugar, salt and nutmeg in large bowl. Beat at medium speed of electric mixer until creamy. Beat in sweet potatoes, until well mixed. Beat in eggs. Beat in milk and vanilla slowly. Spoon into 3 unbaked pie shells, using about 4 cups filling per shell.
4. Bake at 350°F for 50 to 60 minutes or until set. Cool to room temperature before serving. Store in refrigerator.

Three 9-inch pies

Dr. Dorothy I. Height, President/CEO
National Council of Negro Women, Inc.

HERITAGE RECIPE

Variation: Bake filling as a pudding in greased 12½ X 8½ X ¾-inch glass baking dish. Bake for about one hour or until set. Sprinkle with 2 cups miniature marshmallows. Return to oven 5 to 10 minutes or until marshmallows are lightly browned.

CLASSIC CRISCO CRUST

8, 9 or 10-inch Single Crust

1⅓	cups all-purpose flour	½	cup Crisco Shortening
½	teaspoon salt	3	tablespoons cold water

8, or 9-inch Double Crust

2	cups all-purpose flour	¾	cup Crisco Shortening
1	teaspoon salt	5	tablespoons cold water

10-inch Double Crust

2⅔	cups all-purpose flour	1	cup Crisco Shortening
1	teaspoon salt	7 - 8	tablespoons cold water

1. Combine flour and salt in bowl.
2. Cut in Crisco using pastry blender (or 2 knives) until all flour is blended in to form pea-size chunks.
3. Sprinkle with water, one tablespoon at a time. Toss lightly with form until dough will form a ball.

For single crust

4. Press dough ball between hands to form 5 to 6-inch "pancake." Flour rolling surface and rolling pin lightly. Roll dough into circle.
5. Trim 1 inch larger than upside-down pie plate. Loosen dough carefully.
6. Fold into quarters. Unfold and press into pie plate.
7. Fold edge under and flute.
8. For recipe calling for unbaked pie shell, follow baking directions given in that recipe. For recipe calling for baked pie shell, heat oven to 425°F. Prick bottom and sides thoroughly with fork (50 times) to prevent shrinkage. Bake at 425°F for 10 to 15 minutes.

For double crust

4., 5., 6. Divide dough in half. Roll each crust separately and transfer bottom crust to pie plate as described above in Steps 4 - 6.
7. Trim edge even with pie plate. Moisten pastry edge with water.
8. Add desired filling to unbaked pie shell. Lift top crust onto filled pie. Trim ½ inch beyond edge of pie plate. Fold top edge under bottom crust and flute. Cut slits in top crust for escape of steam.
9. Bake according to filling recipe.

Alternate Rolling Technique: Roll each dough "pancake" between unfloured sheets of waxed paper or plastic wrap. Peel off top sheet. Flip into pie plate. Remove other sheet.

CALIFORNIA CUSTARD PIE

Crust

1¾	cups all-purpose flour	¾	cup shortening
½	teaspoon salt	3	tablespoons ice water

Filling

2	eggs	2¼	cups milk, divided
1¼	cups sugar, divided	¾	cup half and half
1½	teaspoons vanilla	3	tablespoons unsalted butter
2	tablespoons cornstarch	½	cup shredded coconut
1½	teaspoons all-purpose flour	½	cup slivered almonds, toasted

Topping

Whipped cream   Toasted coconut

1. For crust, combine flour and salt in medium bowl. Cut in shortening until mixture resembles coarse crumbs. Sprinkle water around edges. Blend with fork until dough will form a ball. Wrap in plastic wrap. Chill one hour.
2. Heat oven to 400°F.
3. Flour rolling surface and rolling pin lightly. Roll dough into circle. Trim one inch larger than upside-down 9-inch pie plate. Loosen dough carefully. Fold into quarters. Unfold and press into pie plate. Fold edge under and flute.
4. Prick bottom and sides thoroughly with fork (50 times) to prevent shrinkage. Line with parchment paper or greased aluminum foil. Spread with dry beans or rice to weight down.
5. Bake at 400°F for 20 minutes. Remove from oven. Remove beans or rice carefully. Peel off paper or foil. Bake about 10 minutes or until crust is golden. Cool.
6. For filling, place eggs in medium bowl. Beat one minute. Add ½ cup sugar and vanilla. Beat until smooth. Add cornstarch and flour. Beat until smooth. Add ¾ cup milk gradually. Beat until smooth.
7. Place remaining 1½ cups milk and half and half in large saucepan. Add remaining ¾ cup sugar. Do not stir. Bring to a boil on medium heat. Beat in egg mixture slowly with wire whisk. Beat in while mixture comes to a boil for 30 seconds. Pour into medium bowl. Beat in butter until melted.
8. Combine coconut and toasted almonds. Fold into custard. Pour into baked pie shell. Cover completely with plastic wrap. Refrigerate 3 hours.
9. For topping, peel off plastic wrap. Top with whipped cream and toasted almonds.

One 9-inch pie

Dionne Warwick, Entertainer
1991 NCNW Black Family Reunion Celebration Chairperson

HARVEST APPLE PIE

Sweet Potato Pie Tradition

My grandmother, Mattie Blackshear, was a great cook; for the first year of my marriage I didn't cook a single Sunday dinner because everybody gathered at my grandmother's for dinner or we'd eat with my mother, Mattie Stewart. This tradition continued until Grandma died in 1980, then we carried on at Mom's until she got sick. Everybody who was living in town would stop by on Sunday's to visit as well as eat. Now family members who live outside Detroit come back for holidays and my sister and I prepare family meals for the holidays and birthdays, but we don't do it every Sunday the way our mother and grand-mother did. Grandma's sweet potato pie was a favorite of mine. I never learned to make it the way she did, but my son, Keith, learned how from hanging

Continued on next page

Crust

Unbaked 9-inch Classic Crisco Double Crust

Filling

½	cup firmly packed brown sugar
½	cup granulated sugar
2	tablespoons all-purpose flour
½	teaspoon cinnamon
1	tablespoon Butter Flavor Crisco
6	cups peeled, sliced tart baking apples (about 2 pounds or 6 medium apples)
3	tablespoons apple cider or juice

Glaze

Milk
Granulated sugar

1. Heat oven to 375°F.
2. For filling, combine brown sugar, granulated sugar, flour and cinnamon. Cut in Butter Flavor Crisco with fork until crumbs form. Toss apples with crumb mixture. Spoon into unbaked pie shell. Sprinkle with apple cider. Moisten pastry edge with water.
3. Roll top crust same as bottom. Lift onto filled pie. Trim ½-inch beyond edge of pie plate. Fold top edge under bottom crust. Flute. Cut slits in top crust for escape of steam.
4. For glaze, brush with milk. Sprinkle with granulated sugar.
5. Bake at 375°F for 40 to 50 minutes or until filling in center is bubbly and crust is golden brown. Cover edge of pie with foil last 10 minutes, if necessary, to prevent overbrowning. Cool until barely warm or to room temperature before serving.

One 9-inch pie

BANANA CREAM PIE

Crust

　　Baked 9-inch Classic Crisco Single Crust

Filling

3	tablespoons cornstarch
¼	teaspoon salt
1⅔	cups water
1	can (14 ounces) sweetened condensed milk (not evaporated milk)
3	egg yolks, beaten
2	tablespoons butter or margarine
1	teaspoon vanilla
3	medium bananas, divided
	Lemon juice

Topping

1	cup whipping cream, whipped

1. For filling, dissolve cornstarch and salt in water in medium saucepan. Stir in condensed milk and egg yolks. Cook and stir on medium heat until thickened and bubbly. Remove from heat. Add butter and vanilla. Cool slightly.
2. Slice 2 bananas. Dip in lemon juice. Drain. Arrange on bottom of baked pastry shell. Pour filling over bananas. Cover. Chill 4 hours or until set.
3. For topping, spread whipped cream over filling. Slice remaining banana. Dip in lemon juice. Drain. Garnish top of pie. Refrigerate leftover pie.

One 9-inch pie

Continued

around the kitchen to lick the bowls when he was little. He began making sweet potato pies like Grandma's for our family dinners when he was 18 and continues to make them whenever he comes home. If Keith doesn't make the sweet potato pies, we don't have any.

Mary Helen Morris
Supreme Basileus
Chi Eta Phi Sorority
Detroit, MI

CLASSIC LEMON MERINGUE PIE

Crust

Baked 9-inch Classic Crisco
Single Crust

Filling

1½	cups sugar	2	tablespoons butter or margarine
¼	cup cornstarch		
3	tablespoons all-purpose flour	1½	teaspoons grated lemon peel
¼	teaspoon salt	⅓	cup plus 1 tablespoon fresh lemon juice
1½	cups hot water		
3	egg yolks, beaten		

Meringue

½	cup sugar, divided	4	egg whites
1	tablespoon cornstarch	¾	teaspoon vanilla
½	cup cold water		

1. Heat oven to 350°F.
2. For filling, combine sugar, cornstarch, flour and salt in medium saucepan. Add water gradually, stirring constantly. Cook and stir on medium heat until mixture comes to a boil and thickens. Reduce temperature to low. Cook and stir constantly 8 minutes. Remove from heat. Add about one-third of hot mixture to egg yolks. Mix well. Return mixture to saucepan. Bring mixture to second boil on medium-high heat. Reduce temperature to low. Cook and stir 4 minutes. Remove from heat. Stir in butter and lemon peel. Add lemon juice slowly. Mix well. Spoon into baked pie shell.
3. For meringue, combine 2 tablespoons sugar, cornstarch and water in small saucepan. Stir until cornstarch dissolves. Cook and stir on medium heat until mixture is clear. Cool.
4. Combine egg whites and vanilla in large bowl. Beat at high speed of electric mixer until soft peaks form. Beat in remaining 6 tablespoons sugar, one tablespoon at a time. Beat well after each addition. Combine meringue with cornstarch mixture. Beat until stiff peaks form. Spread over filling, covering completely and sealing to edge of pie shell.
5. Bake at 350°F for 12 to 15 minutes or until meringue is lightly browned. Cool to room temperature before serving.

One 9-inch pie

SOUR CHERRY PIE

Crust

Unbaked 9-inch Classic
Crisco Double Crust

Filling

2	cans (16 ounces each) pitted red tart cherries	1	tablespoon butter or margarine
1½	cups sugar, divided	¼	teaspoon almond extract
⅓	cup cornstarch	3 - 4	drops red food color
⅛	teaspoon salt		
1	cup liquid drained from cherries		

Glaze

Milk   Granulated sugar

1. For filling, drain cherries, reserving 1 cup liquid. Combine ¾ cup sugar, cornstarch and salt in medium saucepan. Stir in reserved cherry liquid. Cook and stir on medium heat 3 to 4 minutes or until mixture thickens. Remove from heat. Stir in cherries, ¾ cup sugar, butter, almond extract and red food color. Refrigerate one hour. Spoon into unbaked pie shell. Moisten pastry edge with water.
2. Heat oven to 400°F.
3. Roll top crust same as bottom. Lift onto filled pie. Trim ½-inch beyond edge of pie plate. Fold top edge under bottom crust. Flute. Cut slits in top of crust for escape of steam.
4. For glaze, brush crust with milk. Sprinkle with sugar.
5. Bake at 400°F for 10 minutes. Reduce temperature to 350°F. Bake for 40 to 45 minutes or until filling in center is bubbly and crust is golden brown. Cool until barely warm or to room temperature before serving.

One 9-inch pie

**Milton,
Supercaterer
to the Stars**

In Memoriam

Milton F. Williams was buried on August 30, 1991. His career spanned forty-three years. Williams rose through the ranks from houseboy to the late actor, Edward G. Robinson, to become one of Hollywood's foremost caterers. I remember his telling culinary students at the Los Angeles Trade and Technical College, "You can be as much of an artist with food, as you can with a canvas...the pluses being instant gratification by guests with what you've created." He credited such benefactors as Rella Factor, a cosmetic heiress, Sybil Hartsfield, department store heiress, the late Danny Thomas and his wife Rosemarie, and art patrons Sally Gulck and Ethel Frend, with his success. Milton F. Williams made an indelible contribution to the African-American food experience.

Libby Clark, Food Editor
Los Angeles Sentinel
Los Angeles, CA

DEEP DISH PEACH COBBLER

Pastry

2	cups all-purpose flour
½	teaspoon salt
⅔	cup butter or margarine
4 - 6	tablespoons water

Filling

2	cans (29 ounces each) peach slices in syrup
½	cup firmly packed brown sugar
2	tablespoons all-purpose flour
½	teaspoon cinnamon
¼	teaspoon nutmeg
⅛	teaspoon allspice
	Dash of salt
½	cup reserved peach syrup
1	tablespoon lemon juice
1	tablespoon butter or margarine

1. Heat oven to 400°F.
2. For pastry, combine flour and salt in medium bowl. Cut in butter until mixture resembles coarse crumbs. Sprinkle with water while mixing lightly with fork. Form into ball. Roll two-thirds of dough into 13-inch square on lightly floured surface. Place in 8-inch square baking dish.
3. For filling, drain peaches, reserving ½ cup syrup.
4. Combine brown sugar, flour, cinnamon, nutmeg, allspice and salt in large bowl. Add peaches, reserved syrup and lemon juice. Mix lightly. Spoon into pastry shell. Dot with butter.
5. Roll remaining dough into 9-inch square. Cut into eight strips. Place strips across fruit to form lattice. Seal and flute edges of pastry. Bake at 400°F for 40 to 45 minutes or until golden brown.

8 servings

*The Late Milton F. Williams,
Caterer & Cookbook Author*

**HERITAGE
RECIPE**

BUTTERMILK PEACH PIE

Crust

Unbaked 10-inch Classic Crisco Double Crust

Filling

1	can (1 pound 13 ounces) yellow cling peaches in heavy syrup
3	tablespoons cornstarch
1	cup sugar, divided
3	tablespoons reserved peach syrup
3	eggs
1/3	cup buttermilk
1/2	cup butter or margarine, melted
1	teaspoon vanilla

Glaze

2	tablespoons butter or margarine, melted
2	tablespoons sugar

1. Heat oven to 400°F.
2. For filling, drain peaches, reserving 3 tablespoons syrup.
3. Cut peaches into small pieces. Place in large bowl.
4. Combine cornstarch and 2 to 3 tablespoons sugar. Add 3 tablespoons reserved peach syrup. Add remaining sugar, eggs and buttermilk. Mix well. Stir in melted butter and vanilla. Pour over peaches. Stir until peaches are coated.
5. Pour filling into unbaked pie shell. Moisten pastry edge with water.
6. Roll top crust same as bottom. Lift onto filled pie. Trim 1/2-inch beyond edge of pie plate. Fold top edge under bottom crust. Flute. Cut slits in top crust for escape of steam.
7. For glaze, brush top crust with melted butter. Sprinkle with sugar.
8. Bake at 400°F for 45 minutes or until filling in center is bubbly and crust is golden brown. Cool to room temperature before serving.

One 10-inch pie

A Peach Cobbler of My Own

When I was a young girl, my aunt would make my favorite dessert, peach cobbler, on special days. There was one problem—we always had company on these days and I would be the one to receive less when it was my turn to be served. One day I vowed I would learn to make peach cobbler, so that when I grew up I could eat all I wanted. I kept my vow. My friends think I am one of the best peach cobbler makers and that I should market my pies.

Meda Chamberlain
Executive Director,
Southern California
Area
NCNW
Los Angeles, CA

PINTO BEAN PIE

Crust

Unbaked 9-inch Classic
Crisco Single Crust

Filling

2	eggs, lightly beaten	¾	teaspoon cinnamon
1	cup evaporated milk or light cream	¼	teaspoon salt
		¼	teaspoon ginger
2	cups mashed pinto beans, home cooked* or canned	¼	teaspoon nutmeg
		¼	teaspoon cloves
⅔	cup sugar		Whipped cream (optional)

1. Heat oven to 425°F.
2. For filling, combine eggs and evaporated milk in large bowl. Stir until well blended. Add pinto beans, sugar, cinnamon, salt, ginger, nutmeg and cloves. Beat at low speed of electric mixer until well blended. Pour into unbaked pie shell.
3. Bake at 425°F for 15 minutes. Reduce oven temperature to 350°F. Bake for 35 minutes, or until knife inserted in center comes out clean. Serve warm or at room temperature. Top with whipped cream, if desired.

* Home preparation of beans. Rinse pinto beans. Place in large saucepan. Cover with cold water. Cook 3 to 5 minutes, covered, or until water is hot. Remove from heat. Set aside for 1 hour. Return to range. Simmer 1 hour 30 minutes or until soft enough to mash. Drain. Mash.

One 9-inch pie

HERITAGE RECIPE

GEORGIA APPLE BETTY

1¼	cups firmly packed brown sugar, divided	1	teaspoon cinnamon
1	cup water	4	cups peeled, diced apples
¼	cup light corn syrup	4	cups whole wheat toast cubes
1	tablespoon lemon juice	¼	cup Butter Flavor Crisco
			Whipped topping

1. Heat oven to 475°F.
2. Combine 1 cup brown sugar, water, corn syrup, lemon juice and cinnamon in large saucepan. Bring to a boil. Add apples. Boil 5 minutes. Remove from heat. Add toast cubes. Mix lightly until liquid is absorbed. Spoon into 1-quart casserole. Press lightly. Sprinkle with remaining sugar. Drizzle with Butter Flavor Crisco.
3. Bake at 475°F for 10 to 12 minutes or until top is crisp. Serve warm with whipped topping.

4 servings

SYNOVIA'S BLACKBERRY PIE

Crust

Baked 9-inch Classic Crisco Single Crust

Filling

1	package (4 serving size) peach or berry flavor gelatin (not sugar free)
1	cup boiling water
1	pint vanilla ice cream, softened
1¾	cups fresh or frozen dry pack blackberries, partially thawed

1. For filling, combine gelatin and water in large bowl. Stir until dissolved. Cut ice cream into small chunks. Add to gelatin mixture, a spoonful at a time. Blend with wire whisk after each addition.
2. Dry blackberries between paper towels. Fold into gelatin mixture. Spoon into cooled baked pie crust. Refrigerate or freeze several hours before serving.

One 9-inch pie

HERITAGE RECIPE

Celebrating Achievements

In our family my mother Peggy Hardy, was into celebrating achievements. She cooked the favorite dish of each child whenever we accomplished a goal we had set. Although she was concerned about nutrition, she would make an exception and fix whatever we liked most if we did something special. My celebratory dish was blackberry pie. There was nothing like coming in from school and breathing in the sweet, tart smell of a freshly baked blackberry pie and knowing that it was for me. Recently, I received my master's degree and my mother came out from Milwaukee for the graduation. She almost missed her plane because she was making a blackberry pie to bring with her. None of the accolades I received that day were as special as my mother bringing me a blackberry pie.

Synovia Hardy
Youngblood
Regional Coordinator
NCNW Black Family
Reunion Celebration
Los Angeles, CA

VINEGAR PIE

Crust

Unbaked 8-inch Classic
Crisco Single Crust

Filling

2	tablespoons Butter Flavor Crisco	½	teaspoon cloves
		½	teaspoon allspice
½	cup sugar	1	cup water
3	tablespoons all-purpose flour	1	egg
2	teaspoons cinnamon	2	tablespoons cider vinegar

1. Heat oven to 350°F.
2. Bake crust partially at 350°F for 3 minutes.
3. For filling, combine Butter Flavor Crisco and sugar in medium bowl. Mix at low speed of electric mixer until well blended. Add flour, cinnamon, clove and allspice. Add water, egg and vinegar. Stir until well blended. Transfer to double boiler.
4. Cook and stir over simmering water until thick. Pour into partially baked crust.
5. Bake at 350°F for 45 minutes or until filling starts to bubble. Cool to room temperature before serving.

One 8-inch pie

HERITAGE RECIPE

MOTHER'S OLD FASHION EGG PIE

Crust

Unbaked 9-inch Classic
Crisco Single Crust

Filling

1	cup sugar	1	teaspoon vanilla
½	teaspoon salt	3	eggs, well beaten
2	teaspoons flour	1	cup milk
1	tablespoon butter or margarine, melted		

1. Heat oven to 350°F.
2. For filling, combine sugar, salt and flour. Add buter, vanilla, and eggs. Add milk and mix well.
3. Pour into unbaked pie shell.
4. Bake at 350°F for one hour (until firm).

One 9-inch pie

CHOCOLATE ALMOND PIE

Crust

Baked 9-inch Classic Crisco
Single Crust

Filling

1	package (8 ounces) cream cheese, softened	1	package (6 serving size) chocolate flavor pudding or pie filling mix (not instant)
¼	cup chocolate flavor syrup		
½	teaspoon almond extract	1	tablespoon Crisco Oil
		¼	cup sliced almonds

1. For filling, combine cream cheese, chocolate syrup and almond extract in large bowl. Beat at medium speed of electric mixer until well blended.
2. Prepare pudding mix following directions for pie filling. Add to cream cheese mixture. Beat at medium speed until smooth. Scrape side of bowl as needed. Pour into pie crust.
3. Heat Crisco Oil in small skillet. Add nuts. Cook and stir on medium heat until nuts are golden brown. Drain on paper towels. Cool. Sprinkle over pie. Refrigerate 2 to 3 hours, or until set.

One 9-inch pie

EDNA'S GERMAN CHOCOLATE PIE

Crust

Unbaked 9-inch Classic
Crisco Single Crust

Filling

1	package (4 ounces) German's sweet chocolate	1⅓	cups flake coconut
		3	eggs, lightly beaten
¼	cup butter or margarine	½	cup sugar
1	can (12 ounces) evaporated milk		

1. Heat oven to 400°F.
2. For filling, melt chocolate and butter in medium saucepan. Add milk and coconut. Combine eggs and sugar. Stir into chocolate mixture. Pour into unbaked pie shell.
3. Bake at 400°F for 30 to 40 minutes. Cool completely.

One 9-inch pie

DOUBLE CRUST BLUEBERRY PIE

Crust

Unbaked 9-inch Classic
Crisco Double Crust

Filling

⅔ - ¾	cup sugar	5	cups fresh blueberries, divided
3	tablespoons cornstarch	1	tablespoon plus 1½ teaspoons
⅛	teaspoon salt		butter or margarine
¼	cup water	1½	teaspoons lemon juice

1. Heat oven to 425°F.
2. For filling, combine sugar, cornstarch, salt, water and 3 cups berries in saucepan. Cook on medium heat until mixture thickens and comes to a boil. Remove from heat. Cool slightly.
3. Place remaining 2 cups berries in unbaked pie shell. Stir butter and lemon juice into cooked filling. Spoon cooked filling over fresh berries. Moisten pastry edge with water.
4. Roll top crust same as bottom. Lift onto filled pie. Trim ½-inch beyond edge of pie plate. Fold top edge under bottom crust. Flute. Cut slits in top crust for escape of steam.
5. Bake at 425°F for 30 to 40 minutes or until filling in center is bubbly and crust is golden brown. Cool until barely warm or to room temperature before serving.

One 9-inch pie

PINEAPPLE-COCONUT CHESS PIE

Crust

Unbaked 9-inch Classic
Crisco Single Crust

Filling

1⅔	cups sugar	1	teaspoon vanilla
½	cup Butter Flavor Crisco	1	can (8½ ounces) juice packed
3	eggs		crushed pineapple
1	teaspoon yellow corn meal	½	cup flake coconut
1	teaspoon all-purpose flour		

1. Heat oven to 325°F.
2. For filling, combine sugar and Butter Flavor Crisco in large bowl. Beat at medium speed of electric mixer until light and fluffy. Add eggs one at a time, beating well after each addition. Add cornmeal, flour and vanilla. Mix well.
3. Combine undrained pineapple and coconut. Fold into creamed mixture. Pour into unbaked pie shell.
4. Bake at 325°F for 45 to 50 minutes or until knife inserted in center comes out clean.

One 9-inch pie

OLD SOUTH MOLASSES CRUMB PIE

Crust

Unbaked 9-inch deep dish
Classic Crisco Single Crust

Filling

2	tablespoons Crisco Shortening	¼	teaspoon ginger
¾	cup all-purpose flour	¼	teaspoon cloves
½	cup firmly packed brown sugar	¼	teaspoon baking soda
¼	teaspoon salt	¾	cup boiling water
½	teaspoon cinnamon	½	cup molasses
¼	teaspoon nutmeg	1	egg, beaten

1. Heat oven to 425°F.
2. For filling, cream Crisco at low speed of electric mixer. Add flour, brown sugar, salt, cinnamon, nutmeg, ginger and cloves. Mix until crumbs form.
3. Add baking soda to boiling water. Stir in molasses and egg.
4. Sprinkle bottom of unbaked pie shell generously with crumbs. Cover with molasses mixture. Repeat, finishing with crumbs on top.
5. Bake at 425° for 10 minutes. Reduce temperature to 350°F. Bake for 25 minutes. Cool to room temperature before serving.

One 9-inch deep dish pie

HONEY CRUNCH PECAN PIE

Crust

Unbaked 9-inch Classic
Crisco Single Crust

Filling

4	eggs, lightly beaten	2	tablespoons butter or
¼	cup firmly packed brown sugar		margarine, melted
¼	cup granulated sugar	1	tablespoon bourbon
½	teaspoon salt	1	teaspoon vanilla
1	cup light corn syrup	1	cup chopped pecans

Topping

⅓	cup firmly packed brown sugar	3	tablespoons honey
3	tablespoons butter or margarine	1½	cups pecan halves

1. Heat oven to 350°F.
2. For filling, combine eggs, brown sugar, granulated sugar, salt, corn syrup, butter, bourbon, vanilla and nuts. Mix well. Spoon into unbaked pie shell.
3. Bake at 350°F for 15 minutes. Cover edge of pastry with foil. Bake 20 minutes. Remove from oven.
4. For topping, combine brown sugar, butter and honey in medium saucepan. Cook about 2 minutes or until sugar dissolves. Add nuts. Stir until coated. Spoon evenly over pie. Cover edge of pastry with foil. Bake 10 to 20 minutes or until topping is bubbly and golden brown. Cool to room temperature before serving.

One 9-inch pie

MAMA'S APPLE DUMPLINGS

Pastry

    Dough for 9-inch Classic Crisco Double Crust

Filling

6	baking apples (about 3 inches in diameter) peeled and cored
⅓	cup chopped pecans
⅓	cup raisins
½	teaspoon cinnamon

Syrup

2	cups firmly packed brown sugar
1	cup water

Topping (optional)

    Whipped cream

1. Heat oven to 425°F. Grease 11½ X 8 X 2-inch baking dish.
2. For crust, roll out two-thirds of pastry into 14-inch square on lightly floured surface. Cut into 4 squares. Roll remaining pastry into 14 X 7-inch rectangle. Cut into 2 squares.
3. For filling, place one apple in center of each pastry square. Combine nuts, raisins and cinnamon. Spoon into center of apples.
4. Moisten corners of each square. Bring 2 opposite corners of pastry up over apple and press together. Repeat with other corners. Press pastry seams together along sides of dumpling. Place dumplings in prepared baking dish.
5. For syrup, combine brown sugar and water in medium saucepan on low heat. Stir until mixture comes to a boil. Pour carefully around dumplings.
6. Bake at 425°F for 40 minutes or until apples are tender and pastry is golden brown. Spoon syrup over dumplings several times during baking. Serve warm with whipped cream, if desired.

6 servings

HERITAGE RECIPE

Making a Family Tradition

When I was 13 and living in Sanford, Florida, my father taught my sister and me how to make Apple Duby. Apple Duby is a dessert of cooked apples and dumplings. I can still remember the aroma of nutmeg and cinnamon in the air. This was a meaningful experience because of the intimacy my sister Audrey and I shared with my father while learning to prepare this special dish. The apples had to be just right, not too sweet and not too tart, so we would carefully measure all of the ingredients. I can now fully appreciate how this activity brought our family together. The tradition of making Apple Duby is in my family even today.

Dr. Oswald P. Bronson, Sr. President, Bethune-Cookman College Dayton Beach, FL

FRIED PIES

Crisco Shortening or Crisco Oil for deep frying

Filling

1	can (16 ounces) cling peach slices, drained
2	tablespoons sugar
1	tablespoon cornstarch
⅛	teaspoon nutmeg

Pastry

2	cups all-purpose flour
1	teaspoon salt
½	cup Crisco Shortening
½	cup cold water

1. Heat 2 to 3 inches Crisco Shortening or Crisco Oil to 365°F in deep fryer or deep saucepan.
2. For filling, place peaches on paper towels. Dry. Combine peaches, sugar, cornstarch and nutmeg in small bowl.
3. For pastry, combine flour and salt in medium bowl. Cut in Crisco using pastry blender (or 2 knives) until all flour is blended in to form pea-size chunks. Sprinkle with water, one tablespoon at a time. Toss lightly with fork until dough forms ball.
4. Flour rolling surface and rolling pin lightly. Divide dough in half. Roll each half to 1/16-inch thickness. Use lid from 3 pound Crisco can as pattern. Cut 6 circles (about 5¼ inches) from each half. (Reroll as necessary.)
5. Place several peach slices on each dough circle. Moisten edges with water. Fold in half over filling. Seal with fork.
6. Fry, a few at a time, for 3 minutes or until golden brown. Turn once. Remove with slotted metal spoon. Drain on paper towels. Serve warm or at room temperature.

12 fried pies

HERITAGE RECIPE

A Special Way to Say "I Love You"

My mother used to make the best fried apple pies. She would make the dough from scratch. Sometimes she would even dry the apples herself and then season them with sugar, cinnamon and allspice. Then she would place the mixture on the dough she had cut into pieces and fry them. They were delicious! She would only cook them on special occasions, so we didn't get them very often. But when we did, we knew she was happy. It was her way of letting us know she loved us. I can't make them the way she did, but fried pies will always remind me of my mother and her love.

Annette Cowan
National President
Las Amigas, Inc.
Charlotte, NC

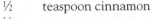

PANDOWDY

Filling

5	cups sliced, peeled cooking apples, pears or peaches
½	cup pure maple syrup or maple-flavored pancake syrup
2	tablespoons lemon juice

½	teaspoon cinnamon
¼	teaspoon nutmeg
2	tablespoons Butter Flavor Crisco

Crust

Dough for 9-inch Classic Crisco Single Crust

Glaze

2	teaspoons milk	1	teaspoon sugar

Topping (optional)

Cream, whipped cream, ice cream

1. For filling, toss apples with maple syrup, lemon juice, cinnamon and nutmeg in large bowl. Spoon into 8-inch square glass baking dish. Dot with Butter Flavor Crisco.
2. Heat oven to 400°F.
3. For crust, roll dough into 8½ to 9-inch square between lightly floured sheets of waxed paper on dampened countertop. Peel off top sheet of waxed paper. Flip dough over on top of apples. Remove other sheet of waxed paper. Press dough down along insides of dish. Trim pastry along inside edge. Cut large vents to allow steam to escape.
4. For glaze, brush with milk. Sprinkle with sugar. Bake at 400°F for 25 to 30 minutes or until crust is light golden brown. Remove from oven.
5. Cut pastry into 2-inch squares. Spoon juice from bottom of dish over entire top of pastry. Return to oven. Bake 20 to 25 minutes or until top is deep golden brown. Serve warm with cream, whipped cream or ice cream, if desired.

8 servings

HERITAGE RECIPE

JACKSON FAMILY RICE CUSTARD

2	cups cooked rice	¾	cup raisins
1	cup milk	½	teaspoon vanilla
3	eggs, lightly beaten		Dash nutmeg
¾	cup firmly packed brown sugar		Whipped cream
3	tablespoons melted butter or margarine		

1. Heat oven to 350°F.
2. Combine rice, milk, eggs, brown sugar and butter in 1-quart casserole or baking dish. Place casserole in baking pan. Fill pan with enough water to go halfway up side of casserole.
3. Bake at 350°F for 30 minutes. Remove from oven. Stir in raisins and vanilla. Sprinkle with nutmeg. Return to oven. Bake for 30 minutes. Serve hot or chilled, topped with whipped cream.

6 to 8 servings

Katherine Jackson, Mother of "The Jackson Five" and Michael Jackson

BANANA PUDDING

⅔	cup sugar	3	tablespoons butter or margarine
⅓	cup cornstarch		
½	teaspoon salt	2	tablespoons vanilla
3	cups milk	2	cups vanilla wafers
2	eggs	2	cups sliced ripe bananas

1. Heat oven to 350°F.
2. Combine sugar, cornstarch, salt and milk in a large saucepan. Cook and stir on medium heat until thickened.
3. Beat eggs lightly with wire whisk. Add a little hot mixture to eggs and blend well. Pour eggs into mixture in saucepan.
4. Continue cooking for a few minutes, stirring constantly. Add butter and vanilla. Blend mixture well. Cover pudding. Cool slightly.
5. Place layer of vanilla wafers on bottom of casserole dish. Alternate with layers of banana slices and pudding, ending with pudding on top.
6. Put dish in the center of preheated oven of 350°F. Bake for ten minutes.

6 servings

Johnetta B. Cole, President
Spelman College

HERITAGE RECIPE

COCONUT PUDDING

| 3 | tablespoons sugar | 2 | cups coconut milk, divided |
| 3 | tablespoons cornstarch | ¼ | teaspoon salt |

1. Combine sugar and cornstarch in small bowl. Blend in ½ cup coconut milk and salt.
2. Heat remaining 1½ cups coconut milk in medium saucepan. (Do not let it come to a boil.) Add cornstarch mixture. Cook and stir until thickened. Pour into 8-inch square dish. Refrigerate until firm.
3. Cut into squares. Serve cold.

4 servings

Anna Marie Horsford, Television Star

GRANDMA SELDON'S THREE BREAD PUDDING

6	slices day old wheat bread, crust trimmed	1	cup raisins
		1	cup sugar, divided
6	slices day old white bread, crust trimmed	3	teaspoons cinnamon
		3	cups milk
6	slices day old raisin bread, crust trimmed	6	eggs or egg substitute equivalent
1	cup Butter Flavor Crisco, melted	2	teaspoons vanilla

1. Heat oven to 350°F. Grease 1½ to 2-quart casserole or baking dish with Butter Flavor Crisco.
2. Brush both sides of bread lightly with Butter Flavor Crisco. Cut into quarters. Arrange half each wheat and white in layer in casserole. Sprinkle with ½ cup raisins, 2 tablespoons sugar and 1 teaspoon cinnamon. Repeat. Use raisin bread for top layer.
3. Combine milk, eggs, remaining ¾ sugar and vanilla in large bowl. Stir until sugar dissolves. Pour over bread. Place casserole in pan containing 1-inch hot water.
4. Bake at 350°F for 55 to 60 minutes or until knife inserted in center comes out clean. Serve warm or chilled.

8 to 12 servings

BAKED LEMON PUDDING

2	eggs, separated	2	tablespoons melted Butter Flavor Crisco
¼	teaspoon salt		
¾	cup sugar, divided	3	tablespoons all-purpose flour
1	tablespoon grated lemon peel	1	cup milk
5	tablespoons lemon juice		

1. Heat oven to 350°F. Grease 1-quart casserole.
2. Combine egg whites and salt. Beat at high speed of electric mixer until moist peaks form when beaters are raised. Add ½ cup sugar gradually. Beat until stiff.
3. Beat egg yolks, lemon peel, lemon juice and Butter Flavor Crisco in small bowl until blended, using same beaters.
4. Combine remaining ¼ cup sugar and flour. Stir into egg yolk mixture. Stir in milk. Fold in egg whites by hand. Pour into casserole.
5. Pour ½ inch hot water into baking pan. Place casserole in pan.
6. Bake at 350°F for 55 to 65 minutes or until top is firm and browned. Serve warm or at room temperature.

4 to 6 servings

SWEET POTATO & FRUIT PUDDING

4	medium sweet potatoes or yams	¼	cup melted butter or margarine
½	cup apple juice	1	tablespoon honey
½	cup pineapple juice	1	teaspoon nutmeg
½	cup flake coconut		Dash cayenne pepper
		¾	cup chopped pecans

1. Heat oven to 350°F. Grease 1 to 1½-quart casserole.
2. Cook sweet potatoes until tender. Remove skins. Place in blender or food processor.
3. Add apple juice, pineapple juice, coconut, butter, honey, nutmeg and cayenne. Process until smooth. Spoon into casserole. Sprinkle nuts over top of sweet potatoes.
4. Bake at 350°F for 45 minutes.

4 to 6 servings

MAMA JOHNSON'S SWEET POTATO PONE

6	medium sweet potatoes or yams	1	cup biscuit baking mix
½	cup Butter Flavor Crisco	½	teaspoon baking powder
1	cup sugar	1	teaspoon vanilla
4	eggs	½	teaspoon cinnamon
½	cup milk	¼	teaspoon nutmeg
			Cinnamon sugar

1. Heat oven to 300°F. Grease and flour 12 X 8 X 2-inch baking dish.
2. Cook and peel sweet potatoes. Cut in small pieces.
3. Combine Butter Flavor Crisco and sugar in large bowl. Beat at medium speed of electric mixer until well blended. Add eggs and milk. Beat until well blended. Add biscuit mix and baking powder. Beat until well blended. Add sweet potatoes, vanilla, cinnamon and nutmeg. Beat until blended. Pour into baking dish. Sprinkle top generously with cinnamon sugar.
4. Bake at 300°F for 1 hour to 1 hour and 15 minutes or until pone pulls away from sides of dish and center is lightly springy. Cool to room temperature. Cut into 2-inch squares to serve.

24 servings

HERITAGE RECIPE

An Example to Live By

I long ago realized I would never enter the annals of great cooks. Those places are reserved people like my grandmother, Nellie Holmes, who died when I was 14. Some of the things Grandmother made are beyond my comprehension. She actually made doughnuts! And her bread—I remember it especially. It started out flat, then magically rose. I would peek under the dishtowel, but I never could catch it in motion.

It was in my grandmother's kitchen that I first developed the taste for raw dough. Today I would rather eat dough than bread, cake batter than cake. I'm sure it comes from having a grandmother whose cooking was so amazing that I simply could not wait. Although my grandmother was not able to teach me her skills as a chef, I am grateful for the more important lesson of her example—whatever you do, do your very best!

Congresswoman Eleanor Holmes Norton, Washington, DC

GOLDEN YELLOW CAKE

2	cups all-purpose flour
1⅔	cups sugar
1	tablespoon plus ½ teaspoon baking powder
1	teaspoon salt
1¼	cups milk, divided
⅔	cup Crisco Shortening or Butter Flavor Crisco
3	eggs
1	teaspoon vanilla

1. Heat oven to 350°F. Grease and flour two 9-inch round cake pans or 13 X 9 X 2-inch pan.
2. Combine flour, sugar, baking powder and salt in large bowl. Mix dry ingredients at low speed of electric mixer until thoroughly combined.
3. Add ¾ cup milk and Crisco Shortening or Butter Flavor Crisco to dry ingredients. Mix at low speed until moistened, about 20 seconds. Beat at medium speed 2 minutes. Scrape sides of bowl as needed.
4. Add eggs, remaining ½ cup milk and vanilla. Mix at low speed for 20 seconds. Beat at medium speed 2 minutes*. Scrape bowl as needed. Pour into pan(s).
5. Bake at 350°F: two 9-inch for 30 to 35 minutes, 13 X 9-inch for 35 to 40 minutes or until toothpick inserted in center comes out clean. Cool on cooling racks 10 to 15 minutes. Remove from pan(s). Cool completely on racks before frosting. Frost as desired.

* Use high speed if using hand-held mixer.

One 2 layer cake or 13 X 9-inch cake

PICNIC CHOCOLATE CAKE

2	cups all-purpose flour
2	cups sugar
½	cup unsweetened cocoa powder
2	teaspoons baking powder
½	teaspoon salt
½	teaspoon baking soda
1½	cups milk
½	cup Crisco Shortening
1	teaspoon vanilla
2	eggs

1. Heat oven to 350°F. Grease and flour two 9-inch round cake pans.
2. Combine flour, sugar, cocoa, baking powder, salt and baking soda in large bowl.
3. Add milk, Crisco and vanilla. Beat at low speed of electric mixer until combined. Beat at medium speed 2 minutes. Add eggs. Beat 2 minutes. Scrape sides of bowl as needed. Pour into pans.
4. Bake at 350°F for 30 to 35 minutes or until toothpick inserted in center comes out clean. Cool cakes on cooking rack 10 minutes before removing from pans. Cool completely on rack before frosting. Frost as desired.

One 2 layer cake

Aunt Cora Raised Me

My aunt, Cora L. Burston, who raised me was a professional cook, and she made everything delectable and delicious. During the week she would sometimes bring rolls home from work, but on the weekends I was treated to the smell of homemade yeast rolls baking. We had lots of company; our relatives would stop by to eat because there was always plenty of excellent food. She told me that what made her sweet potato pie so tasty and smooth was her generous use of butter, and that plenty of eggs gave her cakes that rich flavor. Ironically, the only thing I learned how to cook was her banana pudding which I always bring to our annual family reunion in Luthersville, Georgia. In 1990, 107 family members attended our reunion. We always have a short formal program introducing family members so each one can bring the group up to date on what has happened in the past year.

Louise Strozier
Regional Coordinator
NCNW Black Family
Reunion Celebration
Atlanta, GA

AUNT NARVA'S APPLE CAKE

3	cups sifted all-purpose flour
1	teaspoon baking soda
1	teaspoon cinnamon
1	teaspoon salt
2	cups sugar
1	cup vegetable oil
3	eggs
3	cups cored and sliced apples
1	cup walnuts (optional)

1. Heat oven to 350°F. Grease and flour 13 X 9 X 2-inch pan.
2. Combine flour, baking soda, cinnamon and salt in medium bowl.
3. Combine sugar, oil and eggs in large bowl. Add dry ingredients. Stir until well blended. Fold apples and nuts into batter (batter will be stiff). Spread in pan.
4. Bake at 350°F for one hour or until toothpick inserted in center comes out clean.

Narva Parker Van Dunk
Gloucester, Virginia

The Best Possible Gift

Narva Parker Van Dunk's family in Gloucester, Virginia, considers "Aunt Narva's Apple Cake" to be the best possible gift on all holidays and special occasions. Rarely can a guest get a slice of the cakes that are sent for the many family celebrations, because all the family members rush to claim a half (or a whole if no one is looking) to take home with them. We hope your family will enjoy this recipe as much as the Parkers, Poes, Clarks and Van Dunks.

Dr. Mabel Phifer,
Director
Black College Satellite Network
Washington, DC

CLASSIC WHITE CAKE

2	cups all-purpose flour
1	tablespoon baking powder
½	teaspoon salt
1½	cups sugar
¾	cup Crisco Shortening
2	teaspoons vanilla
1	cup milk
4	egg whites

1. Heat oven to 350°F. Grease and flour two 8 or 9-inch round cake pans.
2. Combine flour, baking powder and salt in small bowl.
3. Combine sugar, Crisco and vanilla in large bowl. Beat at medium speed of electric mixer until fluffy. Add flour mixture alternately with milk, beating well. Scrape sides of bowl as needed.
4. Wash and dry beaters thoroughly. Beat egg whites in another large bowl until stiff peaks form. Fold egg whites gently into batter. Pour in pans.
5. Bake at 350°F about 25 minutes or until toothpick inserted in center comes out clean. Cool cakes on cooling racks 10 minutes before removing from pans. Cool completely on racks before frosting. Frost as desired.

One 2 layer cake

Balanced Meals

My motivation to cook and try new recipes was obtained from my mother. I am from a family of eight children, so there was always the smell of food, lots of food, in our house. Dinner was always ready when we came home from school, and we had homemade desserts practically every day. My mother enjoyed cooking and you could see it in the love that went into her preparation of our daily meals. Thanks mother for preparing all of those balanced meals.

Glenda A. Brown
Union City, GA

OLD-FASHIONED DATE CAKE

1	package (8 ounces) chopped, pitted dates
1	cup boiling water
1½	cups all-purpose flour
1	teaspoon baking soda
¼	teaspoon salt
½	cup Crisco Shortening
1	cup sugar
1	teaspoon vanilla
2	eggs
¾	cup chopped walnuts
	Raisin-Nut Frosting (see page 185)
	Walnut Halves (optional)

1. Combine dates and boiling water in small bowl. Cool to room temperature (about 1 hour). Do not drain. Mash dates slightly with fork.
2. Heat oven to 350°F. Grease 13 X 9 X 2-inch pan.
3. Combine flour, baking soda and salt.
4. Place Crisco in large bowl. Beat at medium speed of electric mixer for 30 seconds. Add sugar and vanilla. Beat until fluffy. Add eggs, one at a time, beating about one minute after each addition.
5. Add flour mixture alternately with date mixture, beating at low speed of electric mixer after each addition until just combined. Stir in chopped nuts. Spread batter in pan.
6. Bake at 350°F about 35 minutes or until toothpick inserted in center comes out clean. Cool cake completely on cooling rack. Frost with Raisin-Nut Frosting. Garnish with nuts, if desired. Store in refrigerator.

One 13 X 9-inch cake.

She Beamed Over Her Flock

My mother, Candy K. H. Streater, was a great cook. When she baked cakes they came out perfectly. We would watch her carefully waiting for our favorite part. She always left some of the batter in the mixing bowl and would spoon out a teaspoon to each of her children standing nearby. I can still see the big smile on her face as she beamed over her flock.

Loretta Streater
McNeal
Chesterfield, SC

MCRAE'S GINGERBREAD

1½   cups all-purpose flour
¾   teaspoon cinnamon
¾   teaspoon ginger
½   teaspoon salt
½   teaspoon baking powder
½   teaspoon baking soda
½   cup Crisco Shortening
¼   cup firmly packed brown sugar
1   egg
½   cup light molasses
½   cup boiling water

1. Heat oven to 350°F. Grease and flour one 9-inch round cake pan.
2. Combine flour, cinnamon, ginger, salt, baking powder and baking soda in large bowl. Beat in Crisco at medium speed of electric mixer about 30 seconds.
3. Add brown sugar. Beat until fluffy. Add egg and molasses. Beat one minute. Add flour mixture alternately with water, beating at low speed after each addition just until combined. Spread in pan.
4. Bake at 350°F for 30 to 35 minutes or until toothpick inserted in center comes out clean. Cool gingerbread on wire rack 10 minutes before removing from pan. Serve warm.

One 9-inch layer

Baking Gingerbread

One of my fond memories of my childhood is making candy and baking gingerbread. All I needed was for one of my brothers to say, "Sis, you surely can make good treats," and I headed for the kitchen. I always helped keep the pantry full of pies or at least something sweet.

Gingerbread was one of my favorite cakes and the way I made it has stayed with me through the years. This is how we made gingerbread at our house, and the aroma was a dead give-away that we would be having gingerbread for supper!

Even though gingerbread today doesn't taste like the gingerbread grandma made, here's the recipe I used that Mama used.

Thelma McRae
Caldwell
Asheville, NC

CARROT CAKE

Cake

2¼	cups all-purpose flour	3	eggs
1½	cups sugar	½	cup milk
2	teaspoons baking soda	2	cups shredded carrot
1½	teaspoons cinnamon	1½	cups flake coconut
½	teaspoon nutmeg	¾	cup chopped walnuts
½	teaspoon salt	½	cup currants or raisins
1	cup Crisco Oil		

Cream Cheese Frosting

2	packages (3 ounces each) cream cheese	2	teaspoons vanilla
½	cup butter or margarine, softened	4½-4¾	cups confectioners sugar

1. Heat oven to 325°F. Oil and flour 13 X 9-inch pan.
2. For cake, combine flour, sugar, baking soda, cinnamon, nutmeg and salt in large bowl. Add Crisco Oil, eggs, milk and carrot. Beat at low speed of electric mixer until ingredients are moistened, scraping bowl constantly. Beat at medium speed 2 minutes, scraping bowl occasionally. Stir in coconut, nuts and currants. Pour into pan.
3. Bake at 325°F for 55 to 60 minutes, or until toothpick inserted in center comes out clean. Cool completely.
4. For frosting, combine cream cheese, butter or margarine and vanilla in large bowl. Beat at medium speed of electric mixer until light and fluffy. Add 2 cups confectioners sugar gradually. Beat until well blended. Beat in enough of remaining confectioners sugar gradually to make frosting of desired spreading consistency.
5. Frost cooled cake.

One 13 X 9-inch cake

JAMAICAN BANANA CAKE WITH BROILED TOPPING

Cake

⅔	cup Butter Flavor Crisco	2¼	cups all-purpose flour
1¼	cups sugar	1	teaspoon baking powder
1	teaspoon vanilla	1	teaspoon baking soda
2	eggs	½	teaspoon salt
1	cup milk	½	cup chopped walnuts
1	cup mashed bananas (about 2 medium)		(optional)

Broiled Topping

¾	cup firmly packed brown sugar	1	cup flake coconut
⅓	cup Crisco Shortening	⅓	cup chopped walnuts or
2	tablespoons milk		pecans

1. Heat oven to 350°F. Grease 13 X 9 X 2-inch pan with Butter Flavor Crisco. Flour lightly.
2. For cake, combine Butter Flavor Crisco, sugar, vanilla and eggs in large bowl. Beat at medium speed of electric mixer until light and fluffy. Add milk, bananas, flour, baking powder, baking soda and salt. Beat at low speed until blended, scraping bowl constantly. Beat at medium speed 3 minutes, scraping bowl occasionally. Stir in nuts. Pour into pan.
3. Bake at 350°F for 40 to 45 minutes or until golden brown and toothpick inserted in center comes out clean. Cool for 5 minutes.
4. For topping, heat broiler. Combine brown sugar, Crisco and milk in small saucepan. Cook and stir on medium heat until Crisco melts and mixture comes to a boil. Stir in coconut and nuts.
5. Spread over warm cake. Broil 4 inches from the heat for 2 to 3 minutes or until golden brown, watching closely. Cool completely.

One 13 x 9-inch cake

FESTIVE FRUIT CAKE

1	cup Crisco Shortening
1	cup granulated sugar
1	cup firmly packed brown sugar
4	eggs
2	cups applesauce
4	cups all-purpose flour, divided
1	teaspoon salt
1	teaspoon baking soda
2	teaspoons cinnamon
1	teaspoon mace
2	teaspoons nutmeg
2	tablespoons unsweetened cocoa powder
1	pound raisins
1	pound mixed candied fruit
½	pound candied cherries
½	cup chopped English walnuts
½	cup chopped pecans
	Juice and peel of ½ fresh orange
	Juice of 1 lemon

1. Heat oven to 275°F. Grease and flour 3 loaf pans or 1 large tube pan.
2. Combine granulated sugar, brown sugar and Crisco Shortening in large bowl. Cream until well blended. Add eggs, one at a time. Add applesauce. Mix lightly.
3. Sift 3 cups flour, salt, baking soda, cinnamon, mace, nutmeg and cocoa together. Combine with applesauce mixture. Stir until blended.
4. Coat raisins, fruit and nuts with remaining 1 cup flour. Stir mixture into batter. Mix thoroughly.
5. Stir in orange juice, orange peel and lemon juice. Pour into pans.
6. Bake at 275°F for 2½ to 3 hours.

Dr. Mabel Phifer, Director
Black College Satellite Network

A Winning Recipe

This Festive Fruit Cake recipe was given to me when I was a freshman majoring in Home Economics at Barber Scotia College. My mother, Winifred Parker Poe, gave me the recipe as a possible entry in the Department's annual Christmas Baking Contest. The Festive Fruit Cake won first place in the contest for three consecutive years. I would bake this cake for Dr. L. S. Cozart, the President of the college. Dr. Cozart would buy all the ingredients and still pay me $15. It seemed like a fortune to a college student.

Dr. Mabel Phifer
Washington, DC

CLASSIC POUND CAKE

⅔	cup butter or margarine
1¼	cups sugar
1	teaspoon grated lemon peel
1	tablespoon lemon juice
½	cup milk
2	cups all-purpose flour
1¼	teaspoons salt
1	teaspoon baking powder
3	eggs
	Confectioners sugar

1. Heat oven to 300°F. Grease 9 X 5 X 3-inch loaf pan.
2. Beat butter at medium speed of electric mixer in large bowl until creamy. Add sugar slowly. Beat until light and fluffy, about 3 minutes. Beat in lemon peel and lemon juice. Add milk. Beat until well blended.
3. Sift together flour, salt and baking powder. Add to creamed mixture at low speed. Beat until smooth, about 2 minutes. Scrape sides of bowl as needed.
4. Reduce mixer speed to low. Add eggs, one at a time, beating well after each addition. Scrape bowl as needed. Transfer to pan.
5. Bake at 300°F for 1 hour and 25 minutes or until toothpick inserted in center comes out clean. Cool on cooking rack 10 minutes before removing from pan. Cool completely. Dust with confectioners sugar.

Variation: Eliminate lemon peel and lemon juice. Replace with 2 teaspoons water and 1 teaspoon vanilla. Add dash nutmeg.

One 9-inch loaf

Aunty's Specialty

My three brothers and I thought it was a big deal when Aunty baked a cake—especially her pound cake. It was extra special because she was creative with her toppings. Aunty was our great aunt with whom we lived. While mother worked, Aunty prepared the meals. When she started to bake, the four of us would sit and watch. As she finished with a bowl, a spoon or the mixer beaters, we'd get to lick them clean. The bowl was always my favorite, because she seemed to leave more batter in it! Whenever I eat a piece of "old fashioned" butter pound cake, I remember Aunty baking and singing, and then I want strawberries and whipped cream on top.

Mrs. Dorethea Nelson Hornbuckle
National President
Iota Phi Lambda
Sorority, Inc.
Montgomery, AL

LEMON YOGURT POUND CAKE

2¼	cups all-purpose flour	1½	teaspoons finely shredded
1¼	cups sugar		lemon peel
1	cup Crisco Shortening	1	teaspoon vanilla
1	carton (8 ounces) lemon	½	teaspoon baking soda
	yogurt	¼	teaspoon salt
3	eggs		Confectioners sugar (optional)

1. Heat oven to 325°F. Grease and flour 10-inch Bundt pan.
2. Combine flour, sugar, Crisco, yogurt, eggs, lemon peel, vanilla, baking soda and salt in large bowl. Beat at low speed of electric mixer until blended. Beat at medium speed for 3 minutes. Scrape sides of bowl as needed. Spread in pan.
3. Bake at 325°F for 60 to 70 minutes or until toothpick inserted in center comes out clean.
4. Cool on cooling rack 15 minutes before removing from pan. Cool completely. Sprinkle with confectioners sugar, if desired.

One 10-inch tube cake

SIMPLY SENSATIONAL CHEESECAKE

1¼	cups graham cracker crumbs	3	eggs
½	cup Crisco Shortening, melted	3	tablespoons lemon juice
¼	cup sugar	1	container (8 ounces) dairy
2	packages (8 ounces each)		sour cream, at room
	cream cheese, softened		temperature
1	can (14 ounces) sweetened	1	can (21 ounces) cherry pie
	condensed milk (not		filling, chilled
	evaporated milk)		

1. Heat oven to 300°F.
2. Combine crumbs, melted Crisco and sugar. Press firmly on bottom of 9-inch springform pan.
3. Place cream cheese in large bowl. Beat at medium speed of electric mixer until fluffy. Add condensed milk gradually, beating until smooth. Add eggs and lemon juice. Beat at low speed just until combined. Pour into pan.
4. Bake at 300°F for 45 to 50 minutes or until center appears nearly set when shaken. Remove from oven. Spread sour cream carefully over cheesecake. Return to oven. Bake 5 minutes. Cool cheesecake on rack 10 minutes. Loosen from sides of pan. Cool 30 minutes. Remove sides of pan. Cool completely. Refrigerate. Spread pie filling over top. Refrigerate leftovers.

One 9-inch diameter cake

BLACK WALNUT POUND CAKE

⅔	cup butter or margarine
1¼	cups sugar
1	teaspoon vanilla
½	cup milk
2	cups all-purpose flour
1¼	teaspoons salt
1	teaspoon baking powder
3	eggs
1	cup finely chopped black walnuts
	Confectioners sugar

1. Heat oven to 300°F. Grease 9 X 5 X 3-inch loaf pan.
2. Beat butter at medium speed of electric mixer in large bowl until creamy. Add sugar slowly. Beat until light and fluffy, about 3 minutes. Beat in vanilla. Add milk. Beat until well blended.
3. Sift together flour, salt and baking powder. Add to creamed mixture at low speed. Beat until smooth, about 2 minutes. Scrape sides of bowl as needed.
4. Add eggs, one at a time, beating well after each addition, at low speed. Scrape bowl as needed. Add chopped nuts, mixing well. Transfer to 9-inch loaf pan.
5. Bake at 300°F for 1 hour and 25 minutes or until toothpick inserted in center comes out clean. Cool on cooking rack 10 minutes before removing from pan. Cool completely. Dust with confectioners sugar.

One 9-inch loaf

My Favorite Dessert

My fondest food memories go back to my childhood. Growing up in a small East Texas town and coming from a large family, times were hard. But the holidays seemed to bring our family even closer. Thanksgiving and Christmas were special times and my mom would begin her cooking several days in advance. There were always so many different aromas coming from her kitchen. But my favorite was the smell of her fresh baked Black Walnut Pound Cake. It was my favorite dessert because as children we had a part in preparing it by hand-shelling the nuts.

Loretta S. McCullough
Jacksonville, TX

AUNT EDITH'S HONEY CAKE

2½	cups all-purpose flour
2½	teaspoons baking powder
½	teaspoon cinnamon
¼	teaspoon salt
¼	teaspoon baking soda
⅛	teaspoon cloves
¾	cup Crisco Shortening
½	cup sugar
1	teaspoon vanilla
¾	cup honey
1	beaten egg
1	cup hot water
1¾	cups chopped walnuts, divided
	Whipped cream

1. Heat oven to 350°F. Grease 13 X 9 X 2-inch pan.
2. Combine flour, baking powder, cinnamon, salt, baking soda and cloves in small bowl.
3. Combine Crisco, sugar and vanilla in large bowl. Beat at medium speed of electric mixer until fluffy. Add honey and egg. Beat well. Add flour mixture alternately with hot water, beating well after each addition. Stir in 1 cup of the nuts. Spread in pan. Sprinkle with remaining ¾ cup nuts.
4. Bake at 350°F for 30 to 35 minutes or until toothpick inserted in center comes out clean. Cool cake on cooling rack. Serve warm or at room temperature with whipped cream.

One 13 X 9-inch cake

COCONUT PINEAPPLE UPSIDE-DOWN CAKE

Topping

¼	cup Butter Flavor Crisco	½	cup flake coconut
½	cup firmly packed brown sugar		
1	can (8 ounces) juice packed crushed pineapple, drained, 2 tablespoons juice reserved		

Cake

1	cup all-purpose flour	1	teaspoon baking powder
¾	cup granulated sugar	¼	teaspoon salt
½	cup milk	2	tablespoons reserved pineapple juice
⅓	cup Butter Flavor Crisco		
1	egg		

Garnish (optional)

Maraschino cherries

1. Heat oven to 350°F.
2. For topping, blend Butter Flavor Crisco and brown sugar in 9-inch round cake pan. Place in oven 5 minutes to soften. Remove from oven. Add pineapple and coconut to melted mixture in bottom of pan. Mix and spread in even layer.
3. For cake, combine flour, sugar, milk, Butter Flavor Crisco, egg, baking powder, salt and reserved pineapple juice in medium bowl. Beat at low speed of electric mixer until blended, scraping bowl constantly. Beat at medium speed for one minute, scraping bowl occasionally. Pour over pineapple mixture.
4. Bake at 350°F for 35 to 40 minutes, or until toothpick inserted in center comes out clean. Invert on serving plate. Garnish with maraschino cherries, if desired. Serve warm or at room temperature.

One 9-inch cake

MISSISSIPPI MUD CAKE

Cake

1	cup (2 sticks) butter or margarine, softened
2	cups sugar
2	tablespoons unsweetened cocoa powder
4	eggs
1	teaspoon vanilla
1½	cups all-purpose flour
1½	cups nuts
1½	cups flake coconut

Topping

1	jar (7 ounces) marshmallow cream

Icing

1	box confectioners sugar
½	cup unsweetened cocoa powder
½	cup evaporated milk
½	cup (1 stick) butter or margarine, softened

1. Heat oven to 350°F.
2. For cake, combine butter, sugar, cocoa, eggs and vanilla in large bowl. Mix until creamy. Add flour, nuts and coconut. Mix thoroughly.
3. Bake at 350°F for 45 minutes.
4. For topping, remove cake from oven and immediately spread marshmallow cream on top. Let cool.
5. For icing, combine confectioners sugar, cocoa, evaporated milk and butter. Mix thoroughly. Spread on top of marshmallow cream.

One 13 X 9-inch cake

Birthday Memory Mississippi Mud

For my ninth birthday my mother's best friend, Madeline, surprised me with a Mississippi Mud Cake. I was so glad because that meant I could have as much of the chocolate, gooey, sweet, crunchy cake as I wanted. Whenever we visited Kortney and Madeline my mother would only let me have two small pieces, but the cake I got for my birthday was all mine!

Later, we were planning a party at my school and I volunteered to bring Mississippi Mud. The other kids said they didn't want anything made out of mud, but when I brought it to school, everybody liked it so much they all wanted the recipe. Here's the recipe Madeline gave me.

W. Kamau Bell
Philadelphia, PA

PEANUT BUTTER FROSTING

⅓	cup Crisco Shortening	¼	cup milk
⅓	cup peanut butter	1½	teaspoons vanilla
4½	cups confectioners sugar		Milk

1. Combine Crisco and peanut butter in medium bowl. Beat at medium speed of electric mixer until fluffy. Add about half of confectioners sugar gradually, beating well.
2. Beat in ¼ cup milk and vanilla. Beat in remaining confectioners sugar gradually. Beat in additional milk, if necessary, to make desired spreading consistency.

Fills and frosts two 8 or 9-inch round layers or frosts one 13 X 9-inch cake or 24 cupcakes

PRALINE FROSTING

¼	cup Butter Flavor Crisco	½	teaspoon vanilla
½	cup chopped pecans	3 - 3½	cups confectioners sugar
¼	cup milk		

1. Combine Butter Flavor Crisco and nuts in small saucepan. Cook on medium heat until shortening melts. Remove from heat. Blend in milk and vanilla.
2. Transfer to medium mixing bowl. Add confectioners sugar, 1 cup at a time, beating at medium speed of electric mixer until frosting is of desired spreading consistency.

Frosts one 13 x 9-inch cake

RAISIN-NUT FROSTING

1	package (8 ounces) cream cheese, softened	4	cups confectioners sugar
⅔	cup Crisco Shortening	½	cup raisins
½	teaspoon vanilla	½	cup chopped pecans

1. Combine cream cheese, Crisco and vanilla in medium bowl. Beat at medium to high speed of electric mixer until fluffy.
2. Add sugar gradually, beating well. Chill about 30 minutes or until of desired spreading consistency.
3. Stir in raisins and nuts. Store in refrigerator.

Fills and frosts two 8 or 9-inch round layers or frosts one 13 X 9-inch cake

Spiritual Vibrations

In the spring of 1991, the second of our three sons, a jazz drummer and student, announced that he was presenting a performance which he called Spiritual Vibrations. It was in the Howard University Fine Arts Building, so we summoned family and other long term participants in our Love Circle to join us for another ceremony of life. One of our guests was a treasured friend and my former professor at the Howard University School of Social Work, Evelyn Greene. She arrived with a gift that created food memories like cellular life multiplying itself. The nucleus of the food memory—the edible part—was in a Garfinkel's tin. The historical documentation was written on a carefully selected note featuring a j. macdonald Henry drawing of an African-American boy, about six years old, wearing a cap and the expression of a dreammaker, much like photos of our son the drummer.

(continued)

FUDGE CUTS

4	squares (1 ounce each) unsweetened chocolate
1	cup butter or margarine
4	eggs
2	cups sugar
1	cup all-purpose flour
	Dash salt
1	teaspoon vanilla
1	cup chopped walnuts

1. Heat oven to 350°F. Grease and flour 11 X 8 X 2-inch pan.
2. Melt chocolate and butter in double boiler over hot water. Cool slightly. Beat eggs until foamy. Add to chocolate mixture. Add sugar gradually, beating after each addition. Stir in flour and salt. Add vanilla.
3. Spread in pan. Sprinkle nuts on top.
4. Bake at 350°F for 30 to 35 minutes. Cool. Cut into squares.

24 squares

PRIZED PEANUT BUTTER CRUNCH COOKIES

2	cups firmly packed brown sugar
1	cup Butter Flavor Crisco
1	cup extra crunchy peanut butter
4	egg whites, slightly beaten
1	teaspoon vanilla
2	cups all-purpose flour
1	teaspoon baking soda
½	teaspoon baking powder
2	cups crisp rice cereal
1½	cups chopped peanuts
1	cup quick oats (not instant or old fashioned)
1	cup flake coconut

1. Heat oven to 350° F.
2. Combine brown sugar, Butter Flavor Crisco and peanut butter in large bowl. Beat at medium speed of electric mixer until blended. Beat in egg whites and vanilla.
3. Combine flour, baking soda and baking powder. Add to creamed mixture. Beat at low speed just until blended. Stir in, one at a time, rice cereal, nuts, oats and coconut with spoon. Drop rounded tablespoonfuls of dough 2 inches apart onto ungreased baking sheet.
4. Bake at 350° F for 8 to 10 minutes or until set. Remove to cooling rack.

3½ to 4 dozen cookies

(*continued*)

The paper she chose was one of a few remaining notes given to her by the late, legendary Dr. Inabel Lindsey, founding dean of the Howard University School of Social Work. These few words she wrote and I share with her permission:

Dear Sonia & Walter, I don't remember if I shared these with you years ago. It's my mother's recipe, before the many Brownie recipes appeared on the chocolate boxes. She called them "Fudge Cuts." They were always on hand for friends. We have kept up the tradition. With love to your family,

Evelyn

The "Fudge Cuts" were rationed with great care, but the spirit that delivered them vibrated without limitations.

Sonia Walker
Regional Coordinator
NCNW Black Family
Reunion Celebration
Memphis, TN

MOLASSES OATMEAL COOKIES

1	cup Butter Flavor Crisco	1	teaspoon baking soda
1	cup firmly packed brown sugar	½	teaspoon baking powder
1	cup granulated sugar	½	teaspoon ground cloves
2	eggs	¼	teaspoon salt
1	tablespoon light molasses	2	cups quick oats (not instant or
1	tablespoon milk		old fashioned)
2	teaspoons vanilla	1	cup coarsely chopped pecans
2	cups all-purpose flour	½	cup raisins
1½	teaspoons cinnamon		

1. Heat oven to 350°F. Grease baking sheet with Butter Flavor Crisco.
2. Combine Butter Flavor Crisco, brown sugar, granulated sugar, eggs, molasses, milk and vanilla in large bowl. Beat at medium speed of electric mixer until well blended.
3. Combine flour, cinnamon, baking soda, baking powder, cloves and salt. Stir into creamed mixture with spoon until well blended. Stir in oats, nuts and raisins.
4. Form dough into 1-inch balls. Place 2 inches apart on baking sheet.
5. Bake at 350°F for 11 to 12 minutes or until edges are lightly browned. Cool 2 minutes on baking sheet. Remove to cooling rack.

3½ to 4 dozen cookies

MOTHER EDNA'S CHEESECAKE COOKIES

⅓	cup butter or margarine	¼	cup granulated sugar
⅓	cup firmly packed brown sugar	1	egg
1	cup all-purpose flour	2	tablespoons milk
½	cup finely chopped pecans	1	tablespoon lemon juice
1	package (8 ounces) cream cheese, softened	½	teaspoon vanilla

1. Heat oven to 350°F.
2. Cream butter and brown sugar in medium bowl. Add flour and nuts. Mix until crumbs form. Reserve 1 cup for topping. Press remaining crumbs into 8-inch square pan.
3. Bake at 350°F for 12 to 15 minutes or until lightly browned.
4. Blend cream cheese and sugar at low speed of electric mixer until smooth. Add egg, milk, lemon juice and vanilla, beating well. Spread over crust. Sprinkle with reserved 1 cup crumbs.
5. Bake at 350°F for 25 minutes. Cool. Cut into 2-inch squares.

16 squares

ULTIMATE CHOCOLATE CHIP COOKIES

1¼	cups firmly packed brown sugar
¾	cup Butter Flavor Crisco
2	tablespoons milk
1	tablespoon vanilla
1	egg
1¾	cups all-purpose flour
1	teaspoon salt
¾	teaspoon baking soda
1	cup semi-sweet chocolate chips
1	cup coarsely chopped pecans*

1. Heat oven to 375°F.
2. Combine sugar, Butter Flavor Crisco, milk and vanilla in large bowl. Beat at medium speed of electric mixer until well blended. Beat in egg.
3. Combine flour, salt and baking soda. Mix into creamed mixture at low speed just until blended. Stir in chocolate chips and nuts. Drop rounded tablespoonfuls of dough 3 inches apart onto ungreased baking sheet.
4. Bake at 375°F for 8 to 10 minutes for chewy cookies (they will appear light and moist—do not overbake), 11 to 13 minutes for crisp cookies. Cool 2 minutes on baking sheet. Remove to cooling rack.

* You may substitute an additional ½ cup semi-sweet chocolate chips for pecans.

Makes about 3 dozen cookies

The Monument of Our Family

My grandmother, Hazel Drew Pratt, was the monument of our family. She, along with my aunt Aimee, took responsibility for raising my sister Benaree and me. She insisted that the family gather for one large meal each evening to discuss the day's events. She was a renowned cook, serving great Southern cuisine. She also enjoyed sending huge boxes of homemade chocolate chip cookies to the summer camps we attended. The cookies were a big hit with everyone at the camps. They all looked forward to receiving those cookies.

Sharon Pratt Dixon, Mayor
Washington, DC

FORGOTTEN TEA CAKES

Dough

½	cup Butter Flavor Crisco	2	teaspoons baking powder
½	cup sugar	¼	teaspoon baking soda
1	egg	¼	teaspoon salt
1	teaspoon vanilla	¼	cup buttermilk
2	cups all-purpose flour		

Topping

1	teaspoon sugar	¼	teaspoon nutmeg

1. Heat oven to 375°F. Grease baking sheet with Butter Flavor Crisco.
2. For dough, combine Butter Flavor Crisco and sugar in large bowl. Beat at medium speed of electric mixer until light and fluffy. Beat in egg and vanilla.
3. Combine flour, baking powder, baking soda and salt. Add alternately with buttermilk to creamed mixture at low speed. Mix well after each addition.
4. Roll dough to ½-inch thickness on lightly floured surface. Cut with floured 2½-inch round cutter. Place on baking sheet.
5. For topping, combine sugar and nutmeg. Sprinkle over top of tea cakes.
6. Bake at 375°F for 10 to 12 minutes. Remove to cooling rack. Serve warm or at room temperature.

1 dozen tea cakes

HERITAGE RECIPE

PRALINE COOKIES

1½	cups firmly packed brown sugar	1	teaspoon vanilla
		1½	cups all-purpose flour
¾	cup Butter Flavor Crisco	1	cup chopped pecans
1	egg		

1. Heat oven to 375°F. Grease baking sheet with Butter Flavor Crisco.
2. Combine brown sugar and Butter Flavor Crisco in large bowl. Beat at medium speed of electric mixer until creamy. Beat in egg and vanilla. Beat until light and fluffy. Add flour and nuts. Stir until well blended.
3. Shape level tablespoonfuls of dough into balls. Flatten to ⅛-inch thickness on baking sheet, allowing 1-inch between cookies.
4. Bake at 375°F for 7 to 8 minutes or until edges are golden brown. Cool on baking sheet for 2 minutes. Remove to cooling rack.

4 dozen cookies

ARTIE'S PECAN TASSIES

Crust

1	package (3 ounces) cream cheese, softened	½	cup Butter Flavor Crisco
		1	cup all-purpose flour

Filling

1	egg, lightly beaten	1	teaspoon vanilla
¾	cup firmly packed brown sugar	⅔	cup pecan pieces
1	tablespoon Butter Flavor Crisco		

1. For crust, combine cream cheese and Butter Flavor Crisco in medium bowl. Beat at medium speed of electric mixer until blended. Add flour. Beat until well blended. Cover. Refrigerate at least 2 hours.
2. Heat oven to 350°F.
3. Shape dough into 2 dozen 1-inch balls. Press balls into bottom and all the way up sides to top edge of ungreased 1¾-inch muffin cups.
4. For filling, combine egg, brown sugar, Butter Flavor Crisco and vanilla in medium bowl. Stir until well blended. Stir in nuts.
5. Fill each cup three-quarters full. Do not overfill.
6. Bake at 350°F for 25 minutes. Cool 10 minutes. Remove carefully from pan. Cool on cooling rack.

2 dozen tarts

Note: Bake in ungreased regular 2½-inch muffin cups if 1¾-inch muffin pans are not available. Line with foil baking cups, if desired. Divide dough into 12 equal balls. Press dough on bottom and up sides to ¼ inch from top. Fill each cup three-quarters full. Do not overfill. Bake at 350°F for 30 minutes. Cool as above.

1 dozen tarts

The Best Eggnog in the World

I lived in Boston from first grade through sixth grade and my best memories of Boston are the holidays, especially Christmas. After we woke up and opened our presents, my mother and I would dress up and take some food over to Reverend Stith's house. Lots of children would be there and we would go upstairs and play with our new toys while the grown-ups talked and prepared all kinds of delicious food. I really liked the eggnog that Percy's grandmother made.

Kortney James Jones, Student, St. Louis, MO

We continue to have "family" holiday dinners on Easter, Thanksgiving and Christmas with those members of our congregation who are away from home, although now we rotate locations. And "Percy's grand-mother," Mildred Boutin Prothrow, still makes the best eggnog in the world.

Charles R. Stith & Deborah Prothrow-Stith, Boston, MA

PROTHROW'S COOKED EGG NOG

6	eggs
¼	cup sugar
¼	teaspoon salt, optional
1	quart milk, divided
1	teaspoon vanilla

1. Heat 2 cups milk to scalding.
2. Combine eggs, sugar and salt in large saucepan. Stir in hot milk. Cook over low heat. Stir constantly until thick and mixture coats a metal spoon.
3. Remove from heat. Stir in remaining 2 cups milk and vanilla. Cover. Refrigerate until thoroughly chilled, at least several hours.
3. Just before serving, pour into bowl or pitcher.

12 (½-cup) servings

AFRICAN-AMERICAN HERITAGE

The Legacy of Mary McLeod Bethune

FAITH, COURAGE, BROTHERHOOD, DIGNITY, AMBITION, RESPONSIBILITY - these are needed today as never before. We must cultivate them and use them as tools for our task of completing the establishment of equality for the Negro. We must sharpen these tools in the struggle that faces us and find new ways of using them. The Freedom Gates are half ajar. We must pry them fully open.

IF I HAVE A LEGACY TO LEAVE MY PEOPLE, it is my philosophy of living and serving. As I face tomorrow, I am content, for I think I have spent my life well. I pray now that my philosophy may be helpful to those who share my vision of a world of peace.

About this fabric

Batik (BA-TEK)

A fabric design from Java created by dipping material into dye. Pattern is created by covering parts with wax or rice paste which resist dye treatment.

GRADUATION CELEBRATION

La Mardi Gras Chicken Breasts
Ambrosia
Perfect Rice
Marion Grace's Smothered Cabbage
Nice and Easy Rolls
Grandma Seldon's Three Bread
Pudding
Edna's German Chocolate Pie

FOURTH OF JULY BARBECUE

Billy's Ribs
Southern Style Barbecued Pig's Feet
Sweet and Spicy Barbecued Chicken
Old South Cabbage Slaw
Classic Potato Salad
Summer Green Tomato Crisps
Heart of the South Fried Okra
Corn Muffins
Old South Molasses Crumb Pie
Deep Dish Peach Cobbler

NEW YEARS EVE PARTY

Chitlins a la California
Pigs Feet Northern Style
Pepperoncini Roast
Corn Relish Salad
Hoppin' John
Collard Greens with Neckbones
Pink Coleslaw
Willette's Yam Casserole
Cornsticks or Muffins
Banana Pudding
Honey Crunch Pecan Pie
Grandma Prothrow's Eggnog

KWANZAA CELEBRATION

Akara or Bean Balls
Deep Fried Maryland Crab Cakes
Jessica's Okra Salad
Vegetarian Blackeyed Peas and Rice
Hoe Cakes
Pandowdy
Double Crust Blueberry Pie

*Editor's Note: Carrot juice or a·ginger
drink is often served.*

THANKSGIVING/ CHRISTMAS FEAST

Roast Turkey in Peanut Butter
Oyster Stuffing
Old-Fashioned Country Beans
Collard Greens with Neckbones
Sweet Potato Bonbons
Macaroni and Cheese Deluxe
Monkey Bread or Corn Muffins
Bethune's Sweet Potato Pie
Black Walnut Pound Cake

FRIDAY NIGHT FISH FRY

Fried Mealed Catfish
Old South Cabbage Slaw
Heart of the South Fried Okra
Buttermilk Hush Puppies or Corn
Oysters
Ndiwo Zampilru Wotendera
(Mustard Greens with Peanut Sauce)
Aunt Narva's Apple Cake

MARTIN LUTHER KING BREAKFAST CELEBRATION

Chicken and Cheese Fritters
Stuffed French Toast
Overnight Breakfast Sausage
Casserole
Marla's Hash Brown Surprise
Bethune Fruit Salad
Emancipation Proclamation
Breakfast Cake

FAMILY REUNION PICNIC

Classic Skillet Fried Chicken
Turkey Wings and Mushrooms
Jambalaya L'Acadien
Baked Ham a la Mom Pan
Katie's Kraut Salad
Medley of Greens with Strawberries
Molasses Muffins
Fried Pies
Aunt Edith's Honey Cake

AFRICAN-AMERICAN FOOD GLOSSARY

by
Jessica B. Harris

The old adage has it that you are what you eat. If that's true, Black Americans are made up of a multiplicity of wonderful things. We're comprised of a dash of cornbread, a hint of chitlins, a rounded tablespoon of biscuit dough, a good measure of molasses and a seasoning piece of fatback. To the mix are added such regional flavorings as a bit of benne from Charleston, South Carolina and a hint of praline from New Orleans. There's a dash of catfish and a pinch of dandelion wine. The recipe is ever- changing with new tastes being brought from "cousins" from Africa and the Caribbean. We're baked, roasted, fried and sautéed and the result has yielded us in all colors of the rainbow from lightly toasted to a deep well done.

It's not at all surprising then that we have developed a language and a vocabulary of food that is uniquely ours. We eat, "grease", "grit" and "nyam" with particular relish around the world. However, whether it's savored on the edge of a wooden spoon straight from a cast iron cauldron or served on heirloom china on a hand crocheted tablecloth, it is all a part of what makes us us. Here then is a glimpse at the wondrous vocabulary of our food from ingredients to eating.

INGREDIENTS

Benne

This is a South Carolina term for sesame seeds which came with the slaves from Africa. In Charleston, the seeds can be found as ingredients in benne seed wafers and benne seed candy. This seed can be purchased in most health food stores and can be toasted for greater flavor. They will keep indefinitely when stored in the refrigerator, but should be used immediately after toasting.

Black-Eyed Peas

Although many would confuse them with beans, these often used legumes are truly peas. In fact, they're one of the most frequently used peas in African and African American cooking. Eaten in Hoppin' John on New Years Day, they're thought to bring good luck for the year. Black-eyed peas are sometimes called field peas as they were at one time planted around the edges of fields. A smaller cousin is known as a cowpea.

These are available virtually everywhere dried or canned and can occasionally be found fresh seasonally in farmers' markets and African American vegetable stores.

Catfish

This scavenger fish is one of the delicacies of southern eating. Traditionally the fish is dipped in cornmeal batter and fried to a crispy turn at summer fish fries.

The popularity of southern food has made catfish readily available fresh and frozen.

Chilies

The African taste for the spicy edge of culinary life has followed her descendants from the continent to just about everywhere we are in the world. Whether they're called hot peppers or, more correctly chilies, these are the little red, green and yellow "devils" that add spice to much of our culinary life. Many lovers of Soul Food would no more think of eating without their thin bottles of hot stuff than they would of having biscuits without sopping the gravy (see SOP below).

Chilies are best purchased fresh when they have no blemishes. They can be refrigerated and will keep for a week or longer. To preserve them, try grinding them and freezing the paste or whipping up one of the numerous hot sauce recipes that exist.

Chitterlings

There's no polite way to describe chitterlings, or chitlins, as they're more frequently called. They're the small intestines of a pig. For this reason, they must be scrupulously cleaned before cooking no matter what it says on the box or tub in which they're purchased.

Chitlins can be purchased at butcher shops and supermarkets in most African-American neighborhoods.

Coconut

While the coconut is used in virtually every course of the meal in Africa, Brazil, and the Caribbean, for most African Americans coconut means dessert. Grated coconut is an ingredient in everything from fruit salads to towering cakes.

While grated coconut can be purchased canned or packaged, this is usually sweetened. It cannot compare in taste with home toasted, freshly grated coconut.

Collards

These are one of the types of leafy greens traditionally eaten in the South. While the greens are not African American in origin, the habit of eating them cooked, "down to a low gravy" and drinking the pot likker (see below) is African in origin.

Fresh collards are available in vegetable markets in African American neighborhoods almost year round. They're best though in the fall and winter after they've been kissed by the first frost. Canned and frozen collard greens are readily available. Other greens are mustard, turnips, kale or a mixture of several.

Cornmeal

This is a gift to African American cooking from the natives of this country. The white or yellow meal is made from corn and used in myriad ways from dredging fish for frying to making a variety of breads from hush puppies to corn pones to cornbread.

White cornmeal is a favorite in many parts of the South, while yellow prevails in the North. Both are readily available.

Fatback

This is the clear fat from the back of a loin of pork. It is salted and or smoked and appears as an ingredient in many southern recipes. When fatback is cut into small pieces and fried, it becomes cracklings or cracklins and is used in such dishes as cracklin cornbread. Rendered fatback is called lard and is traditionally used as an oil for frying chicken or fish.

Hominy

Introduced to American colonists by native Americans, grits are prepared from corn which has been soaked in a weak lye solution and hulled. Readily available grits have become an integral part of a southern breakfast.

Lard (see Fatback)

Okra

These small pods are some of the most maligned vegetables in the western world. However, in African and African inspired cooking, okra comes into its own. The term okra comes from okruma, the term for the vegetable in the Twi language of Ghana. In the Bantu languages, one of the terms used for okra is quingombo from which we get our term gumbo. The pods are valued because of their thickening properties and are used in soups, stews and sauces like Charleston's Okra Soup and Louisiana's gumbos.

Okra is available fresh in vegetable markets and can be readily found canned and frozen. The trick is that the more it is cut or cooked, the slimier it becomes.

Peanuts

A quintessential New World snack, peanuts appear in almost all courses of African and African inspired cooking. For most African Americans, though, the nut is eaten in brittles, as snacks and even raw and boiled.

Roasted peanuts are found everywhere. However, for raw ones, African American vegetable markets are the best source in the North.

Pecans

A classic nut of the American South, pecans make tabletop appearances in pies, chopped on salads and in pralines from New Orleans. Natives of the United States, the nuts are readily available.

Rice

Africans from rice growing regions of West Africa were brought to the southern United States to work in the rice plantations of South Carolina and brought with them their taste for rice. South Carolinians from the Low Country have been known to eat rice at all three daily meals.

Sweet Potatoes

The confusion between what are sweet potatoes and what are yams still reigns supreme in the southern United States. Botanically and elsewhere in the world, a yam is a hairy, white fleshed tuber of the Dioscorea family. So please note that, whatever you choose to call them, Louisiana yams and all other southern yams are members of the Ipomoea batatas family and are really sweet potatoes.

Whether they're called sweet potatoes or yams, these tubers, though are the basis for some of the South's most famous pies and vegetable dishes. A cold weather vegetable, the tubers should be purchased when firm and free from blemishes.

Watermelon

Come summer time, many African American neighborhoods blossom with trucks of watermelon vendors selling what has become a traditional summer dessert or snack. The melon is thought to have originated in West Africa. Today's varieties have sweet flesh that can range in hue from deep red to light yellowish orange. Although many of the current varieties are grown for a thin rind, the rind makes excellent pickles.

EATING

Ashcake

A treat from the time of slavery onward, this is cornbread that has been baked in the ashes of embers of an open fire.

Biscuit

If it's the South, it's breakfast time and it's a round bread, what you're looking at on the plate is probably a biscuit. They're many different types of biscuits: buttermilk biscuits, beaten biscuits, ham biscuits and the like. They should be light and fluffy and butter should melt into delicious yellow puddles when added.

Cobbler

A deep dish fruit pie with a top crust (or occasionally a top and bottom crust) is a cobbler. Blueberry and peach are prime fruits for cobbler making.

Fritters

From West Africa to the New World, African Americans love to nibble and one of the prime nibbles is fritters. These are batter dipped morsels which are fried to a crispy texture. They can be sweet or savory. They can be dipped in sauces or eaten alone or even sprinkled with powdered sugar and served as desserts.

Gumbo

This dish went from Africa to Louisiana with only a slight name change. Quingombo, one of the terms for okra in the Bantu languages, is a main ingredient in gumbo. The dish, which is based on the traditional African concept of a thick soupy stew served over a starch, can have many ingredients and is a classic of Louisiana's Creole cookery.

Hoecake

Originally this was a bread which the slaves baked over open fires in the fields on the blade of a hoe. Today, the term can also be applied to a large biscuit that is traditionally baked and saved for the man of the house.

Hopping John

There are many theories as to how this dish got its name. However, no one disputes the fact that this dish of rice and black eyed peas is traditionally eaten by many African Americans on New Year's Day to bring good luck during the rest of the year.

Pot Likker

When greens have been cooked "down to a low gravy", the cooking liquid that has absorbed all of the nutrients is the pot likker (a corruption of pot liquor). The African habit of consuming the "pot likka" provided the extra nutrients that saved the lives of many slaves and masters alike during the antebellum period.

Red-Eye Gravy

This very special gravy is prepared when a thick slab of country ham has been one of the breakfast meats. The pan juices from the ham are transformed into red-eye gravy with the addition of a bit of the breakfast coffee.

Skillet

This is a southern term for a frying pan. Many will tell you that it is impossible to cook great chicken without a cast iron skillet. They're right. The flavor of food cooked in a well seasoned skillet is unbeatable.

Sop

It's not really a culinary term but a technique of dipping bread into the sauce and juices that are so much a part of African American cooking. Biscuits are sopped in molasses at breakfast and cornbread is sopped in pot likker at dinner. It's all a part of the savoring of every morsel.

CELEBRATIONS

Kwanzaa

An African American cultural holiday created by Dr. Maulana Karenga of Southern California in 1965, it is celebrated December 26 through January 1. Each of these seven days coincides with Dr. Karenga's seven principles for family and community: Umojo (unity), Kujichagulia (self-determination), Ujima (collective work and responsibility), uJamaa (cooperative economics), Nia (purpose), Kuumba (creativity), and Imani (faith).

Karamu

This feast consists of ceremonies, cultural expressions and a magnificent buffet The celebration traditionally occurs on the night of Kuumba (January 31). Everyone dresses in festive African or African inspired attire, exchanges Zawadi (gifts) and enjoys the bountiful feast prepared by all attending.

Juneteenth (19/June/1865)

June 19th is an unofficial holiday observed by thousands of African Americans, primarily in some southern states. The holiday originated in Texas during the Civil War period, when news of the Emancipation Proclamation signed by President Abraham Lincoln in September 1862, to become effective on January 1, 1863, did not reach Texas slaves until June 1865. The slaves immediately left the plantations, congregated in the cities and began celebrating their freedom by praying, feasting, dancing and singing.

Juneteenth originated in Texas and has now become a state holiday there. As Texans of African American descent have migrated across the United States and settled elsewhere, they have taken the observance of Juneteenth with them. More and more descendents of slaves in other states are joining in the celebration and seeking in some instances to make the holiday a legal one in their respective states. Observances are held to a more or lesser degree in Louisiana, the Carolinas, Mississippi, Alabama, Georgia, California and Illinois. Naturally barbecue, prepared Texas style, dominates the feasting. The festivities start at dawn when pits are fired up for the barbecuing and the heady aroma of chili cooking fills the air. The celebrating usually continues until the wee hours of the next morning. Juneteenth is a Mardi Gras without costumes.

NATIONAL COUNCIL OF NEGRO WOMEN, INC.

In 1935, Mary McLeod Bethune, the legendary educator and humanitarian, founded the National Council of Negro Women (NCNW) a national organization of national organizations centered around the concerns of African-American women. Mrs. Bethune said that from her vantage point as Special Advisor to President Franklin Delano Roosevelt, she had come to know the value of collective power.

Today, NCNW is comprised of 33 affiliated constituency based national organizations and 250 chartered community based NCNW Sections, with a combined outreach to 4,000,000 women. The NCNW operates in 42 states with vital programs addressing women's special concerns including: education and career advancement, leadership training, family life, economic opportunity, motor vehicle occupant protection, preventive and service programs in teenage pregnancy, drug abuse, juvenile delinquency, health protection, hunger and malnutrition, child care, and on-the-job training.

The NCNW carried a major role in the Civil Rights Movement. It was the initiator of Turnkey III, a home ownership program for low-income families. It conducted a campaign against hunger and malnutrition. Through direct service, it founded the Women's Center for Education and Development in New York, the Raspberry Child Development Center in Okolone, Mississippi, the Fannie Lou Hamer Child Care Center in Rulesville, Mississippi, and the Bethune Museum and Archives on Black women's history located in the Bethune Council House in Washington, DC. In 1974, in cooperation with the National Park Service, NCNW placed in Lincoln Park the first memorial to an African-American woman or to a woman of any race to be erected in a public park in the nation's capital—the Bethune Memorial.

In 1986, in response to the negative projection of the Black family, NCNW launched the Black Family Reunion Celebrations as positive educational and cultural experience lifting up the values, traditions and historic strengths of the African-American family.

NCNW's International Division conducts development activities throughout Africa in an effort to improve the economic status of women through agriculture and food production, community development and income-generating projects.

The National Council of Negro Women is a member agency of the National Council of Women of the United States, International Council of Women/National Assembly for Social Policy & Development and the N/USA combined Federal Campaign. NCNW maintains non-governmental organizational status with the United Nations.

NCNW Affiliates

Ad Hoc Labor Committee
Washington, DC

Alpha Kappa Alpha Sorority, Inc.
Atlanta, GA

Auxiliary, National Medical
Association
Temple Hills, MD

Chi Eta Phi Sorority
Detroit, MI

Continental Societies
Washington, DC

Delta Sigma Theta Sorority, Inc.
Mobile, AL

Eta Phi Beta Sorority
Milwaukee, WI

Gamma Phi Delta Sorority
San Francisco, CA

Grand Temple Daughters of Elks
Philadelphia, PA

Iota Phi Lambda Sorority
Los Angeles, CA

Ladies Auxiliary, Knights of Peter
Claver
Lafayette, LA

Lambda Kappa Mu Sorority
Syracuse, NY

Las Amigas, Inc.
Charlotte, NC

National Association of Fashion and
Accessory Designers
Washington, DC

National Association of Negro
Business and Professional Women's
Clubs, Inc.
Palisades Park, NJ

National Association of University
Women
Tallahassee, FL

National Sorority of Phi Delta Kappa
Detroit, MI

Pi Omicron Rho Omega Sorority, Inc.
Hyattsville, MD

Sigma Gamma Rho Sorority
Brentwood, TN

Southern Christian Leadership
Conference Women
Atlanta, GA

Supreme Grand Chapter, Order of the
Eastern Star
Brooklyn, NY

Tau Gamma Delta Sorority
Los Angeles, CA

The Chums, Inc.
Washington, DC

The Women's Convention, Auxiliary
to the National Baptist Convention,
USA
Detroit, MI

Top Ladies of Distincton, Inc.
Crete, IL

Trade Union Women of African
Heritage
Baychester, NY

Twinks Social and Civic Club, Inc.
Ashbury Park, NJ

Women's Home & Overseas
Missionary Society, AME Zion
Church
Knoxville, TN

Women's Missionary Council, CME
Church
Berkeley, CA

Women's Missionary Society, AME
Church
Washington, DC

Women Lawyers Division
National Bar Association
Washington, DC

Zeta Phi Beta Sorority
Washington, DC

Communication Workers of America
Cleveland, OH

Recipe Contributors

Adams, Wanda
Aikens, Carolyn E.
Alexander, Maggie
Alexander, Mary Melson
Alli, Esther Napier
Allison, Eula G.
Anderson, Susan
Anthony, Leta
Anthony, Surluta B.
Baker, Clynell
Baker, Helen E.
Baker, Pearlie M.
Baker, Viola
Bamberger, Florence
Bannett, Mauniel
Barbour, Annie Kennedy
Barnett, Shirley L.
Beard, Bertha
Beize, Margaret W.
Bell, Queen Hester
Black, Bobby
Bond, Barbara
Boyd, Lily M. Thomas
Bradley, Ethel
Bradshaw, Melva L.
Britton, Jack
Broomfield, Carrie
Brown, Charlotte G. W.
Brown, Elizabeth Morton
Brown, Glenda
Brown, Mayme L.
Brown, Violet J.
Bryant, Gloria M.
Bryant, Ruth
Caldwell, E. Thelma
  Mcrae
Callaway, Eugenia J.
Callaway, Olivia S.
Campos, Judy
Carlock, Julia Sutton
Carmickle, Lee Dell
Carter, Georgine
Cassell, Florence
Chase, Leah
Chhutani, Carol
Christopher, Lillie M.
Clark, Libby
Clark, Myrtle

Clayton, Cora Faye
  Dixon
Cole, Johnetta B.
Cole, Octavia
Coleman, Katherine
Cook, Ruby L.
Cook, Vivian M.
Cox, Geneva
Cruse, Crystal A.
Cummings, Sylvia
Cunningham, Anne
  Smith
Daniels, Edna
Daniels, Linda
Davenport, Lorrine A.
Davis, Doris W.
Davis, Priscilla
Deveaux, Pam
Dinkins, Joyce B.
Dodson, Marie G.
Dorman, Hattie L.
Douglas, Virginia B.
Downs, Miriam T.
Dozier, Lottie V.
Easton, Eunice
Echols, Marian J.
Falker, Wilmer
Farwell, Laura T.
Felder, Lorraine Perry
Ferguson, Alice
Fields, Lisa D.
Fingers, Diane Cowen
Finigan, Lucille F.
Flowers, Patricia D.
Fortner, Lucy C.
Fulwood, Emma L.
Furtick, Blondena H.
Gaines, Sedalia Mitchell
Gaskill, C. Evelyn Carter
Gates, Jaccquelyn
Gates, Emma
Gibbs, Marla
Gibson, Corinne C.
Gillette, Ms. Franklin J.
Gipson, Tonya
Goodspeed, Ethel Lean
Grace, Marian
Gray, Muse

Gregory, M. Valeria
  Osborne
Gumbel, Marva Tucker
Hall, Mamie Dunston
Hall, Robert A.
Harrington, Margaret H.
Harris, Daisy
Harris, Jessica B.
Harris, Mary Nell Foster
Harris, Robert J.
Harvy, Novella J.
Hawkins, Ayanna S.
Hayes, Pamela
Heard, Barbara T.
Height, Dr. Dorothy I.
Henry, Willie Mae
Hill, Sharl Delon
Hill, Virginia Berry
Hines, Carolyn C. W.
Holston, Rachel
Honeywood, Stephanie
Hooks, Melvin
Hoover, Muriel
Hopkins, Linda
Horsford, Anna Maria
Howell, Lilith
Hoxie, Elizabeth
Hudgins, Vernis I.
Humbles-Liverpool,
  Phyllis
Ingersoll, Zell
Israel, Jr. Rudolph
Ivory, Annie
Ivy, Ernestine Harvey
Jackson, Augusta
Jackson, Katherine
James, Willie L.
Jefferson, Ann
Jenkins, Beverly J.
Jenkins, Elsie
Jenkins, Dorothy
Johnson, Alberta O.
Johnson, Beverly
Johnson, Delia
Johnson, Earlene R.
Johnson, Eleanor
Johnson, Grace
Johnson, Lillie Belle

Johnson, Loretta
Johnson, Marie
Jones, Barbara E.
Jordan, Erdine
Jordan, Mittie M.
Jynes, Marie
Key, Louise
Killion, Hazel M.
King, Odessa M.
Kirk, Ruby
Kirkendoll, Tommie J.
Kitson, Rio
Knight, Elease J.
Knox, Dr. Dorothy H.
LaBelle, Patti
Leake, Steven
Levy, Juanita M.
Lewis, Cordelia
Lilly, Alice V.
Lloyd, Doris Watts
Lopez, Diana L.
Love, Robert O.
Lowe, Lucille R.
Lundy, Roberta R.
Mackerrow, Marjorie
   Robinson
Mallet, Inez G.
Marshall, Joyce T.
Mays, Mae L.
Mays, Mae Louise
McCoo-Davis, Marilyn
McCullough, Loretta
McElroy, Angeline
McEwing, Inez
McKinney, Sarah L.
McKnight, Carolyn
McLeod, Eva M.
McNeal, Loretta Streater
Melancon, Hattie
Mobley, Annette H.
Monroe, Grace E.
Montague, Juanita
Moore, Mable & Benny
Moore, Mary A.
Moore, Geneva
Nays, Connie
Nelson, Helen

Nesbitt, Armentha
Nichols, Betty Faye
Nozizwe, Lena
Owens, Madge Doreen
Palmer, Arviller L.
Parker, Jacquelyn H.
Parker, Judy Wayne
Parker, Vivian B.
Peterson, Elouise R.
Phifer, Dr. Mabel
Plummer, Jessie Mae
Porter, Emma J.
Porter, Jessie L.
Preston, Ms. Mildred O.
Prothrow, Mildred
   Boutin
Pulliam, Laura
Raine, Magie Laine
Randall, Joseph
Rector, Phyllis
Redd, Orial
Reed, Elsie L.
Reese, Delia
Richardson, Mary C.
Richardson, Edna
Rivers, Johnny
Rivers, Edna Henry
Roberson, Eric L.
Robertson, Jean
Robertson, Jean B.
Robinson, Gloria
Robinson, Minnie
Rockefeller, Jeanette
Rogers, Idella
Ross, Mary O.
Rudolph, Wilma
Sanchez, Sonja
Sanders, Mable A.
Scales-Taylor, Madeline
Seymore, Philomene
Sherrod, Chef Clayton
Shumpert, Eloise
Simpson, JoAnn E.
Sims, Sharon D.
Skeene, Odessa L.
Smith, Doris Nichols
Smith, Herbuta M.

Smith, Jackie
Stellos, Dr. Marie H.
Stewart, Benny
Stewart, Katherine
Stone, Nevada R.
Stukes, Thelma D.
Sweet, Claudette
   Francois
Taylor, Cynthia J.
Taylor, Susan L.
Thomas, Alice W.
Thomas, Annie R.
Thomas, Audrey
Thomas, Donna
Thomas, Jennifer
Thompson, Margaret
   Anne
Thompson, Bettye B.
Townsend, Mildred
Turner, Jeri
Vary, W. Joe
Vaughn, Alma Lee
Vaught, Marva D.
Vinson, Queen E.
Walker, Joe Willie
Wallace, Jeni
Warwick, Dionne
Washington, Sharon L.
Waters, Maxine
Watkins, Marlene
Welton, Marie
White, Ella B.
White, Katie Kinnard
White, Margaret
   Sweeting
White, Marlin M. Hall
Williams, Francis
Williams, Mary L.
Williams, Milton F.
Williams, Nancy
Williams, Nellie R.
Williams, Zerline
Wilson, Emma D.
Wilson, Nancy
Young, Roberta M.

Index